To my dear
brother Nadia,
          A belate
I just realised I
already given you — love,
                  ~~Ismat~~ "Lindblad"
                  24 April 2014
                  (Anno's
                    birthday)

UNBECOMING DAUGHTERS
of the Empire

To the women who taught us

UNBECOMING DAUGHTERS
of the Empire

edited by
Shirley Chew and Anna Rutherford

Dangaroo Press

ACKNOWLEDGEMENTS

Margaret Atwood, 'Empire Bloomers' is an excerpt from *Cat's Eye* (London: Bloomsbury, 1989).

Isabel Huggan, 'End of the Empire' was first published in an earlier form in *Soho Square*, edited by Alberto Manguel (Bloomsbury Press, 1990), was broadcast by BBC Radio 4 as a 15-minute story in 1991, and is the opening story in *You Never Know*, a new collection to be published in Spring 1993 by Alfred A. Knopf Canada and Viking/Penguin USA.

Daphne Marlatt, 'Difference (em)bracing' first appeared in *Language in her Eye: Writing and Gender*, edited by Libby Scheier, Sarah Sheard and Eleanor Wachtel (Toronto: Coach House Press, 1990).

Grace Nichols, 'The Duke Coming' is an excerpt from *Whole of a Morning Sky* (London: Virago, 1986).

We wish to thank Penguin Books for permission to reprint the photo of Grace Nichols; The Women's Press for permission to reprint the photo of Ama Ata Aidoo. We wish to thank all the photographers whose names appear on pp. 205-207, where the captions and credits for the photos are listed. Other people we would like to thank are Coral Ann Howells and Kirsten Holst Petersen who attended our first 'think tank' meeting; Sister M. Dominic, O.P.; Christiana Keane and Ronald Warwick of the Commonwealth Institute. Anna Rutherford would also like to thank the Staff of Ward 60, Aarhus Amtssygehus, who not only looked after her broken leg but arranged 'an office' around the bed to allow work to continue. Above all, we would like to express our gratitude to Tim Caudery and Glenda Pattenden who helped to make the seemingly impossible possible.

First published in 1993 by Dangaroo Press
Australia: G.P.O. Box 1209, Sydney, New South Wales, 2001
Denmark: Pinds Hus, Geding Søvej 21, 8381 Mundelstrup
UK: P.O. Box 20, Hebden Bridge, West Yorkshire, HX7 5UZ

ISBN 1-871049-97-0 (Paperback)
ISBN 1-871049-62-8 (Cloth)
Printed in Great Britain by Villiers Publications, London N3

Contents

Marion Halligan *(Australia)*
Regirdling the Earth   1

Lyn Innes *(Australia)*
Unpacking the Trunks   11

Anna Rutherford *(Australia)*
Another Empire   19

Ama Ata Aidoo *(Ghana)*
Male-ing Names in the Sun   29

Buchi Emecheta *(Nigeria)*
Head Above Water   37

Lauretta Ngcobo *(South Africa)*
My King and Another King   47

Cherry Clayton *(South Africa)*
Buried Treasure   55

Jane Bryce *(Tanzania)*
White Child – Black Nation   63

Lauris Edmond *(New Zealand)*
Membership of the Club   71

Dorothy Jones *(New Zealand)*
The Antipodes of Empire   79

Jean Arasanayagam *(Sri Lanka)*
School Memories: The Missionaries   85

Yasmine Gooneratne *(Sri Lanka)*
Family Histories as Post-colonial Texts   93

Shashi Deshpande *(India)*
Them and Us   101

Meenakshi Mukherjee *(India)*
Growing up by the Ganga   107

Nayantara Sahgal *(India)*
The Schizophrenic Imagination   113

Ishrat Lindblad *(Pakistan)*
The Irresistible Anglo-filiation of Ishrat   121

Shirley Chew *(Singapore)*
'and there's another country I've heard of'   129

Shirley Geok-lin Lim *(Malaysia)*
Chinese Ba/British Da: Daughterhood as Schizophrenia   137

Grace Nichols *(Guyana)*
The Duke Coming   145

Velma Pollard *(Jamaica)*
Frog of Britain Proudly Waving   151

Olive Senior *(Jamaica)*
Colonial Girls' School   159

Margaret Atwood *(Canada)*
Empire Bloomers   163

Isabel Huggan *(Canada)*
End of the Empire   171

Daphne Marlatt *(Canada)*
Difference (Em)bracing   179

Maggie Butcher *(UK)*
Fireworks in May   185

Helen Niven *(UK)*
When the Sun was Setting: Individual
Connections in a British Girlhood   191

Marina Warner *(UK)*
Between the Colonist and the Creole:
Family Bonds, Family Boundaries   197

The idea for the book sprang from a conversation we had while attending a conference on Postcolonial literature at Lecce in April 1990. Late at night, in the bar, we drifted into memories of our personal pasts and were surprised and amused to find that we had a number of experiences in common. This we put down to two facts - first, that we had been colonials and, second, convent girls! Other people were soon drawn into the conversation and so we went on to sound a few differences. We then discovered that though we were all erstwhile colonials (and, indeed, it was this shared history which had brought us together into the field of Postcolonial literature), there were divisive factors at work which we had not always taken into consideration. Thus when two Australians related the stories of their childhood, we could hardly believe that they had grown up in the same period, in the same continent, albeit several hundred miles apart. If this could happen in their case, then, we went on to speculate, how many more factors there must have been to divide, say, a colonial person in Singapore from one in Trinidad, or a person in Canada from an Indian on the subcontinent.

The narrative of Empire was constructed in terms of sameness (we could all recite Wordworth's poem about daffodils and most of us celebrated Empire Day in our schools). It was always careful to conceal the tremendous diversities among the colonies. What prompted the book was our desire to investigate further the common ground which we shared and, more importantly, to uncover the differences. To that end, we met in London in the summer of 1991 and drafted a list of possible contributors as well as a list of the points they might take into account when they wrote their pieces. We received an enthusiastic response from most of the people we contacted and the articles soon followed, some keeping close to the suggested Guidelines and other blithely ignoring them. We also began to encourage our contributors to send in photos of themselves and of places important to them when young. All in all, it has been an exciting and interesting venture, and our only regret throughout is that we received no positive response from French Canadian writers nor from indigenous Australian, New Zealand, and Canadian writers.

That briefly is the story of the inception of this book. The book itself, however, would not have been possible without the generous co-operation of its contributors, the women for whom writing their memories of what it was like to be 'daughters of the Empire' was also a means of writing themselves out of that history, of 'unbecoming daughters'.

SHIRLEY CHEW
ANNA RUTHERFORD

I wandered lonely as a cloud,
That floats on high o'er vales and hills,
When all at once I saw a crowd,
A host of golden daffodils;
Beside the lake, beneath the trees,
Fluttering and dancing in the breeze.

Continuous as the stars that shine
And twinkle on the milky way,
They stretched in never-ending line
Along the margin of a bay:
Ten thousand saw I at a glance,
Tossing their heads in sprightly dance.

The waves beside them danced; but they
Out-did the sparkling waves in glee.
A poet could not be but gay,
In such a jocund company:
I gazed—and gazed—but little thought
What wealth the show to me had brought:

For oft, when on my couch I lie
In vacant or in pensive mood,
They flash upon that inward eye
Which is the bliss of solitude;
And then my heart with pleasure fills,
And dances with the daffodils.

WILLIAM WORDSWORTH

Marion Halligan

Marion Halligan was born in Newcastle on the east coast of Australia and grew up by the sea. She now lives in Canberra with her husband and (occasionally) two children, and has spent some time in France. Her books have won several prizes, including the Steele Rudd Award for *The Living Hothouse* in 1989, and the Geraldine Pascall Prize for Criticism. Her other books are the novels *Self-Possession* (University of Queensland Press, 1987 & 1992), *Spider Cup* (Penguin, 1990), *Lovers' Knots* (Heinemann, 1992, Minerva, 1993); two more collections of short stories, *The Hanged Man in the Garden* (Penguin, 1991) and *The Worry Box* (Minerva, 1993); and a collection of essays about food and other things entitled *Eat My Words*. She has published over sixty short stories in journals and magazines, and has been widely anthologized. She reviews for *The Canberra Times*, *The Australian*, *The Age*, *Australian Book Review* and ABC Radio. She has received a number of fellowships from the Literature Board of the Australia Council, and has recently been appointed Chairperson of that Board.

MARION HALLIGAN

Regirdling the Earth

10th December 1991

I am lying in bed thinking. Outside a large green garbage truck is emptying nine large green garbage bins. They are so large it takes a long time for their noisy contents to fall into the truck, which must then thump them into a small space. The garbage truck means it is twenty-three minutes to seven. And it's Paris. The cleanest city in the world. And one which I love dearly.

If it weren't for this garbage truck I would be lying in bed sleeping. But since it's woken me up I am thinking. Improving the shining hour. Though I think that was meant to apply to something more visibly productive. I'm thinking about last night's television news. Since this is Paris it was in French, so I wouldn't like to be in a position of having my fingernails pulled out if I got a detail or two wrong. But of its general tenor I have no doubt; it was talking about the ex-USSR. Byelorussia and the Ukraine have seceded. The Evil Empire is no more. We should not panic, says one of the various experts brought in as always on French news – they've not entirely come to grips, apart from trying to employ handsome people and the weather map, with the notion that television's got pictures – we should not panic, says the historian. Probably nothing will really change much. But of course psychologically and linguistically it has. When a phrase like *evil empire* totally loses currency then a lot has changed. We live in historic times.

The ex-ness of the USSR was not at all expected to be the headline news. That was supposed to be the meeting at Maastricht. Will that go down in history as one of those significant document-place names, like the Council of Trent, the Treaty of Versailles, the Union of Utrecht? The Accord of Maastricht, or maybe the Discord. For out of twelve European countries who were to vote on the question of a single currency one was in disagreement. England, of course. Ah, I said to Cosmo. It's not too late to retrieve the situation. Come home Mum, all is forgiven.

He having nearly three decades' practice in decoding such remarks knew how to take it. Namely, with a certain if interim seriousness. And of course he is a New Zealander. Generally a nice type of person, New Zealanders. A bit more English than us Australians, perhaps, a bit closer to the old country, maybe it's something to do with the size of the islands, they're very green aren't they. They don't have our space and dryness. A girl could do worse than marry a New Zealander. I had a cousin who did, in the fifties, he was a sheep farmer, very posh (now there's a good Empire word) but all this is a long time ago and a new generation has ditched its classy English vowels and invented an accent that proclaims it's all its own work.

Don't draw too many conclusions from the surname, mine and Cosmo's. Certainly it once was Irish. It transmutes to Hooligan. There's a rumour that it's a version of Cuchulain, coming from the ancient kings of Ireland. Is there anybody not descended from the ancient kings of Ireland? Caesar's dust stopping a bunghole is one thing, I'd like to know are there any veins (why do we say veins when we ought to mean arteries? Are veins more poetic? Or is it the used blood we mean to refer to?) so, are there any veins in which royal blood does not flow? Maybe in China where there are

3

a lot of people? But in small places, along with the viruses and maladies and hereditary diseases, the cholesterol building up and blocking, there must be many a drop of royal blood. Diluted of course. What is royalty? One of your ancestors having a stronger will and longer ambition than all his fellows, that's what. If that didn't work of course he could've become a convict and got transported to a penal colony, and many of us must have that sort of blood as well.

Apart from legendary giants and heroes the Halligans were the unromantic sort, the Protestant kind. They even chose a part of New Zealand called Belfast to live in. And they married with various Anglo-Saxon people so that Cosmo is only five-eighths Irish. You can still say that, though he and both his parents were born in New Zealand. It's as though the colonial parts don't count.

I shouldn't be surprised if one day having an Irish surname were to get me into trouble. Either being taken for a descendant of the old country in circumstances where that isn't admirable, or else for not being so derived and thereby guilty of false pretension. I once did a reading during Warana Writers' Festival in Brisbane at the Irish Club, in Tara House, a superb old building with painted plasterwork and Gaelic inscriptions and shamrocks and when I admitted the Halligan was by marriage there was a sigh of disappointment. In Australia you are never just Australian, you are always from somewhere else, even if it is out of 40,000 years of history.

But this Irishness is a digression. I'm back at Maastricht, or rather, in bed in Paris thinking about Maastricht. Of course I'm not actually writing this in bed, I'm on a train going to Belgium, or at least I was as far as Belfast, some paragraphs back, now I'm in Australia and it's early April and even more of relevance has happened. But before I leave the train: there I was deep in Europe, and Belgium is as deeply European as you can get, being full, at least on fast trains, of Eurocrats: polished, blinkered, and luxuriously funded. But at least the people in my compartment are real. Opposite is a family who look as though they come from somewhere in the Pacific. The daughter has a still and dreaming Gauguin face. She's cold. She's pinching her toes through her boots. She's a noble savage, tall, brown, handsome, delicately missing her warm homeland. I doubt she knows she's got a Gauguin face. It's the painter's perception and my recognition of it that give her that. She's reading an Asterix comic book, *La Rose and La Glaive*, and smiling over it, even though she's huddled in her shawl. I mention her coldness because the carriage is heavily heated. Her parents are murmuring together in French. My neighbour is an elderly thin woman with an aristocratic air, a mink coat and pearls, reading *L'Actualité*. Gorbachev has understood nothing, it says.

So, on a train, deep in Europe, thinking about Maastricht. That *Come home Mum all is forgiven* has a morsel of truth in it. It refers to one strand in the complicated knot of feelings I have for England. A strand that is a little tight twist of abandonment. While I was growing up England was the Mother Country; my grandparents and my aunts, though not my father, always referred to it as Home, all capitals intended, as indeed it had been for varying parts of their lives. My father on the other hand deliberately cultivated an Australian accent and consciously made this country his own. If you left your birthplace and went to a new world then that was what you had to make of it, a new world, and not hanker after the old. Though that did not prevent his sense of betrayal when that cove Niemeyer, Sir Otto Niemeyer from the Bank of England, came out here and gave us bad advice and England went off the gold standard and nobody over there gave a damn what happened to our country. This is a diatribe I remember from my childhood; several decades had not softened its anger. I feel a similar disappointment when the Mother Country abandons her children and goes soliciting a concubinage of convenience in Europe. Logic and common sense and desire and will all tell me that this is the best thing for both of us, and yet there is that thread-thin sense of abandonment.

For I was, during much of my childhood, a most becoming daughter of Empire. I was ardent. I got a lump in my throat when I looked at the red bits on the map – what an achievement of ours this was. What an intrepid race we Britishers were. How proud was our heritage. The greatest empire the world has ever known. A fourth of its population. A girdle round the earth. The phrase 'on which the sun never sets', when I finally worked out what it meant, could bring a mist to my eyes. (I've only just found out that it was Philip II of Spain who invented the boast and then the Dutch used it, but, says my 1920s encyclopedia, their claims were laughable compared to ours.) Proudly I recited the school pledge, honouring, serving, saluting, my God, my King and my Flag. And then there was Empire Day.

Empire Day. Queen Victoria's birthday. A half holiday. In the evening there'd be fireworks. School in the morning was marching, and pageants. Considering these pageants now, I am struck by how static they were, how hieratic. No action, no tension, no conflict. Nothing at all dramatic. Of course it is not the nature of pageant to be dramatic; the interesting thing is that this was the chosen form, this the tradition. A matter of being, not becoming. An affirmation. A celebration. We dressed in the native costumes of the peoples of Empire, formed tableaux, stepped to the front of the stage when it was our turn to make a speech reiterating what everybody already knew. Being in these pageants was immensely desirable.

I didn't do as well as my friend Geraldine. She got to be Britannia. No words to say, just sit and receive the homage of her subjects. In a white net dress and a trident made of a broom handle with gold cardboard prongs. And a fireman's helmet, one of those florid brass affairs. She still remembers the weight of it on her seven-year-old neck. She had a shield too made of a Union Jack which photographs show her to be holding upside down; at the time nobody noticed. Or knew.

I did manage to play India. Some places were more glamorous than others, because of the costumes. New Zealand was good, you could wear a grass skirt and beads and be a Maori. Canada and South Africa on the other hand were never represented by their indigenous peoples, nor was Australia. You just wore a nice dress, the one you had for Sunday School. Once I was South Africa; I had some doggerel verse to say, which I've forgotten except for the last line: 'There blooms my own white heath' (you can hear how thumping the metre is). I needed a bit of white heath to wave at this point so I made the family go for a walk in the bush the Sunday before in order to find some suitable local flowers (in those last glorious days of Empire it was okay to pick native flora too). Anything scrubby and white would do, since neither teachers nor parents had any idea what South African heath looked like.

I don't recall needing a floral emblem for India, I don't recall much about it at all, since I was about six at the time, but I did have a costume. A length of blue cotton my mother was planning to make into a dress was wrapped around me and pinned in imitation of a sari. I remember this because of my huge and terrible chagrin at being made to wear a jumper under it (very pretty it was, white wool in a feather and fan pattern, but that was no help) because even sunny Newcastle can get quite cold on the 25th of May. A jumper under a sari! It was probably the most mortifying thing that had ever happened to me. It destroyed my pleasure in this plum role. And of course the irony is, it was just what a real Indian woman would have done, what the doctor who came to live next to my parents twenty years later did in fact do.

By high school pageants had disappeared and somewhere along the way Empire Day became Commonwealth Day. We sang 'Land of Hope and Glory' and I got a lump in my throat. I still think it's a great song, and enjoy a wallow in it now and then, at the same time as I am perfectly cynically able to see how it manipulates me, as well as recognize its bizarre jingoism. And I can laugh when people parody it, without my pleasure in the real thing being in any way diminished. Maybe it was growing up being fervently Australian and patriotically British at the same time that made me able to appreciate several layers of meaning at once. An early training in ambiguity is an excellent thing.

As well as looking up to England, old Mother Britannia over there ruling the waves, we looked sideways at our fellow ex-colonies, our siblings. Especially the Dominions. Somebody said to me recently that the English these days don't care at all for the places they settled (however bloodily), only for those they conquered, with whom they are still locked in a passionate and unendable dialogue. Perhaps. But those settled places always had a lot of communication with one another. There was a certain sense of their interchangeability, and of the arbitrariness of the choice that had taken people there. My father's parents had thought of going to New Zealand; Australia may have depended on a decision as idle as the tossing of a coin. My mother had great aunts in New Zealand, her mother wrote to them regularly, they sent us magazines, and there were other relations in South Africa. There were faded mysterious pictures of them in photograph albums. This grandmother of mine lived in a house called Pretoria. We lived quite close and I passed it going to school; day after day I read this name on the gate and not for years did I realize it was a town in South Africa; I thought it was just a pretty word. My father's mother was one of ten children of an English sea captain and a woman he met when she took passage on his ship to New Zealand; one of her brothers went to South Africa when my mother-in-law was a girl and she never saw him again. Canada does not seem to have been quite so much on the circuit; maybe it was a matter of the hemisphere; you picked south or north and if it was south the exact country didn't matter all that much. The sibling affection remains; look at the pleasure with which South Africa has been received back into the cricketing fraternity.

There's something admirable in this new world seeking. You chose a place and off you went and made your life there and your children and their children were natives of that place. What started to complicate the whole gallant saga of intrepidity and resourcefulness was the realization by those children that their forbears' chosen places already had natives inhabiting them who were happy with the way things were. Colonial pasts are murky and messy and impossible to clear up but you have to try to achieve some clarity for present and future. If that sounds vague it's because it is and nobody's sure how to do it and fortunately it's not the subject of this essay. And, ambiguity again, the wrongness of those old acts is one thing, the spirit with which they were carried out another.

But I do confess to moments of malicious glee in observing the red bits on the map coming home to roost – or, rather, going. In England in her turn being colonized by her colonies. As France is, leading to the unedifying desire of the far right to send the country's blacks home. The blacks, naturally, think that after a generation or two home is France.

In 1953 I was one of millions of schoolchildren to cheer the Queen. We meant it. We were amazed by her; she confounded our blasé expectations. Land of Hope and Glory made flesh. But the enthusiasm wore out, and was finally if inadvertently given the *coup de grâce* by Mr (Pig Iron Bob) Menzies' fatuous quotation: 'I did but see her passing by/ Yet shall I love her till I die.' Well, he's dead, and it's other times, other manners. At the moment, Australia is in very bad odour with the Brits. We're accusing them of ditching us in Singapore, fifty years ago but in living and very lively memory. Our current prime minister put his arm around the Queen. His wife did not curtsy. A comedian whose claim to skill was imitating the ineffable Joh Bjelke Petersen, and there's no longer much call for that, tried to impersonate the monarch as a comedy turn and English cricketers walked out. (Mind you, it was the Australian-owned English gutter press that shrieked most loudly over this.) She's Queen of Australia, is the reply from down under. We treat her in our own way. I doubt she will be for long. Republicanism is a matter for passionate argument, not the least that it's a red herring to distract attention from the parlous state of the Australian economy. But soon, I think, it will be a matter of course. However foolish the antics of much of the Royal Family, however anachronous the institution, Britain needs to hang on to the monarchy for the sake of the tourist trade. Australia doesn't. Maastricht may have seen Britain quibbling over the details of her alliance with Europe but it's a *fait accompli* (and seen from outside, quite often a disturbing, complacent and exclusive fact). The ancient feuds, rivalries, love and hate affairs with France and Germany are ultimately more relevant than the rump of Empire. She doesn't even care about New Zealand butter. Mum won't come home to us and we don't want to go home to her. But our own grown-up siblings, as is often the way, are our good friends and that won't change. Britannia, come to think of it, was always pretty much a cipher in the pageant. It was the children of Empire who did the talking.

And when it came to the point, our country was Australia, not England. I might have been a British subject, I was most importantly an Australian citizen, and the country that one was a subject of was not quite the same as that Britain across the sea, which often sent us large numbers of migrants, who were nearly as different from us as Greeks and Italians. Who claimed to speak English but did so quite strangely. These were people to be kind to, help get used to our ways, to send food parcels to during the war. They weren't the might of Empire made flesh. Our England was a country of the mind, a construct put together from history and films and paintings and ceremonies and wonderful jamborees like the 1951 Festival of Britain and above all books. The books available to an Australian child in the forties and fifties told you more about the streets and monuments of London or Bath than about Sydney or Melbourne; the geography and scenery of woods and downs were more read about than the trees and coasts of the countryside I lived in. (That's part of the excitement of Australian literature in the last several decades; at last we can read about our own place as a matter of course, rather than in a look at me aren't I full of local colour fashion.) The result of all this was that when you got to England it could be a disappointment. Not the way you'd imagined it. Like coming across the picture book of a much-loved story you knew only in words; the illustrations weren't the way you'd seen them in your head. And of course, looking back, that British Empire patriotism: it was basically words. Poetic, ceremonial, nobly cadenced, loaded words: a girdle round the earth, the sun never setting, Britons never never never being slaves. How shall we extol thee, who are born of thee ...

Australia was a country that coined the phrase *cultural cringe* to describe its attitude to the rest of the world. I think that phrase now has only historical validity. These days we think very subtly about the nature of our country, but curiously can be given little credit for this. I was talking to the Czech ambassador (a writer too) recently and she said, You Australians, you are so uncertain of yourselves, so insecure. This was because I was explaining to her that I could not say 'We Australians ...'. I could speak for educated white Anglo-Saxons, but what was true for us about being Australian wouldn't be for, say, a second generation descendant of migrants of non-English speaking background. She might be as articulate in our language as I am, but her cultural background, Greek, Russian, Latvian, could make her perceptions quite different from mine. And what about a Cambodian boat person, who has all the task of assimilation and language-learning in front of her? What about a black Australian, whose people have been here for 40,000 years as against us newcomers' 200, who has whole scenarios of dispossession to come to terms with. None of these hinder my Australianness, nor the ease with which it fits me, but they do make it a matter of infinite qualification (which is also exhilarating) to talk about Australianness, and this is what my Czech interlocutor, with her historical patriotism reinforced by repression, mistook for insecurity. I think the subtlety and the conscientiousness required to think Australian these days are a great gift. And maybe being once upon a time a good daughter of Empire was a useful practice in making something of such a gift.

When I was in Bergen a Norwegian man who spoke very good English with an American accent asked me what it was like to be stuck with being the speaker of an international language. This annoyed me. International language, I said. I don't speak an international language, I speak my native language, my mother tongue, as it was my parents' and their parents' before them. (I have an ancestor called Jane Austen who lived from 1770 to 1828, at Wye in Kent and then in Godmersham when she married William Crothall, which was my maiden name.) If people want to regard it as an international language that's their business, not mine. For me it's a language that belongs to me, and I love it with a passion immeasurably beyond any patriotic leanings, a passion which springs, entirely selfishly, from what it does for me, from what I can read in it and write in it. The language is my heritage. Jane Austen the novelist belongs to me much more surely than Jane Austen my ancestor, just as she belongs to anybody of whatever national extraction who has the language to read her. I once taught a girl who told me the story of her father having his tonsils out when he was twelve, back home in his village in Greece. He was given a slug of brandy, laid out on the kitchen table, and the tonsils snipped out with scissors. He passed out for a day or two but was finally all right. He came to Australia as a young man, went into the fish trade, became a pillar of the local Greek community and was now educating his daughter in a private school. She thought 'Emma' was the most fabulous book she'd ever read. It belonged to her.

Once I was indeed a becoming daughter of Empire. A model child, as was my habit in those days. I grew out of it; I became critical, and cynical. Though I don't regret it, or feel harmed by it. And it would be most unbecoming of me not to be grateful for this gift of its language. Which has made me what I am. Among other things, a connoisseur of ambiguities.

You may wonder how I come to be thinking these things in Paris, and writing them down on a train to Belgium. The daughters of Empire were the children of people who upped their traps and took off into the unknown. Often widow women with teenage children, like mine and Cosmo's maternal grand- and great-grand-mothers, embarking on many-monthed voyages to uncertain destinies on the other side of the world. They weren't very rich; most of their baggage was metaphorical. Cultural, in part. With reservations – for we could doubtless have done without certain prejudices and preconceptions – it was baggage to be grateful for. Not the least of it was this desire for other worlds. There aren't any new ones available, but the old ones are seductive. So off we go, with more speed and comfort and safety than our foremothers. And more leisure to learn.

As for France ... what if ... what if ...

8

Laperouse had got to Botany Bay before Captain Cook and we were the daughters of another empire, of a peasant society and not the Industrial Revolution, of a thrifty and cunning people who could have known how to husband our fragile soils, who might have learned from the Aborigines instead of exterminating them ...

What if, indeed.

Lyn Innes

Lyn Innes was born in Mudgee, Australia, in 1940 and studied and taught in Australia, the USA, and England. She was an Associate Editor for *Okike* Magazine, which was founded and edited by Chinua Achebe, and is currently Associate Editor for *Wasafiri,* a journal of African, Asian and Caribbean Literatures in English. Her recent books include *The Devil's Own Mirror: The Irishman and the African in Modern Literature* (Three Continents Press, 1990), and *Chinua Achebe* (Cambridge UP, 1990). She co-edited *African Short Stories* (Heinemann, 1985) and *Contemporary African Short Stories* (Heinemann, 1992) with Chinua Achebe. Her book on *Woman and Nation in Irish Literature and Society 1880-1935* will be published by Simon and Schuster in 1993. She now teaches English Literatures at the University of Kent, Canterbury, England.

Prize Essay Winners

THE NAWABZADA MISRAT ALI MIRZA OF MURSHIDABAD

Prize-winners in an essay competition entitled "The Importance of the Confirmation Pledge," photographed with the Rev. Father T. Kerr after His Eminence Cardinal Gilroy had presented the girls with their prizes at the recent annual meeting of the Legion of Catholic Women. First prize was awarded to 15-year-old Nancy Casey (right), of Holy Cross College, Bellevue Hill; second prize went to Lynette Innes, left (15), of St. Scholastica's College, Glebe Point; and third to Robyn Hearn (11), of St. Joseph's Convent, Penrith. The competition was organised by the Catholic Women of Australia and conducted in Sydney by the Legion of Catholic Women.

Unpacking the Trunks

Wherever we moved, the trunks accompanied us. In the house in Bobbin Head Road on the outskirts of Sydney, where we stayed while my father served in the army, they towered above me, large rectangular obstructions, somewhere for my father to put his tin hat out of reach when he came home on leave. At night they loomed in the darkened house, with its blinds firmly closed in the blacked-out city, while search lights swept the sky outside for the Japanese planes which never arrived. After 1944, they cluttered the small rooms and took one corner of the verandah of the slab hut which was our first home on the farm my parents returned to on a mountain range some sixty miles from Mudgee, New South Wales. With his repatriation money, my father had a new fibreboard house built for his growing family (now five small children, and soon to be six). There the trunks settled permanently, it seemed, and took on more distinct identities.

The biggest of the trunks was made of wood, brass studded, with a high hinged lid which opened to reveal layers of drawers. These were lifted out, one by one, until the lowest and deepest layer appeared – exquisite baby clothes, hand sewn and embroidered in cream silk, a seed pearl necklace, white lace tablecloths, a crepe silk evening dress and a fan which had belonged to my mother, and sepia photographs: my mother as a girl in fur hat and muff clutching an English collie, a large grey stone house in Wales, my grandmother in a dashing wide-brimmed hat, my uncle as a small boy in oriental costume, my mother's nanny in Edwardian dress. These things were taken out and looked at on rare occasions before being carefully packed back amid layers of tissue paper. They were never used, but lay like tangible and inherited memories inside the trunks which still wore their torn P. & O. labels. They belonged to another world, incongruous beside the dungarees and shorts and flannel shirts which we children handed down from one to the other, the unglamorous routine which was demanded by sheep and vegetable farming. Equally incongruous was the kilt packed away in the small brown trunk in my father's study, the Gordon clan kilt he had worn as a member of the 52nd Highlanders' Regiment in the First World War. The full dress kilt, he proudly told us, had eleven yards of material.

In my English grandmother's house, some fifty miles away, were other trunks. Once she opened for us the black and brass trunk which held my grandfather's 'court' dress. We marvelled at the brightness of the green muslin shirt, the dress sword with a huge square emerald ornamenting the hilt, the gold-braided tunic, the kilt so much lighter and brighter than my father's. There were more sepia photographs, including one from *The Times* showing my grandfather in full 'costume'. It read: 'The Nawabzada Misrat Ali Mirza of Murshidabad who attended court on June 5th. The Prince is the son of his Highness the late Nawab Nazim of Bengal, Behar and Orissa and is the Uncle of the present Nawab of Murshidabad.' (*sic*) My grandfather had died when I was one year old and the words meant little to me at the time except as signs of an unacceptable foreignness, although much later I sought to untangle the strands of history that lay entwined in that caption. But for the time being the clothes and photograph were locked away in the trunk, and the only reminders of my grandfather's cultural past were the crescent seal my grandmother used on important letters and packages and a huge leather bound Koran in my grandmother's library. The Koran we treated with cautious reverence because we were told that it could cost us our weight in gold if we ever dropped it.

My mother's parents had left England in 1924 to start a new life for their oldest son, who was not doing well at Harrow, as a gentleman farmer in Australia. The new life involved changing their names from Prince and Princess Nusrat Ali Mirza to Norman Alan and Elizabeth Mostyn, while their son's name changed from Said to Savile (later he changed it to Stan). Only my mother's first names, Myriam Sara, remained as they had been. Neither my grandfather nor my uncle had ever had any experience of or liking for farming; my grandfather eventually moved to the city, and lived near Manly Beach where he watched with wry humour the attempts of Anglo-Australians to turn themselves browner than the Asians the white Australia policy was designed to keep out. My uncle became a car salesman. Only my grandmother stayed on to run the property, where she created her own demesne which she supervised until her death at the age of 83. A visit to my grandmother's house was for us children a visit to a museum, an idea of England painstakingly recreated and preserved amidst the red ants and red gravel which somehow marked for us the difference between the landscape she inhabited in the Capertee Valley and the richer dark soil of our mountain farm.

At my grandmother's house we left behind the egalitarian ethos of our own home, where age and size rather than sex determined the tasks we were assigned and the authority we could assume, and became ladies and gentlemen. My grandmother always wore a long taffeta gown and diamonds for festive days such as Christmas or Easter, and thus dressed for her part, she arranged the scene and assigned us our roles. I would watch with amazement my brothers stand awkward and subdued till my grandmother was seated, opening doors and carrying trays for her, tiptoeing cautiously in their newly polished shoes over the wooden parquet floor. Crystal glassware and gold-rimmed china replaced the pretty but sturdy apple blossom crockery we used at home. Careful to avoid making moist hand marks on the gleaming copper tables and walnut furniture which had been brought from England, we children would spend hours leafing through old copies of *Punch* and *The Sunday Times* while the grown-ups talked. After dinner, we gathered round the piano to sing ('John Peel' was my grandmother's favourite), and in the late afternoon sat on the verandah overlooking the garden to the blue mountain peaks beyond. My grandmother had created the nearest she could to an English cottage garden: roses over archways twined with fragrant jasmine, periwinkle covering the ground, grape vines which turned a rich gold at Easter. (Many years later I was reminded of my grandmother's garden when I read Doris Lessing's 'The De Wet's Come to Kloof Grange'.) When we left, we often took with us small treasures from this other world – a pair of silver buckles, a gold tie pin, a bunch of grapes, and perhaps one of my grandmother's watercolours, for in imitation of her great hero, Winston Churchill (for whom she claimed once to have been a secretary), she had taken up painting in her sixties.

From the artificial and theatrical world of my grandmother's house, it was always a relief to return home and resume our 'real' lives again. Here the variously accumulated books for all ages were well-thumbed and could be read as we lolled on the floor in front of the open fire. (We particularly loved following through, section by section, the twenty volumes of Arthur Mee's *Children's Encyclopedia*.) Here we could lazily play and quarrel over cards, or chess, or even join our parents in a game of bridge. Here the poppies, wallflowers, cornflowers and marigolds which flourished in the garden did not obstruct the magnificent view across the paddocks to the ranges of mountains with their ever-changing patterns of light. Here, at least in our view, our parents had succeeded in blending and merging their cultural worlds naturally with the world of an Australian sheep farm. Hindsight suggests that the merging was not always easy, however. My father had named the property 'Rhu-na-mohr' (Gaelic for 'On the bend of the hill') and occasionally dreamed of building a golf course in the paddocks across the road. He planted birch trees and gorse in the garden, but the cows, sheep, rabbits and wombats constantly invaded and destroyed the young saplings, so that those reminders of his native Deeside never flourished – until after my father died and the house had long been abandoned. (Now yellow gorse covers the slope by the ruined house, there is a graceful birch, and the hawthorn hedge has grown enormous.) Once a week the mail was delivered by Scotty Nicholson, and he and my father would occasionally stand by the roadside and yarn if Scotty had not been delayed by bad weather or a surplus of packages. When I played the piano at home, it was not 'John Peel' but 'The Blue Bells of Scotland', 'Skye Boat Song' and 'Annie Laurie' that seemed appropriate.

Friday was mail day. We children strained to hear the mail truck, and to be the first to see it rounding the bend of the hill a half mile from the house. Then we would race down the home paddock tracks to greet Scotty and receive the bundles – *The Sydney Morning Herald*, with the Sunday comics and children's pages containing the latest exploits of Ginger Meggs, Prince Valiant, and Bluey and Curley; letters from Sydney, and sometimes from England; very occasionally a parcel from our Aunt Emily in Scotland with an exotic Scots doll, dried heather, and a bundle of *Beano* comics sent by our Scots cousins; clothes ordered from the David Jones or Grace Brothers catalogue; and always, for each of the children over six, a packet from the Correspondence School.

Until I was ten, all my formal schooling was channelled through the series of leaflets and exercise books sent every week by Blackfriars Correspondence School in Sydney. Each morning after we had milked the cows, checked the rabbit traps, chopped and brought in wood for the kitchen stove, and done whatever other chores were thought appropriate to our age and size, we sat at the kitchen table to do our school work for the day. From practising strokes and letters with ink pens, we moved on to copying sentences and nursery rhymes, and then composing our own stories and essays. The verses and rhymes we read were about magpies, robins, or bluebells, and it was only when I came to England twenty-five years later that I discovered that these were not identical with the animals, birds and flowers which had been so named in Australia. We were encouraged to write about our own experience, although sometimes the teachers' written comments on our essays suggested that they preferred us to be less explicit about the details of butchering sheep, marking lambs, or trapping rabbits, which we children regarded as normal farm activities. Our written lessons were supplemented by radio broadcasts with music, song, poetry and stories, almost all of which were of English origin, and were read or announced in the nearest possible approximation to the standard English expected by listeners to the 'serious' networks, 2FC and 2BL.

In May of the year I was eight, we children all received with our correspondence lessons red, blue, and white ribboned Commonwealth medals, marking the formal end of Empire. Although we had annually looked forward to Empire Day on May 24th, which our family celebrated with a huge bonfire and fireworks, the significance of 'Empire' had never troubled my mind. The arrival of the medals suddenly made me aware of some distant centre which seemed almost sinister in its efforts to reach out to all those isolated children in the bush, and I had the first inklings of a community of children all over Australia, and possibly England and Canada too, who were being included, willy nilly, in this 'Commonwealth'. We were not fooled by the change of name, however; Empire Day remained Empire Day as far as we were concerned, and continued primarily to signify bonfire night. And for years, England, Australia and Canada remained the extent of that imaginable community to which the King and later the Queen spoke on the wireless each year at Christmas. Wales was also included, because my mother had grown up in Wales and, despite her attachment to the Welsh landscape, was clearly English. Scotland remained outside, however. When Australia played cricket against England, we children cheered the Australian side, and teased our mother as an assumed supporter of the English team. Australia's champion batsman Donald Bradman was our hero. My father refused to take sides, and his and Scotland's separate identity seemed to us most clearly demonstrated in his lack of interest in the Test Matches. Nevertheless, we knew that the Scottish regiments and the Australians had been the bravest of all soldiers, and had won 'the war' for England.

For England was both our mother's country and the Mother Country. As such, it needed and deserved protection, and as such it disseminated true culture, softening the raw edges and accents of her sons. Australia, Scotland, Canada and, as we became faintly aware of the 'Mau-Mau', Kenya, were male dominions. Did not the 'Australian national anthem', played before each reading of the national and international news, begin, 'Australia's sons let us rejoice/ For we are young and free'? None of the Australian literature or history I began to encounter suggested a role for women; all were stories of lone men – the man from Snowy River, Lassiter's last ride, Burke and Wills, Leichhardt, Stuart, Eyre. My mother read to us every evening from A.A. Milne, Kipling, Robert Louis Stevenson, Kenneth Grahame, and we loved them all, but here too the action was for men and boys only. At the same time the absence of women from these stories allowed a certain freedom in imagining a girl's future. But it was the American radio serials for children which inspired our play. My brothers and I played cowboys and Indians, pretending to be Red Ryder and Little Beaver, Tom Mix, Hopalong Cassidy. My younger brother was nick-named Tom Mix by our nearest neighbours, two miles away at the foot of the mountain. On hot days, we walked all the way down the mountain to visit and be offered some of the rich, cold ice-cream made by Mrs. George, and while we ate first, second and third helpings, we listened to Mr. George's stories of Mrs. Hicks, the woman leader of a cattle rustling gang which used to take the stolen cattle past his cabin on the mountain while he hid in fear in the darkened hut. He told us many stories about her exploit and her escapes from the police with the aid of the black trackers, but although Mrs. Hicks had lived and died in a cave near our farm, it never occurred to us to play at being cattle rustlers or bushrangers, let alone female ones. But women were allowed, even expected to participate in culture; while my brothers imagined they might become farmers, soldiers or engineers, my sisters and I might become writers like my mother and grandmother, or musicians, or artists, or attend university.

My parents worried that I lacked the company of other girl children (my oldest sister was at boarding school, the youngest still an infant), and decided that I should join 'The Brownies' group in the nearest town. So for several Wednesday afternoons we drove in our battered 1928 Dodge the 21 miles of dirt road to Rylstone, where the doctor's wife was Brown Owl. I thought the Brownie uniforms ugly and cumbersome, and refused to wear one; the activities and games seemed boring and pointless, and I was soon demoted from a sprite to a boggart. By common agreement, and to everyone's relief, I stopped attending Brownies after the first six weeks and settled back happily into following my father around the farm, or

16

exploring and playing in the bush with my brothers once our school lessons had been hastily finished (usually well before lunch).

But our happy isolation came to an end when I was ten. My father's increasingly crippling arthritis took us from the damp mountain farm to the drier climate of my grandmother's farm. From there it was possible to catch a school bus to the cement and coal-mining town of Kandos, twenty-five miles away. My parents had both become converts to Roman Catholicism in the late 1930s, and decided we should attend the convent school. My two years there were overshadowed by my father's illness and death, highlighted by my mother's courage as she struggled to keep the family physically and psychologically whole. Despite the kindness of the nuns who took me under their wing, my first experience of 'normal' schooling filled me with dismay: the early morning rush down two miles of track to catch the seven o'clock bus; the crowded, swaying bus, with children who jeered in strange accents at my own English/Scots one; the grey, cement-dust covered town; the big hard play-ground where other children played incomprehensible games; the ever-changing cliques and alliances among the school children; the shock of being caned by the nuns when I failed to understand mathematical concepts or when the accents of my classmates made me confused about spelling; the discovery that Protestants and Catholics must never mix, much less marry; the odour of loneliness and despair that haunted the 'New Australian' men who occasionally came to the convent door to beg for food and clothing. Above all, I resented and feared the children who lived on nearby farms and who sneered about 'the black princess', my grandmother, and all the 'little black tar-babies', her grandchildren. I learned that 'black' was not a colour, for my grandmother was English and very fair, and indeed my grandfather's photograph showed him to be lighter-skinned than many of my classmates; 'black' was an epithet attached to us because it referred to all Indians, and thus linked us to 'the blacks', the aborigines whose decorated caves we sometimes saw when we were riding in the valleys. We had listened to an elderly neighbour tell my mother how she watched the men hunt down the last aboriginal in the area, remembering how 'he bounded across the field like a kangaroo with the dogs after him'. I learned also that the ultimate national sin was to deny the Australian norms of colour and class by linking 'blackness' with an aristocratic title. I felt it my responsibility to protect my younger brothers and sisters, and indeed my parents, from those sneers and from knowledge of the furious fist fights and hair-pulling which daily took place between myself and the sneerers.

At the convent school we studied Church History, which was largely Irish nationalist history, from the preaching of St. Patrick and founding of monasteries in Ireland and Iona to the proscriptions against Catholicism by the English. We learned to revere Daniel O'Connell as the Emancipator, and to sing 'Faith of Our Fathers', a resoundingly anti-English hymn. The Parish Priest, Father O'Byrne spoke with a strong Irish accent, and several of the nuns had come as missionaries from Ireland. I reacted by becoming strongly anti-Irish and pro-English, although I devoutly avoided mixing with the Protestant children who attended the State school and was secretly bored by the little princesses, Lilibet and Margaret, who featured in the picture books an aunt gave me each Christmas. My brothers took a different tactic, adopted protective accents, and became aggressively anti-English and anti-'culture'. Back at home, my grandmother rebuked them for speaking like Irish labourers.

A Diocesan bursary sent me at the age of twelve to a convent boarding school in Sydney. There St. Patrick's Day far overshadowed any Commonwealth or Queen's birthday celebrations, for it was on March 17th that all the children of Sydney's Catholic secondary schools paraded in uniform and were addressed by the cardinal, or once the Papal Nuncio, at the Sydney Showground. Nevertheless, our school was shocked by the news of King George VI's death in February 1952, and we spent the day in prayer for his soul and in decorous mourning. Our grief was relieved, however, by the information, solemnly relayed to us by one of the nuns, that the King had secretly converted to Catholicism, and had been able to make his confession and receive communion on his deathbed. Such deathbed scenes, we were reliably informed, were customary among English royals, most of whom privately acknowledged the superiority of Catholicism but were forced to pretend an adherence to the Church of England.

My secondary schooling began with the death of King George VI; it ended with the Suez Crisis and with a military coup in Pakistan. At school, except for one year devoted to Australian history and geography as a self-contained unit, we had studied British and European history only, and apart from tales of Clive of India, Cecil Rhodes and General Gordon, knew nothing about Egypt, Africa and India. Officially, we knew that Nasser was a dangerous man, a Communist who must be stopped, and few questioned Prime Minister Robert Menzies' whole-hearted support for British intervention. The coup in Pakistan passed unnoticed. But when I went home for the Christmas holidays, a series of letters from my great-aunt Vaheedoonissa, my grandfather's sister in Murshidabad, suggested other perspectives. Speaking only Urdu, my great-aunt had dictated her letters to a scribe who then translated them into English and sometimes added his own footnotes and comments. Great-aunt Vaheedoonissa spoke with polite caution about Suez and the diplomatic misunderstandings; her scribe wrote that the English were outrageous and should long since have learned their lesson. My aunt vigorously defended Pakistan's Prime Minister Iskander Mirza, her nephew and my mother's cousin, from the charges of corruption and incompetence levelled at him by his successors; the scribe had his reservations about the Sahib. Those letters stirred my curiosity and opened tiny cracks in the sealed world in which my convent school had wrapped me, and which, safely distanced from my home community, had allowed me to keep my Indian ancestry a guilty secret.

The following year, I began studying for an Arts Degree at the University of Sydney. Packed in my trunk were the books I would need for my first year English course – Sweet's *Anglo-Saxon Primer*, Chaucer, my mother's copy of Milton's collected poems, Joyce's *Portrait of the Artist as a Young Man*, and, the one concession to our Australianness, D.H. Lawrence's *Kangaroo*. Beside them lay my school prize books, *The Imitation of Christ* and the poetry of Gerard Manley Hopkins. Wrapped carefully in the new circular skirt I had made during the summer holidays, I took with me as a kind of talisman the tiny bottle of perfume my Aunt Vaheedoonissa had sent as a gift from Murshidabad.

Anna Rutherford

Anna Rutherford is a graduate of the University of Newcastle, NSW, and since 1966 has taught at the University of Aarhus, Denmark. She was founding editor of *Commonwealth Newsletter*, later to become *Kunapipi,* and in 1986 she was elected International Chairperson of ACLALS (the first woman to be elected to this post). She has published widely in the field of Commonwealth Literature and is founder/director of Dangaroo Press.

ANNA RUTHERFORD

Another Empire

As a matter of fact I never was a daughter of Empire, or not 'that' one. I was born an Australian, and that was more than good enough for me. I resented the fact that on my first AUSTRALIAN passport there was also stamped, 'British Subject'. Further salt was rubbed into the wound when I turned up for work at my first school in London and announced to the headmistress that I was the new supply teacher. 'Oh,' she said, 'you're a colonial.' 'No,' I replied, 'I'm an Australian.' What was all this 'subject' and 'colonial' nonsense? Why, I'd never even been a Brownie. So when it came to writing this piece I asked myself a question rather like the one asked of Miss Mattie in Louise Bennett's poem 'Back to Africa'.

> Back to Africa, Miss Mattie?
> Yuh no know what yuh dah seh?
> Yuh haffi come from somewhe fus
> Before yuh go back deh![1]

How do I unbecome what I never was? I posed my problem to Shirley Lim and she replied 'Ah, but you had another Empire'. This made me think again, and in the end I was forced to agree with Shirley. I did, and do, have another Empire. Being born a Catholic, or if not exactly born one, baptized one just seven days later, meant that almost automatically in the Australia of that time (the 1940s) one would have a Catholic school education. I was no exception. I received all my primary and secondary education from the Dominican nuns.

The nun who taught us religion was an Irish Dominican called Sister Reginald. She was a strict disciplinarian and I think it would be fair to say that most of us were terrified of her. I always said it was easier to get up and go to daily Mass than to tell Sister Reginald why I didn't. Her task as she saw it was to instruct us in our religion, to make us realize how grateful we must be to God because we were lucky enough to have been born Catholics, and above all, to ensure that we would remain faithful all our lives to that One, True, Faith. From time to time we became bored hearing about our good luck and tried to divert her from what she saw as her mission in life, but try as we might we always failed. Nothing seemed capable of taking her mind off making sure we remained saved. But it is a rare person who has not a single chink in her armour, and, remarkable woman as she was, Sister Reginald was also human, and at last we found her chink: it was called Henry Parkes. At the mention of his name our salvation was temporarily suspended whilst she burst into a tirade of abuse (not charitable we thought, but later agreed justified) against this man who sounded like the devil incarnate. What was wrong with Henry Parkes?

To answer that question one must look at the history of education in Australia. In the early history of the Australian colonies, education was essentially in the hands of the various denominational churches. As the population increased there was an increased demand for education, which liberal-minded thinkers thought should be in the hands of the State. In New South Wales, in spite of opposition from the churches, in particular the Catholic church, two acts were passed: the Educational Act of 1866, to be followed in 1880 by the Public Education Act, which abolished all

21

aid to denominational education and established a state school system which would be free, secular and compulsory. The person behind these two acts was none other than Henry Parkes. In the State schools he may be known as the Father of Federation, but in the Catholic schools and community he was known as the man who introduced 'an infidel system of education'. The education issue 'became the centre of what was probably the most passionate, fundamental and continuing ideological conflict in Australia's history'.[2] It was designed to further the bigotry and sectarianism that already existed in the colony and to strengthen the divisions between Catholic and Protestant. The education of Catholic children became a battlefield.The Catholic hierarchy decided that rather than submit their children to a Godless, secular system, bent on the destruction of the Catholic faith, they would go it alone and set up their own schools staffed by priests, brothers and nuns recruited from Ireland. As a consequence of this a dual system of education came into existence. In real terms this meant that

> [t]he Protestant and the State-school boy [girl] grew up to believe in the contribution of the British to the freedom of men and the progress of the world; the Catholic boy [girl] grew up to nurse in his [her] mind the melancholic history of the Irish people and a conviction that the British by great barbarity and cruelty had contributed to the oppression and degradation of the ancestors of his people in Ireland.[3]

It was an act which caused deep resentment in the Catholic population, which at that time, and until much later, were generally to be found in the working class section of the society. It was yet another example of British injustice. We paid taxes to the state government, but not a penny of those taxes went to our schools, which were in dire need of support.

The battle over State Aid (Protestant version)/State Justice (Catholic version) was, as I said, one of the fiercest in our history and was to remain so until the 1960s, when legislation was passed and we got what we believed was our right. But such memories die hard, and I was reminded of this when in July, 1992 I spoke to a former teacher of mine, Sister Dominic, who must be in her eighties now. I mentioned Henry Parkes, and some days later I received a letter from her, concerning Henry Parkes. I quote from it.

> I presume I am not misquoting Henry Parkes, but I remember my parents saying lots of harsh things about him and quoting that pronouncement of his. He is said to have held in his hand the newly passed Education Act in 1880 and to have said with great jubilation 'I hold in my hand what spells death for the priesthood of Rome.' ... My mother was at boarding school at Bathurst when Parkes was Premier, and he visited the school. I remember she said that even at the age of fifteen or sixteen her Irish-Australian soul rebelled when she saw the arch-enemy being treated with courtesy by the nuns! Maybe she thought they should throw stones – which is probably what they felt like doing.

I grew up in Mayfield, a working class suburb of Newcastle, which is THE industrial working class city of Australia. My first school was a two room weatherboard wooden shed, officially known as the Hanbury Street Annex of the St.Columban's parish school, but known by all and sundry as Snake Gully. In many ways it was representative of the rickety, unpainted and overcrowded Catholic schools of the working class population which relied on the 3d and 6d a week school money to keep them going. Some tried to outwit the opposition and get something out of 'them'. The most ingenious instance I can remember occurred when I was in fifth class. It was first day of the year and the nun was calling the roll. She came eventually to the name of a boy who was one of a family of seven and whose parents were staunch Catholics. She called his name and there was no reply. Another pupil then volunteered the information that all seven children had gone to the 'publics'. He might as well have announced that Archbishop Mannix had joined the Royal Empire Society. A second child then informed the teacher that the mum of the defectors had told his mum that they'd all be back when 'they'd got what they could'. In a week's time they returned armed with the exercise books, pens, pencils, rulers, etc. that were supplied free to the children in the State schools but which the Catholic school children had to buy. In times of strikes, which were plentiful in the forties, even the 3d's and 6d's dried up. The chief source of income was gambling. Raffles were as much a part of our lives as prayers. Added to the weekly ritual of Confession, Benediction and Mass was one more – housie. We could all of us recite the litany of housie (bingo): legs eleven – one one, the devil's own – thirteen, clickety-click – sixty-six, with as much ease as we could the litany of the Saints. Actually, I think that if I was asked, at around the age of eight, who was a good person, I'd reply 'Anyone who'd buy a raffle ticket from me.'

We grew up in divided worlds where Catholic and Protestant rarely met and where we each eyed one another with suspicion and mistrust. We knew what 'they' thought of 'us'. We only had to study the history of the settlement to know that they had refused to let us have Catholic priests to tend to the Catholic convicts, that they flogged the latter for refusing to attend the Protestant services, and that they believed that it was only the shade of skin that separated us from the Aborigines. The surgeon to Port Phillip Association, Dr Alexander Thomson, claimed that the Irish were 'utterly useless ... intellectually inferior even to the aborigines'. The South Australian Government, in its promotion campaign for migrants, emphasized that it was a state 'free from Papists and Pagans', whilst Governor Arthur begged the Colonial office not to send Irish convicts to Australia, as they would lead to the impoverishment of the colony's intellectual and spiritual life. Of course we knew the terms of abuse like 'ignorant as Paddy's pigs' or 'Irish curtains' (cobwebs), but we didn't mind, for *we* were quite sure *we* had God on our side and that their Empire was a piddling nothingness compared to ours! We countered 'Land of Hope and Glory' with 'Faith of our Fathers living still/ In spite of dungeon, fire and sword'. In games against other schools, just to make sure of victory, we'd put a medal under our goal post, surreptitiously moving the medal to the other end when we changed at half time. We didn't really ponder the philosophical implications of this when we were playing against other Catholic schools, even though we were certain they would be doing the same thing.

We had our own dances – on Sunday evenings, to the horror of the Protestants, who were scandalized at this desecration of the Sabbath. We each had our own basketball teams, Mayfield Catholics, Adamstown Methodists, etc. We didn't join the Boy Scouts or Girl Guides, Baden Powell's Imperial child army. Instead, we became children of Mary, blue capes, white veils, daughters of that other Empire.

What did we have in common? In the primary schools both State and Catholic used Spaull's History and Geography books. In the secondary school there was a set curriculum for the state examination, but even here there were choices, and you could be certain that Gerard Manley Hopkins and G.K. Chesterton would feature large in the Catholic schools and not in the State schools. When it came to state exams we were always reminded not to put JHS or AMDG on our examination papers as that would give us away to the examiners, who were certain to be Protestant.

What we really had in common were the Australian fictional characters that became part of our everyday life: Ginger Meggs, Blinky Bill, Snugglepot and

Cuddlepie, the Banksia man, Australian characters to whom we *all* could relate as AUSTRALIANS.

That other Empire rarely entered into our school life except on the occasion of the visit of the school inspector. We all knew that he would be a protestant, because, even though the percentage of Catholics in the N.S.W. Education Department was much higher than any other denomination, no Catholic was an inspector. 'They' were determined to keep 'us' out. He was there, we knew, to spy on us, to find faults, and we were equally determined that he should find none. One of the tests that was particularly popular with the State school inspector was to hand out stencilled sheets of the map of the world plus red pencils and ask us to 'fill in the Empire'. We, and our teachers, knew that it was a trick meant to test our loyalty, and for weeks before we used to practice 'filling in the Empire'. So on the actual day we were not only prepared for the test but we were also prepared to answer the question that was sure to follow, namely 'And what does that red mean to us?' to which we would sweetly reply, 'It means *we belong* to the Great British Empire, Sir'. I was reminded of the significance of the verb 'belong' not so long ago when I was watching a British film, set in the same period, the 1940s. The teacher had a map of the world on the blackboard and with a long stick she pointed to the various countries coloured red and asked the same question, 'What does all that red mean?' to which a young boy replied, 'It's the Empire, Madam. It means it's *ours*.' I also remember that in order to please the inspector I happily filled in the Irish republic as well as Northern Ireland. This is bound to please him, I thought. It may have done so, but it didn't please my teacher. If we occasionally made mistakes when we were on trial so too did the inspector. I can always remember the time he was testing our spelling ability. One of the words he chose was *candle*. 'Not something we use now' he added jokingly. He must have noticed us looking at him curiously and then turning our glances to the various shrines and statues in the room. He suddenly realized where he was, turned beetroot red and said, 'Well, yes, of course we all know about candles'.

Empire Day was passed over without mention. Our substitute was St Patrick's Day. We would practise for weeks for the concert in the city hall and stand when the Bishop arrived and sing, no, not 'God Save the King', but 'God Save Ireland.' At the concert itself the songs were always the same: 'Mother Macree', 'The Meeting of the Waters', etc.

In the State schools, before the children marched into school each day, there would be a ceremony where the flag was raised; the children all turned to it and recited, 'I honour my God, I serve my King (it was in the 40s), I salute my flag'. No such ceremony occurred in the Catholic schools. First of all we had no flag poles. Our substitute was to kneel and recite the Creed, including the words 'I believe in one, Holy, Catholic and Apostolic Church'. For a time religion was the first lesson of the day, being the most important subject. Then it was moved to second period, not because it had been downgraded, but because some pupils came late for school, and they mustn't miss out on religion. I've racked my memory, but I fail to recall any portrait of the King hanging on any classroom wall. But there were plenty of Pius VI!

Apart from the visit of the State School inspector there was only one other occasion when I recall the intrusion of Empire. That was at the 'end of the year' school concert in 1941. Usually the content of the concert was much the same: it was a mixture of Australian and Irish songs, poems, small plays and of course a Nativity tableau. Among the most popular of the Irish songs were 'The Kerry Dance' and 'Dear Little Shamrock'. The Australian element would consist of recitations of 'The

Man from Snowy River', 'My Country' and 'Said Hanrahan'. The most exciting item of all was when we were transformed, with the help of crepe paper and despairing mothers, into May Gibbs characters: gumnut babies (the girls) and wild banksia men (the boys).

What was different about 1941? The Japanese had just shelled Pearl Harbour, and although Australian troops were already fighting in the Middle East the entry of Japan into the battle somehow brought the war much closer to our shores. Like the rest of Australia we had been brought up racist, with a real fear of 'The Yellow Peril'. And now, here they were, pounding on our very doorsteps. This was cause for great alarm, even greater than British domination. Australia had defence-wise always expected Britain to protect it. Now even we felt it was time to give a nod in the direction of England. So what was the main item of the school concert in 1941? The whole school took part, we were dressed as soldiers, sailors and nurses, and we marched up and down and round the stage singing 'There'll always be an England'. When the jingoism of 'Land of Hope and Glory' was mentioned to Elgar he replied, 'It's a damn fine tune.' So too is 'There'll always be an England', and we sang it with great gusto, more perhaps than many of the audience appreciated.

As a postscript to that I can remember that World War II ended on August 15th, which is the Feast of the Assumption, which in turn meant a Catholic school holiday. A group of us went on a picnic to Kotara park. We sensed that the end of the war was imminent and so in a burst of patriotism we decided to sing a song. This time it wasn't 'There'll always be an England'. It was 'There's a brown slouch hat/ With its side turned up'.

We never learned much about the rest of the Empire, though I am not sure the children in the State schools learned much more. India was associated with tigers and the Taj Mahal, New Zealand we knew about because of boot-polish. The most favoured brand was Kiwi, and it had a picture of a Kiwi on the lid. It's a strange combination, I must admit, but we never questioned it any more than present day New Zealanders seem to notice the oddity of Kiwi bacon. We could also sing 'The Maori Farewell'. Our knowledge of Canada was mostly gained from the movies where brave Mounties, usually totally outnumbered, defeated hordes of savage 'red' Indians. Canada's other claim to fame at that time was the Dionne quins. We took a great interest in them, particularly as they were Catholic, even if they weren't Irish Catholic. Africa remained for us mainly what it was for Marlow in Conrad's *Heart of Darkness*: 'a blank spot'. Nearer home we became particularly acquainted with the Papuan New Guineans. They acted as stretcher bearers for the Australian soldiers fighting on the Kokoda Trail and became known, very affectionately, as 'the Fuzzy Wuzzy Angels'. We were not conscious of the tone of racism behind the name we gave them.

If our knowledge of the British Empire was scanty, there was nothing wrong with our knowledge of that other Empire. We knew intimately its daily routine of religious duties, but we also acted out its larger intentions. In his Lenten pastoral of 1881 Cardinal Vaughan wrote:

> Let us, then, often meditate, during these forty days on the great Spiritual Empire to which we belong; encourage in our minds a profound sense of thankfulness that we are members of so glorious a society; and think of how we can do our part towards strengthening its hold and perpetuating its power in this land of our adoption.[4]

This spirit of universality, in which Australia was part of the Catholic world, was notable in all of Vaughan's work. Australia's allegiance should be first to the spiritual; we were to be soldiers of Christ, whose external representative was the

Pope and whose earthly domain was St Peter's in Rome – the Heart of God's Catholic Empire on earth. God came first and then Australia. Britain didn't figure. The other side was accused of toadying to Britain, content with their colonial status; their main allegiance lay not with Australia, but with an English king and an Imperial power. 'Our' allegiance lay with God and Australia.

The virtue I might attach to myself for never being party to the Imperial ambitions of the British Empire I cannot claim in connection with that other colonizing force, the spiritual empire of which Vaughan speaks. I prayed for the Propagation of the Faith, for the Far Eastern Missions, made sacrifices in Lent and duly put the pennies saved in 'mite' boxes to help the missionaries save the black babies. Actually, they weren't black, they were oriental, in particular Chinese. The fact that we wanted to save the Chinese sometimes puzzled me, for whenever we, as small children, went to put any unsavoury thing in our mouths adults would stop us by saying, 'Don't put that in your mouth. A dirty old Chinaman might have touched it.' If they were so dirty why should we try to save them? I could only conclude that baptism would not only purify their souls, but their bodies as well. I told Shirley Chew this, and she told me that I could have saved my pennies; she had no desire to be saved, and as far as being dirty her mother always said that the whites were even dirtier.

Just as we were ignorant of material colonization, so were we ignorant of religious colonization. We never linked one empire with the other. The only thing of which we were certain was that ours was good and theirs was bad. It was a simple as that. And what's more, ours was bigger. Just as we countered 'Land of Hope and Glory' with 'Faith of our Fathers', so did we have our answer to 'Rule Britannia; it was a hymn by Cardinal Wiseman called 'Full in the Panting Heart of Rome'. I quote a few abstracts, for I am sure it is less familiar to most of you than 'Rule Britannia', and it will also give you something of its 'flavour'.

> *Full in the panting heart of Rome*
> *Beneath the Apostle's crowning dome*
> *From pilgrim's lips that kiss the ground*
> *Breathes in all tongues one holy sound:*
> *'God bless our Pope, the great, the good.*
> *God bless our Pope, the great, the good.'*
>
> *It sweeps beyond the solemn plain*
> *Peals over Alps across the main*
> *From torrid south to frozen north,*
> *That wave harmonious stretches forth,*
> *Yet strikes no chord more true to Rome's,*
> *Than rings within our hearts and homes:*
> *'God bless our Pope' etc.*

This notion of linking the internationalism of the Catholic Church with Australian nationalism is nowhere more clearly reflected than in *The Catholic School Paper*, which had its counterpart in the State school in *The School Magazine*. The metaphysical poets' violent yoking together of heterogeneous ideas had nothing on the ingenuity of the yoking of Catholicism and Australian nationalism in *The Catholic School Paper*. One story was called 'The Saint who lived in Flanders' Fields'. I wondered a) who it was, and b) how they were going to avoid the Imperial link and include an Australian link. I discovered it was Father Damian, who was born in Belgium in 1840. We knew him as the saint who looked after the lepers on Molokai, one of the islands in the Pacific. He died in 1889 and fifty years later his bones were buried in

Belgium – in Flanders' Fields. This mix of Catholicism and Australian nationalism could become highly explosive in the prevailing political climate. One obvious and direct provocation was the cover picture of *The Catholic School Paper* vol.13, no.4, 1943. It shows the Virgin Mary standing protectively above Australia. The caption reads 'Our Lady Help of Christians. Patroness of Australia' (May 24). The Catholic hierarchy had deliberately chosen May 24, Empire Day, for the feast-day of 'Our Lady Help of Christians'.

A noticeable feature of 'our' magazine was that it had a much stronger Australian element than the State school magazine. There was more emphasis on Australian literature, natural history, geography etc. which took the place of the British and Imperial content of the State school magazine. However, it goes without saying that this never challenged the prime importance of the faith. For example, an article on 'The Finding of the Opal' was immediately followed by the history of Gregorian Chant. And of course the missionaries loomed large. One item was called 'Black Babies Grow Up'. In it we were told: 'They do not remain babies forever these children you rescue. Here in Central Africa it is very hard to be good Catholics because there are pagans all around them'. But it was not only the Africans who were in need of our prayers. The only reference I could find to England was the 'Story of St Augustine and England' which concluded with the following words: 'Say a little prayer to him [St Augustine] each day that he will ask God, once again to make all the little boys in England Catholics'. I suppose the Queen can be pleased that girls were omitted or it would have been an even more *anno horribilus* for her.

During the Queen's Jubilee a friend of mine received a letter from her mother. She wrote:

> On Tuesday night last they showed us the Queen and her tour of the river and at night 2 hours of pageantry and fireworks and the Royal Family on the balcony and the huge, huge crowd singing Rule Britannia – Land of Hope and Glory – and God Save the Queen, the smiling beautiful girl in bright yellow, what a sight, fantastic in its real sense – I sang with them, had tears in my eyes and anger in my heart that anyone would dare mention a republic only the Catholics, because they'd like the Pope.

She was wrong, I believe, in suggesting that we wanted the Pope, but not much more than a decade later events would indicate that we don't want the Queen either. I am referring to Paul Keating's call for Australia to declare itself a republic, a call that raised his popularity considerably. But a cartoon in an Australian newspaper reminded me that behind the seemingly obvious harmony between Catholic and Protestant in today's Australia lie old divisions. Paul Keating's background is Irish Catholic working class. The cartoon depicted him as an IRA terrorist and the caption read 'Irish Catholic'. It would appear that old enmities die hard.

Empires, as we all know, have a habit of disintegrating. The proud boast that 'the sun never sets on the British Empire' can be made no more. What about that other Empire? It still stands, but is hardly recognizable from the one in which I grew up. That earlier version had a Manichean division as rigid as colonial discourse. White soul/black soul, state of grace/ state of sin, Heaven/Hell. There was no room for doubt. The rules were laid down plainly for all to obey – or disobey, should you dare risk it. At times there seemed no correlation between the sin and the punishment. Murder and eating meat on Friday both carried the spiritual death penalty – mortal sin. The only time I ever heard my mother question the church was when she said she didn't think God would send her to Hell for eating meat on Friday. I pointed out to her that she wasn't game to try, just in case.

Religion governed your complete life. I was given my first bike when I was seven. My father took me for my first practice ride. I was a bit wobbly, and another bike ran into me. I was unhurt but the back wheel of my bike was buckled. I returned home upset. After checking that I was not hurt my mother asked, 'Did you say your prayers this morning?' Not wishing to add a lie to a sin of omission, I had to admit that I hadn't. 'See,' said my mother, 'God has punished you.' I remember that I increased the number of and fervour of my morning prayers for weeks, probably until I was quite proficient on my bike!

It was a hard religion, but it could also be a comfortable and comforting one. All that was asked of you was that you followed the rules. You were not asked to think. Along with total belief and obedience went security.

That certainty and security have both disappeared. The rapid changes that have occurred since the 1960s have left the Church in a state of flux. Once perhaps the Pope could have pronounced that the world was not round but square, and not a voice would have been raised in protest. That is no longer the case. The Pope may still pronounce, but most likely it will be in vain. That is not something I regret.

In her essay Margaret Atwood writes: 'My clothes seem a part of me, even the ones I've outgrown'. In that Empire of mine I outgrew many of the clothes/beliefs a long time ago, but part of them will remain with me. So in some ways I've cheated twice. I have never become a daughter of one Empire, and I have never unbecome a daughter of that other Empire. Instead, it has changed to include me. I have finally become heir to my own Empire.

NOTES

1. Louise Bennett, 'Back to Africa' in *Caribbean Poetry Now*, ed. Stewart Brown (London: Hodder and Stoughton, 1986), p.18.
2. Patrick O'Farrell, *The Catholic Church and Community: An Australian History*, (Sydney: New South Wales University Press, 1992), p.138.
3. Manning Clark, *A Short History of Australia*, (New York: Mentor, 1963), p.149.
4. Quoted by Patrick O'Farrell, p.192.

Ama Ata Aidoo

Ama Ata Aidoo was born in Ghana and is a pioneer in depicting the role of African women. Whilst she was still an undergraduate at the University of Ghana in Lagos she was awarded a prize in a competition sponsored by the Mbari Club in Ibadan. She has travelled widely in Africa, Europe and the USA, and apart from a distinguished academic career she was also Minister for Education in the Ghanian government in the 1980s.

Her writing includes two plays, *Dilemma of a Ghost* and *Anowa* (the latter had a very successful season in London in 1991), two volumes of poetry, *Someone Talking is Sometime* and *An Angry Letter in January* (published by Dangeroo Press in 1992), a collection of short stories, *No Sweetness Here*, and two novels, *Our Sister Kiljoy* and *Changes* (1991). The latter won first prize for the African region in the 1992 Commonwealth Writers Prize. Her writing is sometimes experimental, and combines both African and Western traditions. It has been written that 'she presents us with characters who cannot be viewed as the mere dispossessed "survivors" of colonialism but must be seen, rather, to display an integrity and resourcefulness that colonialism has quite patently failed to impair'.

Ama Ata Aidoo possesses the same qualities as her characters. As Alice Walker wrote: 'Her work reaffirms my faith in the power of the written word to reach, to teach, to empower and encourage.'

AMA ATA AIDOO

Male-ing Names in the Sun

Toli[1] Number One

In May 1949, a young girl stood in the blazing sun on the parade grounds of Dominase, the district capital of Abeadze in the south central region of a country then known as the Gold Coast. She and her schoolmates had been there for at least two hours, waiting for they-didn't-know-whom-but-the-then District Education Officer to come and inspect them. The inspection was part of the main business of the day. The girl had led her school's contingent – in a two-file formation – to march for 4 kilometres between their village and the parade grounds.

The early morning excitement of dressing up for the occasion had died down, although if you had asked the girl and her companions, they would not have confessed to the fatigue, hunger and thirst. And why should they, when they were the chosen few from the whole district? Earlier, they had stood stiffly at attention. Now they were chattering to one another, now squatting, now straightening up, or just generally fidgeting. One or two bold individuals were testing the teachers' patience by breaking free from their own positions to run between the lines.

It was 'Empire Day', the name given to the birthday of a certain English woman called Victoria Alexandrina. The girl was to learn later that this Victoria had been 'the Queen of the United Kingdom of Great Britain and Ireland', and strangely, also 'the Empress of India.' Victoria, alias Mrs. Albert Francis Charles Augustus Emmanuel of Saxe-Coburg-Gotha had been born over one hundred years before this African child was born, and died, in the second year of the 20th Century.

What she was to remember most clearly from the day though, was that she had wanted to scratch her right palm very badly. She had also been aware that she should not. She had been told that as a hyperactive toddler, she had sustained a big and vicious burn when she stumbled, fell and put her palm solidly in the middle of a wood fire on which her mother was cooking. This scar, she had been warned, would itch whenever she felt hot and uncomfortable ... I was that child.

It is a fact that in the south central region of Ghana, there is a division of the Akan nation known as the Fanti. It is also a fact that until quite recently, *Fanti* was an entry in nearly all respectable and scholarly dictionaries of the English language, including those reprinted in the 1960s. The user was informed that as an adjective(!) 'fanti' as in *to go fanti* meant to 'go native' (*sic*), 'wild', 'untamed'... My first language is Fanti.

Nobody spoke well of the Fanti as imperial subjects: and that included Fantis themselves. While the British lamented that 'those damned Fantis' were ungovernable, the Fanti unashamedly boasted of their recalcitrance, their rudeness, their contempt for the imperial set-up, and for the white man. Their language became crammed with proverbs and other sayings attesting to this.

'Aban wotwiw n'adze, wonsoa n'. You don't carry a government (on your head.) You drag it behind you.

Kohwinyi na ose ne dasefo wo Aborokyir. It is a liar who claims his only witness is in Europe. (Who wants to go that far to bring such a witness?!)

31

Fantis called every white man 'Kwesi Buronyi'. Kwesi is a Sunday-born male. And why? White men = missionaries = Christians = Sunday's children (or Sunday workers.) Buronyi is 'corn person'. That is, 'one with cornsilk hair.' There was no equivalent nickname for white women. Maybe they did not exist in the imagination of Fantis.

I also grew up knowing that long before I was born, my father's father had been arrested along with other 'Nkwakwafo'[2] for 'disturbing the King's peace'. They had been sent to the castle prison at Elmina, and tortured. The mode of torture was to force the prisoners to pass cannonballs among themselves, as though they were playing volleyball. Within a week, they were dead, each and everyone of them, including my grandfather. No beatings, no bruising. Very gentlemanly, very civilised.

By the way, the fact that these days, our governments are post-colonially (!) torturing and killing Africans does not lessen or justify colonial crimes. It only goes to show how long our people have suffered.

> God say, God say, God say God say, God say, God say God say, God say ...
> God say, God say,
> God say, God say, God say
> God say, God say, God say
> God say, God say, God say
> God save the King ...

Ghanaians never sang the lyrics of the British Empire anthem as they were taught, instructed, and were expected to. Not if they could help it. Of course, much of the time, most of them could. But why should they sing that anthem correctly? It was too much trouble. 'After all, it isn't our mother's anthem,' is what they would have probably told anyone if challenged. Nothing concerning the Empire was their mother's or their father's. So they took their time to do everything; they did everything halfheartedly or they didn't do anything at all.

Ghanaians have always suspected that Kwame Nkrumah influenced the choice of May 25th as Africa Day. (Also known as 'OAU Day', or 'Africa Liberation Day') The 24th of May had been Empire Day. You do not have to take someone's 'day' over. You only put yours close enough for people to remember 'the good old days', without considering the change spiteful.

These days, Empire Day is supposed to be Commonwealth Day. 'Commonwealth' day? So you ask yourself what on earth you've got to do with Boris Yeltsin? You wonder if it refers to Yeltsin's or Lenin's birthday? However, you also suspect that if there is a Russian whose birthday ought to be celebrated by someone, it should be Vladimir Ilyich Ulyanov, alias Lenin, because in his heyday, he was revered by as many people as Victoria was in hers. Whiteman's tribal politics... All this business of the mind of the African child getting farmed out to different European centres of power was always quite tragic really. It's like suffering from a permanent migraine. No wonder we are amnesiac. Meanwhile everyone expects us, and we expect ourselves, to solve all our problems instantly. Whew!

So then, was W.E. Dubois some malevolent wizard cursing humankind into stupidity and intolerance when he said that the problem of the 20th century was going to be that of race? Or was he just an honest prophet? One thing is certain. Seventy years after he spoke and with only a few years of the century left, the issue of race is still allowed to assume all forms, subsume all controversies and consume every little bit of human energy, vision and imagination. The 21st century is almost upon us, and we are still imprisoned in the colours of our skins. How absolutely awful! How humanly pathetic!!

When we are going about our normal business, we do not stop to wonder whether we might have experienced the whole imperial/colonial wahala differently if we had been white? However, on some idle occasions, we do wonder. Of course the honest answer is a clear 'yes'. After all, we were 'the natives' whose lands and other resources had to be taken and given to the emperor's relatives in Australia, Canada, Kenya and Zimbabwe, no? Why some of them had to leave their homes became irrelevant once they arrived in our neighbourhoods.

> God say, God say, God say
> God save the King...

Toli Number Two: A FRAGMENT FROM A LOST NOVEL

Once upon a time, there was a fisherman who lived in Mowure, a seaside village in the Central Region. As everyone who knows the area is aware, Mowure is really within a stone throw from the town of Oguaa ... ah-h-h ... First, about Oguaa, alias Cape Coast.

Those were the 1920s. Oguaa was the big city of Fantis, who were then congratulating themselves for having used (read 'helped') the British to conquer Ashanti, their more aggressive relatives to the north, whom they were always in mortal fear of! The British had 'pacified' Ashanti, looting Kumasi the capital, especially of its legendary gold arts, and finally exiling the king and other core members of the royal family. Another feat the Fantis had recently accomplished included making Oguaa unviable as the seat of the colonial government.

Now Oguaa was settling down to become the self-appointed, self-conscious fashion centre of the Gold Coast while its people set about the business of Europeanizing themselves with panache. In dressing, they opted for the clothes of the owners of the Empire, as the latter dressed in their cold country. So under the 88 degree sun, the men wore 3-piece *woollen* suits, complete with top hats. The women wore the equivalent long evening gowns, hats, stockinged feet, gloved arms and hands and all.

According to the rest of the country, which came to look upon their antics with a mixture of derision and envy, this was also when Fanti wives started the *haute cuisine*, that became so *haute*, it tipped over into requiring women to light their charcoal and wood fires with butter, and at the end of a cooking session, to extinguish the fires with milk. And that in a region of the world where there had never been dairy farming at all. In fact, one cow seen within a 20 kilometre radius was a spectacle enough for people to name their children after, and for the day to be remembered in historical narratives. So both the milk and the butter were tinned and imported from England, or the Netherlands ...

... may be, it's time to return to the fisherman.

He had been the only surviving child from his mother's six fullterm pregnancies. So as an Ewu-ewu, Abiku or a Kwasamba, and in line with custom, his parents had had to give him a name he would not want to return to his spirit mother with. They chose Srako, the local term for One Shilling. Since he was born on a Wednesday, his full name was Kweku Srako, although everybody conveniently forgot the Kweku and just called him Srako.

Srako and his wife had eight children and thereby proved more fertile than his parents. Their fourth born but first son was Kojo Kuma, named after a revered ancestor of his father's house.

One day, just as Srako was setting out to sea, his wife Esi-Yaa asked him to listen to a thought that had occurred to her. 'What is it?' he asked somewhat impatiently, standing. 'Sit down,' she commanded. Srako could not believe his ears. Was the woman going out of her mind? As if it was not provocation enough to bother him with woman thoughts when he should be on his way. However, he was also thinking that the surest way to bring bad luck on himself and his mates would be to quarrel with her now. He sat down. She sat opposite him.

'Y-e-s?'

'We should send Kojo Kuma to school,' Esi-Yaa said firmly.

'Nyankopon-above and the Gods of our Fathers!' he exclaimed as he jumped up, fetched his sack and dashed out to go and join his mates, who were by then taking the dragnet to their boat.

Srako could not believe that he had heard Esi-Yaa right. How could the same idea occur to him and to her? When a few days earlier, he had realised he should send Kuma to school, he had postponed discussing it with her because he was not sure of how she would react. (Meaning, he had not convinced himself that it was a good idea.) After all, as their oldest son, the child would be expected to go to sea, and in fact, very soon. He was about ten years old. Besides, sending him to school would mean exiling him to go and stay with some of those snobbish and cruel Cape Coast characters. He had decided to give the matter a think-over while he was at sea on this trip. Now he would forever have to give the woman the credit of being the first in bringing up the matter. Ah, ah, ah!

A month later, Srako, his wife Esi-Yaa and their son Kojo Kuma were on their way to Oguaa. It had to be a Tuesday, since that is the sacred day of Nana Bosompo, the god of the sea, and a day on which no self-respecting fisherman would go to sea. A hol(y) day.

They set out quite early. By the time the sun was shaking itself up to be hot, they were on the eastern outskirts of the town. Around half-past eight, they knocked on the door of Isaac Goodful, the circuit minister of the Methodist Church.

Going to the priest instead of any other Oguaa resident was not the result of a random decision made by Srako. Apart from being the immediate leader of his church, the priest was also some kind of a distant relative. Meanwhile, not wanting to take any chances, he had sent a message to the priest to please expect them. Soon Srako, his wife Esi-Yaa, Reverend Goodful and his wife 'Maame Sofo' Mrs. Goodful were seated around a big table. The boy had been deposited with the priest's 'boys' somewhere in the back of the house. The discussion was short and concluded soon enough. Or almost. It was agreed that Kojo Kuma would stay with Osofo and his wife, as one of about half a dozen youngsters, apart from their own children, who lived in the priestly household, getting properly brought up and educated.

Kojo Kuma was sent for. He came and stood before the priest, with his cloth neatly wrapped around his body, and the upper ends tied behind his neck. The presence of his parents gave him some courage, but he was still shaking. The priest looked completely formidable. Even seated, he was much taller than the boy on his feet.

'What is your name?' 'Kojo.'

'Kojo what?'

'Kojo Kuma.'

'I hear you want to go to school?' Kojo nearly said that actually, it was his parents' idea. He liked the thought of it anyway. So he nodded. The four grown-ups jumped on him.

'Hei, that's not done.'

'You cannot use your head to answer questions.'

'You must open your mouth and say: "Please Master, yes."'

The last was from Srako. As for the boy, all he wanted to open his mouth to do was cry. But if he did, everybody will shout at him. That 'a man does not cry.'

'Kojo,' the priest began again, kindly, 'what is your Christian name?'

'Sofo, we have not baptised him yet,' Esi-Yaa cut in.

'So you had not thought of a Christian name.'

'Osofo, no.'

'I can baptise him even this coming Sunday. But we must find him a Christian name.' He paused significantly. Then, 'We shall call him *George*', he said with finality.

As we are all supposed to know, 'George' is nowhere in the Bible. It just happens to be one of the names often given to the men who sit on the throne of England.

'Osofo, we thank you,' Srako and his wife said in unison.

'Thank you, Osofo,' Kojo Kuma piped after his parents.

'Next time, you must say, "Sir ... Thank you, Sir."'

Another pause. 'The child must also have a surname,' the priest pressed on, addressing the parents.

Hardly finding his voice, Srako asked, 'Osofo, what is a surname?'

The man of God chuckled to himself. He cleared his throat, faced the fisherman squarely and explained that 'surname' really meant 'sire's name, a name which you get from your father.'

'Kuma ... Kojo Kuma', the fisherman timidly intervened.

'Ow, said the priest, but that is the boy's *own* name, no?'

'Yes', the mother, the father and the son had all replied. Then Srako added clearly, 'I gave it to him. He was named after his grandfather, my father's father.'

The Reverend had tried to be patient, but all this was taking too long, and getting too far. How could he explain the new system brought by the Europeans to them? He knew that his people's naming system defined each individual clearly, with no ambiguities. However ... but then ... yes, he had to admit it to himself, it was based on some ... eh ... unfortunately primitive matrilineal notions. Whereas the European system of naming people against one singular male line was ... eh ... more ... sensible, Christian and civilized.

His guests watched his face with anxiety. He would have to explain it to them some other time. May be, he could even build a sermon around it, since the question was probably cropping up all over, as people took advantage of the new order and enrolled their children in the white man's schools. This morning though, he doesn't have much time. So barely able to conceal his impatience, he told them that the law from the Europeans said that when children go to school, they must have their father's names as their surname's. So the boy's surname was Srako. He would be registered in school as George Srako.

Another pause. Something had occurred to the priest. Srako is Shilling! He exclaimed into the air. 'Kojo, your name is George Shilling! ... No, since it's your father's name, and you are the son of Shilling! ... Kojo, your name is Shillingson. George Shillingson. George Kojo Shillingson ... G.K. Shillingson!

G.K... G.K... G.K... The priest was very excited. How could he help it? He had just remembered that he had heard there was a distinguished English man called G.K. Chesterton. What he was not sure of was what this other G.K. was distinguished for.

In time. G.K. Shillingson became a distinguished lawyer. He had many children with his lawful Christian wife Mrs. Docia Shillingson, as well as other women: including his receptionists; a young girl from the 'hinterland' who was a servant in his house and at least, one hawker he had lured to his offices. That was to half explain the different kinds of spellings of the name which were passed down over the years.

People also point out that over the years and as an educated, westernized, civilized and a self-consciously developing patriarchy, the Shillingsons spread their male seeds in the countries of Europe. Where, failing to blend their skins into their new environments no matter how hard they tried, they laboured to at least get the family name to conform to the different tribal ways of spelling it.

And so, in time, apart from the original SHILLINGSON, there were SHILLIN-SONS, SHELLINSONS and SHILINSTONS, SHILLINSINS, SHILLINSSONS, SHIL-LINSSENS, SCHILLENSOHNS, SCHIELLINSOHNS, SCHILLEINSENS, SCHIL-LINGSENS, SCHILLENSTEINS and ZWILLENSENS.... They even say that when some got behind the then Iron Curtain – of course, some did! – they became either ZWILLENVITZ, ZVILENSKY or CZVILLENYEV.

Toli Number Three

This is May 1992. We hear that a couple of days ago something interesting happened in Oguaa. A young woman called Achinba was getting married to Dr. Kwesi Shil-lingson. They even say that she is the daughter of one of the schoolmates of the little girl who stood in the sun on Empire Day. We hear that when everything was ready for the wedding, her future mother-in-law called her to her inner chamber to talk to her, woman to woman. That Mrs. Bessie Shillingson had made the mistake of opening the meeting with, 'My Lady, as a future Mrs. Shillingson,...'

'Maa, I shall not call myself Mrs. Shillingson.' Achinba declared.

'Ei,' Mrs. Bessie thought she had not heard right, 'you mean you are not going to marry my son?'

'I am.' Achinba giggled and then continued, 'I am marrying Kwesi. But I want to keep my own name.... I like my name. Besides, you know that as a professional woman, an architect, everybody knows me as Achinba ...'

They say that Achinba need not have bitten back what she was about to say next but had thought better of. Which was that she loved her man, but not his name ... because she had always thought Shillingson sounded funny, and silly.... They say that in fact, Achinba could have said all that and more to Mrs. Bessie. No one would have heard her. Because Mrs. Bessie had decided to faint a long time ago. You know the kind of fainting that only certain women suffer when they do not want to hear, or otherwise deal with, anything unpleasant? ... This kind of fainting, her own son the doctor was later to admit privately to himself, was an art: an art perfected in Europe by the mothers and the wives of the men who built the Empire.

NOTES

1. *Toli* is pidjin for a story. The term is often used to mean 'a tall tale'.
2. The term means 'Youngmen', and refers to a specific group within the Akan socio-political structure.

Buchi Emecheta

Buchi Emecheta was born of Ibuza parentage in Lagos, Nigeria. She came to England in 1962 and now lives in North London. She has written plays for radio and television, articles for journals, four children's stories and ten novels. These include *In the Ditch, Second Class Citizen, The Bride Price* and *The Joys of Motherhood*. Her autobiography, *Head Above Water*, was published in 1986. She has a degree in sociology from London University. In 1980 she was appointed Senior Research Fellow in the Department of English and Literary Studies at the University of Calabar, and she is now a Fellow at the University of London.

In 1983 she was selected as one of the Best British Young Writers, and she is winner of several literary awards, including the *New Statesman* Jock Campbell Award.

She was a member of the Advisory Council to the British Home Secretary on race and equality and also served on the Arts Council of Great Britain.

BUCHI EMECHETA

Head Above Water

I with avowed intent,
To be a Pilgrim...

The lively young voices of the girls at the Methodist High School rang out. Their vibrant silvery echoes burst out of the confines of the school's Assembly Hall, only to reverberate in and among the trees in front of the school compound, and to reach as far as the grey hideous walls that separated the front of the school from the loco-yard opposite. Those grey walls and the elegant trees, all seemed to take up the rhythm of the military Methodist tune in their determination to be like the khakied uniform girls within, pilgrims, pilgrims of Christ.

Hearing those voices from outside the school, the plaintive nostalgic twinge they gave the otherwise orthodox church hymn stood out. The girls did sing in tune, their Welsh Music Mistress, Miss Davies saw to that, yet, and yet, one could tell that those voices were voices from nowhere else than Africa. Because until a few generations back the voices of their grandparents were used in musical village calls, in singing ballads and telling stories in songs, in forest calls and in enhancing the vibrating rhythm of cone-shaped talking drums. Now these girls, the modern girls of twentieth-century Africa, still possess such voices, still with the same strength, still with the same vigour, but now with that added hope and pride, the pride that they were going to be new females of the new Africa. They had been told that their position was unique in history, that they were going to be the black females that would rub shoulders with the types of Miss Davies from Wales, Miss Osborne from Scotland, Miss Verney from England, Miss Humble from Oxford, and Miss Walker from Australia, plus many many other white Missionaries who had left their different countries to come to Lagos, to teach the girls to value their own importance. There were a few black mistresses, one in the Needlework department, and another in the Domestic department, but in the late fifties their influence was still very minimal.

I was late again this morning in leaving my dormitory. I was far from being popular, too shy and too sensitive to be able to forget myself for a while. Because of this; though I craved and bled inwardly for company, yet when in company I was likely to make a fool of myself in doing or saying something wrong, and that wrong thing I would worry about, cry about, bite my nails to the point of almost eating up my fingers. So to be on the safe side I always liked to stay behind deliberately when the others had gone, so that I could read a line of Wordsworth, or a verse of Byron, or Tennyson, then make the short journey from the boarding house, through the trees, that were often still wet from the night dew, with only myself for company, taking my time and walking 'as if next year would do' as our house Mistress, Mrs Okuyemi, often reminded me.

I could deliberate, chew and repeat works of Rupert Brooke, Keats, and Shakespeare, yet I was the daughter of scantily educated parents who came right out of their innocent and yet sophisticated and exotic bush culture. They were innocent to the so-called civilized world. But in communal caring and mutual sharing, in language gestures and music making, they were unsurpassable in their sheer sophistication. But they had to leave all this, my parents, in search of this new thing that was coming from places afar. They left their village homes which had been the habitat of their ancestors so many generations back and came to the city. And there they had me, and they said that I was clever. And they said that because I won something they called scholarship, which my mother used to call 'sikokip', I was to be brought up the new way. That was why instead of being in the village and claying the mud floor of my ancestors, I had to stand there in front of this school compound feeling guilty of having illegally enjoyed Rupert Brooke, and hearing the voices of my already assembled school friends singing.

I sometimes gave the village life a good deal of thought, especially as my people made sure I never lost touch with it. I had to go through all the rituals; tribal marks on the face, clitorization at the early age of eight to give me sexual self control as a young adult and keep me on the straight and narrow, yet I knew even then that, like my parents, I was trapped in this New Thing. But of course to me and all my friends at the Girls' High School it wasn't a New Thing any more, it was becoming a way of life. I was even then feeling like that Prisoner of Chillon, when he cried,

> My very chains and I grew friends,
> So much a long communion tends
> To make us what we are – even I
> Regain'd my freedom with a sigh.

So however much I admired the village life, I knew that for sheer survival I had to make a go of the education the school was offering me free, when almost all the girls in the school were paying. I had to seek more and more the company of myself because I did not pay for my education, and I knew that that made me feel awful, even though I was not given the scholarship out of charity but because I won it. Though to be fair, my parents could not have paid the high fees, how could they, my father had been long dead, and my mother, though a Christian woman, for the sake of survival had gone back to being a native in our village town Ibuza. So though I felt guilty for being on scholarship I was grateful in a way that I had it, because without that good start which those women gave people like me I wonder if I would be here and if you would be reading these horrors. Still, as I was saying, that morning I was late, and I knew I was in trouble. A big Christian girl of fourteen, behaving like a 'bush' girl, irresponsibly. But inside me I knew that I was both a bush girl and a civilized one. I could play both to perfection, depending on the one that was called for. This morning, the humble, quiet Christian was called for, because I was late.

That was why I ran in, stopping by the door, my eyes lowered, my fat navy blue Methodist hymn book clasped to my flat chest (I was a late developer, too skinny). But horror of horrors, I walked into my form Mistress, Mrs Okuyemi. She was black, she was young, she was beautiful, only she never allowed herself to be beautiful. The only day I knew she could smile was when I left school and ran to her house to tell her that I did well in the West African School Examination. She even entertained me. She gave me and my best friend, Kehinde Lawal, a bowl of mixed fruit salad. She treated us like people. So much so that my friend – she was usually more sensible than I was, and I used to copy everything she did because I did not know any other person to copy – said, 'That lady really tried very much to help us, if only we had listened.' Well, it was too late. We had left school by then, and I was already married, even before our school results came out. Anyway all that was still in the future.

This morning Mrs Okuyemi was sitting by the side of our row, as she should, being our form Mistress. She made way for me, not immediately, but kept me waiting long enough for all the subject teachers to see me, standing there. That stupid Ibo girl, with the marks of '10' on her face, had done it again. I stared at the cemented floor. I would not look at anybody's face. Then the other girls all pretended to be disturbed by my lateness. One would have thought that but for my disturbance they would have gone straight away up the imaginary Jacob's ladder in their desire to be the Pilgrim which Bunyan had idealized in his book *The Pilgrim's Progress* on which that hymn was based. I knew they were all being hypocritical, and I was not wrong, because I could see Kofo Olufowokan's perfect teeth flashing behind her hymn book. Then I collided with Bisi, and her chair clattered on the floor, and Miss Davies stopped the piano, and the Head, Miss Walker lowered her glasses, and Miss Humble, a giant of a woman, always in sneakers, stood on tip toe. She was the physical education Mistress and also the head of English and literary studies. I tumbled to the end of the row, to make for the empty seat. Why didn't they allow the empty seat to be near the door, I wondered. But then the late comer would have found life easier that way. Still it was better to be late for an Assembly than not to come at all. Our dear Mrs O would know and would then have a 'word' with the sinner. I would rather disturb the whole school than suffer Mrs O's 'word'. It was Hamlet who boasted that he was going to speak daggers. But our Mrs O's word was sharper than daggers. I know this is difficult to imagine, but that was how we had been conditioned to feel.

The morning service went on, after Miss Davies had put her glasses back on and straightened her already stiff shoulders and had tossed her head back. We soon knelt in prayer and finished the morning assembly by singing the school hymn,

Lord grant us like the watching five,
To wait thy coming and to strive,
Each one her lamp to trim...

I felt this hymn was having a go at me. I was the foolish virgin who did not trim her lamp and was too late and unprepared for the Wedding feast. Some people said this story of the foolish virgins in the bible was symbolic, some of us believed it was real. I remember during one of my school holidays I was explaining the meaning of our school hymn to a distant cousin in Ibuza. She was at school too, but not in a 'big school' like mine. At the mention of the virgin she gasped. 'You mean Jesus Christ refused women, even though they were virgins, simply because they did not trim their stupid lamps?' she asked.

'Not just their lamps, Josephine, they were not ready for the wedding' I began.

'I wish I was there. I can trim and fill twenty million lamps if that is all it will take to be a good woman. Not like this rotten place. You have to be a virgin, a virgin all the time.'

I looked at her, too scared to say a word. We were coming to that age where we were not allowed to say everything that came into our heads. But I suspected that my cousin, Jo, would be in a big trouble on her wedding night. She did not say it, she did not need to. And as if to make me sorrier for her she said, 'One can kill a fowl and pour it on the white cloth you use on your first night with your husband.'

I shook my head. I did not know, but went on, 'My mother said that any other blood would go pale before morning. But the real thing would always be red.'

After an uncomfortable silence, Jo said, 'I can trim lamps. I think Christianity is better. Think of all the beatings and humiliations one would have to go through otherwise. Trimming lamps is easier.'

Jo and I were clitorized on the same day, when we were eight, because we belong to the same age group; yet she was saying this.

I was asking about her the other day, twenty years after this conversation. And I was told she was a nun. Still a nun, when I was writing this. Jo, with the narrow face as the Europeans used to describe her, went into a nunnery because she probably thought God would accept girls who by mistake or curiosity or sheer ignorance had become rather adventurous. The fact that it needs two people to experience such an adventure but it was the girl who had to be penalized, makes one think sometimes. But that was what they said clitorization was supposed to prevent one from doing. I am quite sure I don't know much about that, but if with all that I managed to have five children in five years and all before I was twenty five, imagine what I would have been if I did not have it done. Or is the tradition sheer male brutality? Especially as it was, and still is done in the open, with no anaesthesia of any kind? But I am glad to say all this is slowly dying out. Too slowly perhaps.

Like my cousin Jo, I was taking the school song literally.

But one thing that still surprises me about the discipline of my early school days was our maturity in human relations. No girl reproached you afterwards for disturbing the assembly, not to your face anyway. But the thought of it would die with you. Girls realized even then that that was enough punishment. And that it could happen to them as well. But that they did understand why this kept happening to me, was so humane of them. Or maybe the few people who took the trouble to tell me that I was doing something wrong noticed that I was not confident enough to take any kind of criticism nicely. I still, even now, don't know how people do it. But now I've mastered a beautiful art in which I laugh at myself first, so that when criticisms come, they lose their sharpness and pain. Then I had not mastered the art of masking my emotion. So out of pity, my class-mates would rather not say a word. And because of this, I was ignorant of so many things which the other girls knew and could get away with.

My greatest escape was into literature. I remember clearly the first English story I read by myself. It was Hansel and Gretel, who walked hand in hand and were lost in their bed of flowers in a European wood. I read this book several times in my Primary school, and I knew most of the words by heart. I used to imagine myself lost like that in the bush, so that my relatives with whom I was living at the time would be kinder to me and stop beating me for the slightest thing I did wrong; so that my mother would come and stay with my younger brother and me, like we used to do before our father died; so that my mother would love me so much that she would leave her new native husband, who only had to inherit her and not marry her the way my dead father did. Then the second story was that of 'Snow White'. I used to cry my eyes out with those seven dwarfs. And during the school holidays we used to go home to Ibuza. There I virtually drank in all the old ladies' stories in the village.

Later, towards the end of my school days, my work started to suffer, because the teachers were always intruding into my thoughts, even in the class room. I would build a story in which I was the heroine, and in which I always had enough to eat, and in which I always had a nice bed and not the bug-ridden plank we slept on at Mrs D's boarding house. They used to be such beautiful stories. Thank goodness, I never spoke most of them out. Knowing what I now know of Psychology, I would probably have been certified.

One of the reasons for my imagining my thoughts all by myself happened on the day this story started. After the Assembly, one of the lessons that morning was

English Literature. I always guessed Miss Humble did not like me. There was nothing to like about me, anyway. I was always too serious looking, with formidable glasses, and not particularly clean or clever. My class work was steadily going down, and this was making life more difficult. The position was so circular. It was like this. I was afraid of leaving school, it was not a beautiful life but at least it was safe, it was reliable. Because of this fear, I started to dream of another beautiful world, but the funniest thing about this world was that I was always the mother of many children. And the more I wallowed in my dreams, to the extent even of bringing them into the class room, the more my work suffered, and the greater my fear. Because if one was on scholarship and failed an exam, the scholarship would be taken from that person. I made a good grade in the end, but to achieve this, I drove myself to the brink almost, knowing that it was either that or to die.

Anyway, the tall and broad Miss Humble never liked me. Because I wanted her to like me like she did my friend Kehinde Lawal, I used to really try in her literature lesson. And her subject was my best anyway. I used to dream most in Mrs Osho's Maths lesson, especially when she came to the black board with her horrible looking board compass. Girls who were clever in her Maths class said she was good. But I was not good in her subject. Much much later, how I wished she was with me when I had to take Social Statistics when I was reading for my degree in Sociology.

Anyway, Miss Humble did not like me and that was that. And if she did not like me, she had more excuse after my shameful behaviour in the Assembly that morning. She was reading Coleridge's 'Christabel' and was going

Tu-whit! – Tu-whoo!
And hark, again! the crowing cock,
How drowsily it crew.

My mouth was agape in wonder. I was no longer looking at a young English teacher with an M.A. in English from Oxford, but I was back in the village land of my ancestors. I was listening to the voice of my father's little mother, with her big head covered in white woolly curls, with saliva trickling down the corner of her mouth, with her face sweating and shining in the sweat, and me sitting by her feet, and the Ukwa tree giving us an illusive shade from the bright moon, and the children, the young ones who could not sit still for stories playing Ogbe. I was there in Ibuza, in Umuezeokolo, in Odanta, where all my people came from. I was there in that place and did not hear the young English woman born in the Lake District and trained at Oxford, calling me, calling me. Suddenly somebody nudged me. Then Miss Humble's voice came through. Sharp. Angry.

'Florence! Florence! what are you going to be when you grow up?'

'A writer,' I replied.

Silence.

She stretched herself, standing on her toes as if she was determined to reach the ceiling, and pointed stiffly at me. Then she said in a hoarse low voice, her protruding teeth looking as if they were going to fall out and the white hanky she tied around her watch with the masculine band twitching, 'Pride goes before a fall!'

I was now fully awake. 'I said I would like to be a writer,' I began again, just in case she did not hear me at first.

'Go out, out, and straight to the chapel. Go there and pray, for God to forgive you.'

'Eh?' I said.

'And take a bad Mark!'

I then knew this was serious. I was by the door, ready to run for it. Bad marks were added up and shown in one's school report. Some girls even said they put them in one's leaving school testimonial. But nonetheless I wanted to find out what I had exactly done to warrant this untoward punishment. I hesitated just for a split second, my eyes not leaving her face, as she stood there in her ramrod erectness, her hand stretched straight like a poker. I saw her mouth making the shape of another 'bad Mark'. It was then that I ran, past the large glass window of our class room that faced the verandah in the front part of the school. I did not stop until I was sure Miss Humble could see me no longer. Then I started to walk slowly up the stairs towards the chapel that was on the first floor of our large E-shaped school.

My mind was at first blank, with only Miss Humble's voice ringing in my ears. The voice of authority. The voice one had been taught to associate with correctness. The voice one had never questioned. The voice that had simply to be obeyed. Then as I neared the door of the chapel, my own voice, little and at first insecure, started to filter in. 'What are you going to tell God, eh? What Florence are you going to tell Him, when you go inside there to ask His forgiveness. Are you going to say, "Please dear God, don't make me a writer" ... and then at the same time say, "But dear God, I so wish to be a writer, a story teller like our old mothers at home in Ibuza. But unlike them, I would not have to sit by the moonlight because I was born in an age of electricity, and would not have to tell my story with my back leaning against the Ukwa tree, because now I have learnt to use a new tool for the same art. Now I have learnt a new language, the language of Miss Humble and the rest of them. So where is the sin in that?"'

My voice suddenly grew louder, bolder, and it covered up the voice of Miss Humble. I reached the chapel door, and with my head up, I walked past it. God had more important things to do than punish me for saying my dream aloud. Not only did I not go into that chapel to pray, I did not call the bad mark either. I thought about that for many a night, and I came to the conclusion that Miss Humble probably felt that her language was too pure for the likes of me to want to use it to express myself. Hence to her it was pride to say what I said. But why did she take the trouble to leave her island home and come and teach it to us in the first place? This was one example of the duplicity and near hypocrisy which at that age used to make my head ache so much whenever I wanted to puzzle things out .

But on one point she got me. And that was ordering me out of the class. That kind of action was to us like that meted out to a leper, being excommunicated for just simply being a leper.

I laughed very much when I remembered this scene twenty years later when I was in London, teaching English to English children, and had to order a very difficult and disturbing sixteen-year-old Cockney boy out of the class. I was still new as a teacher. Instead of being ashamed and sorry, the boy was happy and became noisier and started to make faces at the rest of the class through the window. He did not stop at this, but started to bang things against the wall and this brought the school head. I saw him talk to the boy, and with his face purple with anger he asked me in front of the class what I thought I was doing, ordering a boy out of the class. I tried to explain, but the head refused to understand. He made it perfectly clear that in schools like his, the children rule, and teachers have to obey. If you send a child out of the class, you have given him the freedom to go out and vandalize the school, the streets, do all sorts of things. How did those early teachers manage to put such values into us? I soon learnt the ropes in that school. England is a welfare State, one does not need too much education to survive. Nigeria was then and is still now a capitalist state, where you have to work at anything you do to survive. No dole money, no unemployment benefit, and education is highly rewarded. The gap between the rich and the non-rich is very wide. It is nice to be able to travel and sometimes live away from one's native land. I would not be able to know that but for the fact that I was later to live in England.

Anyway, as I was saying, I did not call in my bad mark on the following Friday as one was supposed to do, because I felt that I had done nothing wrong. But for the rest of my school career I made sure never to anger a teacher so much as to send me out of the class. So that when I left school, my head, Miss Walker, said in my testimonial that I was mild, pleasant and placid. And she was sure I would do well in anything I set my heart on. Well she was wrong, about the latter. About the former attributes, I would have been something else, the opposite in fact, if I was only sure of how people would take my outbursts.

I set my mind on making a successful marriage. They taught us at Girls' High School that prayers and devotion could move mountains. Well it did not work out for me that way. And as my marriage neared its end, and I was trying so much to make it work, to make him proud of me, I did again what I did to Miss Humble. That seemed to be my last card in every bad situation. But this time, I did not just say it, I actually wrote it down to prove to him that I was something. He got angry and burnt my first manuscript. And I felt the native, bush independent woman in me come to the fore. I packed my dripping four children and pregnant self and faced the streets of London. The perseverance which one had learnt to go through during one's school days, coupled with reading so many novels and the capability of being able to think and dream, taught me what everybody knows but only sometimes remembers, namely that no situation is permanent. Those babies with wet nappies dangling between their legs are now grown-up young men and women, battling for University places. Children do become adults. And I said to myself that one day, just one day, when they become adults and I am in my forties, then I would be so confident that I would not have to ask anybody's opinion, then I would write. I would then not need Miss Humble to give me a nice smile and say 'Good girl, keep it up,' neither would I need a husband to say, 'But you are such a clever wife, do keep it up, and keep writing.'

As it came about, I started to write when I was still in my mid-twenties, but still as insecure as ever. And somehow I survived, just, my head above water, all those years in England. It reads like a story, even to me, so if it reads like that to you, I won't blame you at all. Because sometimes I don't believe some of the things that happened to me. It is very true that some facts can be stranger than fiction.

Lauretta Ngcobo

Lauretta Ngcobo is a South African by birth. She left South Africa twenty-nine years ago and went into political exile. She spent the first six years of her exile in different countries in Africa and then came to live in Britain. Initially she had left her children in South Africa with her mother. Later they were able to join her, as was her husband, and once that happened, it was possible for all of them to live together as a family for the first time in Britain. Lauretta was a teacher by profession, and worked as such until a year ago when she retired. She has published two novels, *Cross of Gold* (Longman, 1981) and *And They Didn't Die* (Virago, 1990), as well as several essays on the subject of African women and their concerns. She has also edited an anthology of writing by black women, *Let it be Told*.

LAURETTA NGCOBO

My King and Another King

Daughter of the Empire. Ngh ... I am a daughter of the Empire. At least I am supposed to have metamorphosed from its cocoon. Of course I am no longer one. Now I am a creation of another oddity, APARTHEID. But Apartheid has not obliterated all memories of that incubatory stage from which I metamorphosed, the Empire. I remember clearly the absurdities of that earlier period which left me with a strangely bifocal view of life. I perceived it that way even as a child, and had many questions that I could not frame clearly, and which therefore remained unanswered. There was something strangely incongruous about belonging to two countries, having two kings, two languages and a racial barrier down the middle. The spurious notion of England as a motherland for all who lived within an English-speaking world of many peoples was phoney even then.

I was assisted into this questioning frame of mind by my grandmother, more than anyone else. She made it clear to me and my many cousins that our existence was on two planes, very diffused but very real. My grandmother, unlike other people's grandmothers that I knew, never told us a single folk tale. Our fire-side stories were real episodes from history. The live history of the Zulu people. I cannot pretend that at the time these were riveting tales, but we listened carefully, and we imbibed passively what we could. These stories differed markedly from the magical fantasy tales that mother told us. Grandmother brought an uncomfortable awareness to us of a life that had suffered a break, a disfigurement that would have to be put right with time. We experienced a sense of loss even though she made constant references to the deathless power of the Zulus and their history.

It was in school that this sense of displacement was confirmed. In geography classes they told of that country far away which was the epitome of all that was beautiful, powerful, just and perfect in every way. And that country was Great Britain. In brief, we called it England. This, against what was a crumbling system of cultural values, social structure and economic wellbeing under the stress of the Colour Bar, the precursor of Apartheid. There were bound to be questions.

The history of that Kingdom was so paramount that it had to be taught in our schools, to the total exclusion of our own history. If grandmother's heroes were the greatest, how could we have greater kings far away, to whom we owed greater loyalty, I reasoned silently. It was hard to live with these two conflicting versions of history. In class I often asked questions that clearly showed my confusion. These early conflicts put me off the subject of history for the rest of my education. Somehow I could never believe in the authenticity of history as a subject. Buried in it is a deep lie.

Our first lesson in music involved learning the British National Anthem. At the time we spoke very little English. I remember vividly the tortuous exercise hour after hour, day after day, trying to learn the words as well as the tune and to fathom the meaning and relevance of the anthem:

Gad sav ah greshus kin'
Lon' live ah knobble kin',
Gad sav ah kin'.

Sen' heem viktoryus,
Happi an gilory-us,
Lon' to ren over us,
Gad sav the kin'.

I wonder what the inspector who came at the end of that year made of our rendition. I forget his name. But I can never forget the sweating and the finger biting as I stood before him on that hot December day. He had travelled far into the recesses of rural South Africa. At the time I failed to understand why a person of his intelligence and position should put himself through such agony. Of what possible value could our befuddled efforts be to England, I often wondered. Yet today I know that it was all in the service of the Empire; the early effort to sever us from our first loyalty, which should be to our own culture, our language, and our consciousness.

To further enhance the image of the great King of England we had to celebrate Empire Day. All schools were part of this yearly demonstration of loyalty. It was one of the only two national holidays in our school calendar that were set aside to extol any leader or country. (The other being Dingaan's Day, December 16, which was for Africans the day of our mortification.) As children we enjoyed the upheaval, for it threw every school time-table into chaos as we abandoned most classes to practise sports and music for all the inter-school competitions to be held on the day. There would be school outings and picnics in which whole communities took part. For me one of these outings raised more questions than it answered. We were going to the seaside, a prospect that aroused endless dreams as we lived a long way from the sea. When we finally arrived we were awe-struck. The immensity of the sea was unbelievable. The great King lived beyond the vast sea – mega images. It was beyond all our imaginings. We were playing cautiously along the seashore when we saw something that not only diverted our attention but also released our tension. It was a group of white people. Obviously out to enjoy their own picnic on this quiet stretch of the seashore. Perhaps to escape the jollities of the English. Looking back in later life, I concluded that they were unmistakably Afrikaner. Not that we could have known much about such differences at the time. For us one white was like another. They were so awkwardly dressed and all so obese that they looked a spectacle to rural children like us. In those days there were many poor whites among the Afrikaner but we at the time thought no white person had any reason to be poor. Poverty was our prerogative. For some reason, the sight of the massive flesh, spilling over their tight, shabby swimming costumes raised a sudden peal of laughter among us children. We laughed as we pointed at them and for a brief moment they were the butt of our ridicule. By the time our teacher had silenced us, the damage had been done.

Two days later, back in school, the teachers received a letter from the education authorities, forbidding us to use the beach ever again. This raised questions in my young foggy mind. Here we were, coming to commemorate the great white King and his Empire. And now this, from his fellow whites. These were white people and to my young mind this action invested even the poorest of them with immense power. As far as I was concerned, they could have been the King's own cousins. All that benevolence that I had conjured up through the teachings about the great white King was suddenly put to serious doubt. It was hard to dissociate the whites at the beach from the King of England. We all felt terribly aggrieved and sensed rashness if not intolerance in the pronouncement. We learned early that ours was to laud and extol the white man and anything to the contrary was to be punished. It also reinforced in our minds the power and authority of all white people. They owned the beach, and perhaps the sea. They could declare where one could go or not go. We were on the road to learning our place in the scale of things.

Schooldays rolled by and Grandmother's tales slowly faded into a romantic fictionalized history. None of us had seen the King of the Zulus or heard any of his pronouncements. We could not produce proof of his existence. In contrast, Britain slowly materialized as a vibrant entity in our literature lessons, our songs, our history lessons, our Girl Guide Movement and many other manifestations. This was reinforced in 1947 when the King and Queen of England and their daughters came to visit South Africa. After all, weren't the Princesses in the Girl Guide Movement too, like us? Did we not share the same allegiance?

I promise, on my honour,
To do my duty to God,
The king and my country;
To help other people at all times,
And to obey the Guide Law.

Here was irrefutable proof of a living royal family, a thriving reality. Our loyalty was justified. The euphoria swept over us all.

Those of us who were fortunate enough to be in senior classes were dutifully shepherded to see the royal family. Throngs of people filled the Durban Greyville aerodrome. White people on one side, Africans on the opposite, Coloureds and Indians on either side. Milling crowds everywhere, food, drinks, noise and the heat beating down on us all. It all served to heighten the fervent dreams and fantasies of a dispossessed youth. Then big choirs sang to welcome the King and his family. Special tributes had been composed and they were all in the idiom of royal salutations in the Zulu and Xhosa languages. Bitter irony. We actually voiced our own subjection in our own words for the whole world to hear. And saying it, we had enjoyed it. Words that were reserved for no one else but our own King had actually been sung in obeisance to the King of England. BAYEDE, BAYEDE, NKOSI YAMAKHOSI. (Bring them, Bring them, O King of kings. Bring them to come and pay homage.) As night descended we dragged our feet back to school. Shattered. I was walking beside Eunice when I heard her murmur, 'To wash their (the Princesses') feet would be an honour big enough for me.'

For all our deification of the British King, nothing changed for us materially. Nor was there any favourable change in white attitudes towards us as the subjects of their King. In fact it seemed to have made the situation worse, judging by the events of the following year when the Nationalist government came to power with the policy of Apartheid in tow. That King had not lifted a finger to ameliorate the suffering of any of his black subjects. It should not have come as a shock really for most thinking adults. The earlier King of England had been as disappointing after the Anglo-Boer War. Our forefathers had shown great partisanship on the side of the English and had pinned their hopes on the fair-mindedness of the English. But as soon as that war was over, they had gone and agreed to our complete exclusion from the Union of South African States that was formed. The Act of Union became the cradle of Apartheid.

Disillusionment is slow-footed. Many African men had just returned from horrific war service in many parts of the world. In all that searing experience, in all those years, they had been paid a meagre £3 a quarter; a total of £12 a year. Even by South African standards that was low, less than what a miner earned in those days. On their return they were given a bicycle each, as their pension I suppose. The King of the British Empire had come ostensibly to thank his subjects for their patriotic services. A lot of people who returned to great poverty will be forgiven if they entertained great hopes that the King would consider their grievances, and force a change of attitude among white South Africans. After all, if he ruled South Africa he should be able to influence decisions that affected the kingdom. However, one man I knew gained some vital experience while he was overseas. He let it be known, to all and sundry, that he had learned new ways of making love and it had completely changed his life. He became the envy of many men, and his wife was the envy of all women in the neighbouring villages. Nobody trusted him near their women.

These events had a great influence on me, and they helped to shape me into the person that I am now. A host of things that could be defined as political also started to make sense while I was at boarding school. At the same time I had endless questions that I could not even ask anyone about, let alone having them answered. We had a large body of women teachers, both black and white. I had not been very well for some time, showing certain vitamin deficiencies. Miss Cowey, a stern but very kind matron, instructed me to go regularly to their dining-room to get yeast for my diet. I hated the yeast, even though it helped me within a short time. But not before I had observed that white teachers had their meals as a group on their own. The African teachers had theirs in another building. And the quality of food could not have been more different. In later years I rationalized that the African staff could not possibly have afforded all that wonderful food that I saw at Stanwood Cottage. In South Africa, where the colour of one's skin makes such a big difference to one's pay packet, it is quite possible that the African teachers could not afford to live better than they did. However, at that stage, I could not make much sense of it. It simply heightened my feelings of grievance. But these feelings could not find any expression because the African teachers themselves showed no rancour at all.

Boarding school. It is not that I did not like it. In fact, in later years, I acknowledged that this was one of the happiest times of my life. But the idea of boarding schools was very foreign to us. It caused me endless pain in the early years. I was 11 when I went to my first boarding school. At the beginning of every term I cried for days, and few things have given me as much heartache as leaving home for school did. I could hardly eat any of the provisions that my mother had so carefully prepared, because each time I opened the provisions basket, I would burst into tears.

There was the issue of language, in particular the issue of the mother tongue. Having to learn almost every subject in the medium of English, the anxiety of the teachers to make us fluent in English can be understood. It has never occurred to South Africans, even to this day, that Africans can learn, and conceptualize more easily, in their own languages. To further the aims of the school we had to speak nothing but English throughout the week, and our languages only at weekends. It caused a great deal of difficulty and was an incessant source of annoyance at the time. And I was not alone. We resorted to 'dressing' our Zulu/Xhosa/Sotho in English. 'Zuluwising' English, as it was called, means producing sentences that were structurally English, but with most of the vocabulary in Zulu. It didn't matter how often we were punished for this, we all continually did it. Sometimes I am amazed how I finally learned to speak proper English. For every instance of 'Zuluwising', one acquired a bad mark. The penance was paid on Saturdays, in our own free time, when we had to work while the lucky ones (the ones who had not been caught in the act) were enjoying themselves. In the scorching heat we worked in the gardens, planting new flowers and new vegetables, sweeping the leaves or doing other seasonal chores. The language question caused more problems that it was worth. In our school, we were so well guarded that visitors coming to see us were screened carefully. If their direct relationship to the girl in question could not be established, they were often sent away without being allowed to see her. Our letters too were screened, which meant they had to be written in English. Our teachers took the trouble to find out which of us had parents who could not communicate in English. For these, the letters were screened by a black teacher who could read our languages. I was not one of those. I stood no chance, as my mother was known to be an old Inanda girl herself. Not only did my mother tolerate this situation with pleasure but my grandmother did as well, for they were both Inanda girls who had put up with the same rules in their own time. At first I found it most uncomfortable writing to my mother in English. I was always being ticked off for my mistakes.

In the end South Africa was cast out of the British Empire. Of course white South Africans never put it that way. They like to feel that the Empire had degenerated into a jamboree of unthinking, uncivilized new members, and therefore was no longer good enough for them. This was 1960 and the National Party had been in power for about twelve years. Apartheid was in full swing. The 1960s was also the period that saw the liberation of many of the British colonies in Africa. And these newly liberated states found South Africa's policy of Apartheid an affront. They were on a collision course. It is worth mentioning here that the British at home and in South Africa did very little to change the course of Apartheid. One highly respected South African of British extraction, Olive Schreiner, once said the British legacy to the world is their great sense of freedom, personal freedom:

> It is this which we believe and hold to be the peculiar attribute of the English people, our one gift which we have to contribute to the general sum of humanity's wealth – the desire not only to be free, but to make free – the consciousness of the importance of the individual as individual apart from any attributes of sex, nationality, talent or wealth.... It is the profound faith, not in the equal talent, virtues, and abilities of men, but in the equal right of the poorest, most feeble, most ignorant, to his own freedom and to a perfect equality of treatment.

It is this which the Empire failed not only to recognize, but to accord us as a people. But this is not the place to lay bare what it did instead.

Cherry Clayton

Cherry Clayton has produced fiction, poetry and critical essays. Her publications include a collection of essays, *Women and Writing in South Africa: A Critical Anthology* published by Heinemann. Formerly a lecturer at the Rand Afrikaans University, she is now based in Canada.

CHERRY CLAYTON

Buried Treasure

This is dedicated to my parents, Edward Clayton and Joyce McQuade Clayton.

When I think of the late forties and fifties, of how I spent my childhood and adolescence in South Africa, I think of a time of personal and political innocence, though ignorance would be a more accurate word. I was born in a nursing-home in Sea Point in September 1943 (at noon, just in time for my mother to have her lunch, she always says). She sent my father, home from the war 'up north', off in his square black Ford with the wide running-boards, to register their first and only daughter as Anne Clayton. Next to her in the nursing-home a new mother had called her daughter Cherry, which my mother thought a silly name (as it is!). When my father returned he announced that he had registered me as Cherry Ann, an act of male defiance which still calls forth irritated sighs from my mother, almost fifty years later. All of my brothers were named after English cricketers: Keith, Roger and Clive. I often think if the MCC had included women cricketers I might have ended up with a right royal name after all, the one I narrowly escaped. My father had claimed his daughter: an ambiguous inheritance I have spent my life struggling against, like the dubious mantle of Empire.

My English grandfather had left London with his second wife, Alice Cole, and his growing brood of children (five by the first wife and later five boys by the second) in 1913, when my father was 2 years old. My grandfather, a bullying but enterprising man, has always been the focus of family legends and atrocities: his meanness, his attempts to control all of his children even into early manhood and especially womanhood, his abrupt manner and sense of family would be endlessly discussed at family gatherings. At Christmas he would insist on a photograph of the clan, himself wearing a favourite white suit. His children all ran away from home as soon as they could (my father and his brother Jack rode away from home, and would both become well-known South African cyclists, indicating the force of their need for a speedy escape).

The two sons from the first marriage fled to the United States from England, before the South African immigration. The two daughters had less luck: my Aunt Kay, who died in her nineties just after my departure from South Africa in 1990, told me how, as a young woman in her twenties, she had run away from 'the old man', as he was always called, to Johannesburg, hoping to get a job with the firm for which she had worked in Cape Town. One day, walking down the street in Braamfontein, Johannesburg, she suddenly saw her father approaching her. That was it. She went home. There was no escape for young women. If the story has a Dickensian flavour, he was a trifle Dickensian. I tell the stories to show how intertwined the authority of Empire and patriarchal family control were.

I enjoyed my aunt's failed escape story, feeling a solidarity with her which was not often there, because she prided herself on her English accent and use of the language, whereas I saw myself then, and still do, as irredeemably colonial and with a primary loyalty to South Africa, not England. I discovered, like Margaret Laurence when she went to Scotland, that when I went to England it wasn't any kind of home;

that we were 'mock English'; South Africa was home. In Canada, which has become my new home (this article has given me the chance to say that for the first time, unambiguously), some people tell me I sound like an elitist Brit! Perhaps we're all doomed to become our most unappealing ancestors.

Our mock-Englishness consisted of references to my father's birth 'within the sound of Bow Bells', calculated to irritate my mother and any Irish in-laws within hearing; and long, uninformed and pedantic arguments about fine points of English grammar. My grandfather's traditional Christmas gift was an English 'classic' novel, *Treasure Island* or *Robinson Crusoe* or *A Christmas Carol*, meticulously marked up and proof-read by him (he was a proof-reader for The Cape Argus in Cape Town, and apprenticed two of his sons, Ted, my father, and the aforementioned Jack, to the printing trade). I can still see those first reading books with his careful corrections. There's always been some ink in my blood.

My first years were spent on Clifton beaches: my parents lived in a bungalow on Fourth Beach, and then in Johannesburg after my father was demobbed, from 1945 to 1947. My grandfather owned a bungalow on First Beach until his death. The feel of gritty sand on the legs, the sunny outside bathroom, the inside smells of damp and musty age, with my 'grandmother's' watercolours (she was his fifth wife; the others had succumbed or been sacked), I remember from my childhood visits. When I last saw the writer Jack Cope, who took a short story of mine for *Contrast* when I had little hope of publication, he reminded me that he had known my parents at Clifton. I welcomed the memory: there were phases of my life when my interests seemed so remote from my parents' lives that such social connections were later quite startling.

My first memories are from 12 Breda Street in the Gardens of Cape Town, where we lived from 1947 to 1952. Elizabeth Curren, in J.M. Coetzee's *Age of Iron*, drives down Breda Street at one point, and thinks of setting herself alight after driving down the oak-lined Government Avenue, which was part of our familiar walk. Walking up it you passed the bastions of the Mount Nelson Hotel, and you could buy wonderful ice-cream and frozen milk suckers on Mill Street. The house had an oak tree at the front gate, more memorable than the house; in the front room we had gentle and courteous Polish refugees as boarders; up the road was the Good Hope Seminary where I went to school. Diagonally opposite is the old age home where my Aunt Kay died very recently, and where I last saw her being guided by my father (she was almost blind) along a slightly uneven pavement. Some circle was completed for me at that moment, a different and less final one than hers. Nearby was the lane to the school where I had searched for the 'treasure' of gold beetles under the leaves of the Morning Glory hedge, and the garden of childhood. Later, in another garden in Johannesburg, my son and his best friend would bury glass bottles and treasures under the huge belhambra tree, and later search for them with huge excitement, as if they held the key to their lives.

My family's history is part of the ordinary life of Cape Town, an ancient, unrecorded history of submerged people following the teeming everyday life of need and desire, conflict and gaiety, like Bloom's course through a Dublin day in *Ulysses*. My father knows the streets and byways of the old Cape Town like the palm of his hand; his father had run a boarding-house, Leeds House, and once managed the cafeteria at the top of Table Mountain. My mother's family was even more rooted in Cape Town: she was born there of an Irish father and a South African mother (called Van der Merwe: Van der Merwe jokes, often involving a clan of baboons, always had a wild hilarity in family humour). The tension between snooty English relatives and Irish in-laws reenacted some of the tensions of Empire in my childhood. The family is an empire too.

At Breda Street, the smell of Friar's Balsam and kerosene lamps permeated everywhere: two of my younger brothers were ill with bronchitis as babies; one, Rodney, died in infancy. Motherhood was a time-consuming and anxious occupation in those days. I must have identified with the mother's role: one photograph shows me with plastic handbag and doll's pram, looking anxious about my responsibilities. But the real discovery of those years, and the real link with England, was through reading. Enid Blyton's *Magic Faraway Tree* and *The Wishing Chair* were read to us at school by a Miss Noakes. They offered several layers of magic which I have never outgrown the need for: a transport into another world, an imagined world of infinite possibilities and constant change. To go down the garden and enter that secret and fascinating world: to go up the tree and meet the Saucepan Man and other oddities, to reach the top where the land could magically change! I still stick up for Enid Blyton because of those books. Later I enjoyed the Famous Five books too; people had unlikely names, and the weather was a bit confusing, but I wasn't aware of being patronized, colonized or preached at. I loved school because I loved books, even exercise books; any form of paper, pens, reading and writing materials excited me. And reading seemed to give me licence to dream, to share the dreams of others, to forget daily reality, perhaps, the smell of Friar's Balsam and sick children.

As I was growing up I spent the equally ignorant fifties of my adolescence in Durbanville, then a quiet village with tennis, many churches and ballet lessons. Whatever I knew of 'Empire' came to me and my family in the most ordinary way from England: the *Woman's Weekly*, my mother's journal, with those odious, stodgy photographs of the royal princesses growing up in hats and coats we imitated when we went to church, and my younger brother's *Dandy* and *Beano* comics. The *Woman's Weekly* usually had a demure, pearl-buttoned lady on the cover, with cold-waved blonde hair and a freshly knitted pastel-coloured home sweater over her ladylike bosom. 'Which Twin had the Toni' was a question I thoughtfully pondered; I read the love stories (something inescapable corroded my fantasy life in those years and continues to undermine my feminism). I read the agony columns, which were extremely genteel compared with today's outspoken queries. They generally concerned health and motherhood, household hints and patterns. Their domestic message must have passed me by, because I hated all domestic accomplishments and would hide my grubby pieces of knitting from the domestic science teacher, who would try to tug them away to examine them. Sewing classes were torture. My brother's comics escaped me, too, though I sometimes read them, as I read their *Just William* books and later their *Hardy Boys* and *Biggles* books. I was undiscriminating; and something told me that I should try to do everything that boys did if I was going to get on in the world. Everything I could, that is. Simultaneously I would swoon over a novel called *Strange Rapture* (which I read frequently, in the bath) in which a dark and handsome man has to make up his mind between a young fair woman and a bold woman who paints her fingernails red, always a sign of lax morals. I complacently identified with the adorable and modest winner. I wanted passionate love and I wanted the world of action, which seemed to belong to men. I still do. What I have learned is that they are not so easy for women to reconcile, though I'm still trying. (There's not so much time left before compulsory retirement.) One of the main appeals of Alice Munro's fiction for me, much later (fictions can take you to countries, too), was that she seemed to me to tell the truth about the shoddy compromises and quiet desperations in which girls and women actually live, as opposed to the ideological purity in which the apparatchiks tell us we ought to live. My messy desires and outward unction made me an Alice Munro character before I read her fiction, but I instantly recognized myself.

My voracious reading seemed to have very little to do with Empire (though I'm sure a good Althusserian could make out a case). Where I was affected by the attitudes of Edwardian Empire was in education. One of the unthinking axioms of the English Edwardian family, passed on to my father, was that girls did not need an education. Boys did. Girls would marry, so any education would be wasted. This entertains me now; then I was simply aware that if I wanted an education I would have to struggle for it. I was almost hijacked into a typing pool by my father's prejudices and the educational system of streaming academic and non-academic students from the middle years of high school. The kind intervention of my school principal prevented this; I was too prickly and ungrateful an adolescent (I became a prickly and ungrateful adult later) to see what he did for me then, but I am in his debt.

We seemed to inhabit, in the fifties, an untroubled dream of Empire: I spent my life up on points in ballet classes, at eisteddfods and concerts, on tennis courts, at Presbyterian church services, communion and confirmation. On Sundays the roast chicken sizzled steadily in the oven while we were at church or Sunday school, sticking Jesus and lambs onto green fuzzy backcloth. In the afternoon I would sun my 'naturally curly' hair on the back steps of the house. When not in ballet shoes I was riding around the village on my bicycle, or playing tennis. The thing about these ordinary colonial rituals, I now see, was that they left you free at a deeper level to dream and grow. There was time for reverie, in which the imagination develops, which is the basis of all later transactions with others and with what D.H Lawrence calls 'the circumambient universe'. (I have to recall in the same breath that Bessie Head said she left South Africa because in it black people have no time to dream.) Other countries I knew from my elder brother's stamp collection, if I knew them at all: brightly coloured and exotic squares and triangles, birds, trees, faces and ships. My imagination was caught by the 'penny black', so ordinary, yet rare and valuable, and by the 'black tulip' of the Dumas classic. They seemed avenues to the mysterious, to the paradoxical realm of the imagination.

Of actual black life in South Africa, of racial injustice and dispossession, we knew almost nothing. My family was a part of what Olive Schreiner called the 'lower middle-class Philistines' who made up most of the white population. I no longer think that comment so damning, or quite true. Much of life is lived in that realm, which is also the substance of art. For children like us it was a country of moderate health. We seemed to live out an uncomplicated South-Africanness, with dog, children, family rituals, sport, and a series of generally part-time Coloured servants. (It was only when I moved to Johannesburg in the late sixties that the vast, teeming black life of the country became a visible reality to me.) In our relationships with these servants there was often humour and frankness, sulks and quarrels. We knew about their boyfriends and private lives, as they knew about ours. My parents often struggled for money: poverty lessened the gap between employers and servants.

I suppose what I'm saying is that in South Africa the force of the British Empire was not constraining for people like us, though we lived ignorantly inside its transplanted cultural habits and manners, even its prejudices. My father worked hard to try and make a living; my mother worked hard to supplement his income and raise her children. Her natural talent in caring for people meant there were often lame dogs and hard-up relatives or friends around. Education was not segregated in terms of language groups, so high school years were spent in mingled study and leisure with Afrikaans-speaking students. In the last year of high school I went on a tour to the Victoria Falls with just such a group. We were unpoliticized, ignorant and happy together, though there were earnest discussions about how the different language groups (this meant English and Afrikaans-speakers) should seek closer understanding. It would have been unthinkable for anyone to suggest that this was in order to maintain white power; our history books told us about the Great Trek and the follies of Napoleon; South African trekkers were beleaguered and heroic.

I grew up listening to family stories, which meant mostly my father's stories about the army and sport. He was a bombardier, went to Robben Island to take charge of the Cape Corps, and was then a Staff-Sergeant in the 2nd Anti-Aircraft regiment in Egypt. The war, which took men like him into countries they would never otherwise have visited, gave them a taste of the abuses of power among men but also a sense of comradeship, of a shared and ultimate vulnerability. I thought of the world of his war stories when I first read George Orwell's phrase: 'No bomb that ever burst/ Can shatter the crystal spirit.' The humorous Aussies and the big-hearted Canadians who featured in his war stories were also his comrades in sport: he went to the Empire Games in 1934 and to the Olympics in 1936. I feel some of the same comradeship with other colonials, which is why I felt at my first ACLALS conference that I was meeting the members of a larger family who had been away for a while, and recognizing them for the first time.

What I'm suggesting is that some of the automatically oppressive implications of imperialism are cancelled out, for me, by the implications of the Commonwealth, the shared condition of colonialism. At least this is true of people like myself, a privileged daughter of Empire. I would be hard put to classify myself as one of the oppressed, though I think women, even white women in South Africa, do have subtle forms of indoctrination to struggle free from. No doubt some of them were embedded in the text of my favourite adolescent novel, *Strange Rapture*. The literature which was offered to me, along with the language, was a gift, not an imposition. I do not feel oppressed by it, though I would, these days, naturally mingle all of the literatures in English as a teacher and critic. The abundance and richness of English literature seem to me to cancel out, rather than intensify, any sense of domination from a metropolitan centre. Literature carries us into so many worlds, worlds without end. My perception that this is the case is tied up with my privileged daughterhood in terms of Empire.

South Africa is a special case within the Commonwealth constellation in many ways. One feature often overlooked is that the history of the country has been a history of contestation between two empires: the English and the Dutch. Anglo-Dutch and Anglo-Boer hostility can be seen as the real mainspring of the country's history, a framework within which high apartheid becomes the final Republican kick of the old Dutch Empire at the British who dared to send their liberal messengers out to abolish slavery and force the Boers northward into their conservative Republics. The British Empire contained the seeds of a liberal ethic as well as its own forms of imperialism, no matter how far liberalism may have fallen in reputation in South Africa. At many points in South African history, Britain was seen as a liberal protector from the worst abuses of Afrikaner nationalism. This has diluted the kind of resentment at the British Empire found in other ex-colonies. I sense a more straightforward anger at British imperialism in Australians, for instance, and certainly a much more bitter response to the use of the English language in writers like Jamaica Kincaid. Black intellectuals like Es'kia Mphahlele in South Africa have been far more welcoming of English as a tool of liberation and artistic expression.

I know now that the pain of black life was concealed by my ignorance when I was growing up. In 1959, just before our trip to the Victoria Falls, about 600 African women were in jail in Natal after widespread unrest and riots. Lutuli, ANC President-General, listed the causes as mass removals, influx control, passes for women, increases in rates and taxes, forced labour for women without payment and low wages in relation to the increased cost of living. In March and April, 1960, during my last high school year, the non-violent anti-pass campaign led to the notorious police shootings at Sharpeville and Langa, which left 83 'non-white' civilians dead and 365 injured by police bullets. This suffering, and the typical deep conditions of which it was an expression, came from a South Africa my childhood had hidden from me. I became more aware of its dimensions as I became more aware, as an adult, of other forms of suffering, by witnessing and experiencing them. I had to leave the country, in 1973, in order to return to it with a deeper love and commitment. My final departure has further deepened those bonds, but also my judgment of the abuses of which we were all a part.

What was also concealed from me, because I was living in it, was the tough web of living affections, with family and friends, which I now perceive was the deep treasure of that ordinary life in time, my childhood. I want to hold, remember, and celebrate that time, because I will never have it again.

In 1961 I stood in the street on a windy Cape Town day, a first-year student, and read in the newspaper that South Africa was to become a Republic. Our link with the Commonwealth had ended: there was an outcry and words of dire prophecy and chagrin from English-speakers. I remember standing there and feeling slightly alarmed and abandoned, as if a lifeline of sorts had been cut. The age of innocence was over. Real life was only just beginning, the life we live not just in the buried stream of history, but as human beings who seek a more active part in its changes.

Jane Bryce

Jane Bryce was born in 1951, in Lindi, Tanzania. She read English at Oxford and, after an uncertain career as a teacher, she turned to freelance journalism and academic research in 1981. She worked as a journalist for five years, both for the Nigerian press and British journals, writing mainly features on matters of social, artistic and cultural interest. In 1983 she went to Nigeria to research on Nigerian women's writing and, after gaining her Ph.D. from Obafemi Awolowo University at Ile-Ife in 1988, returned to the UK with her Yoruba husband. In 1992 she was appointed lecturer in African Literature at the University of the West Indies, Barbados. She is currently working on a book on women's writing in Africa.

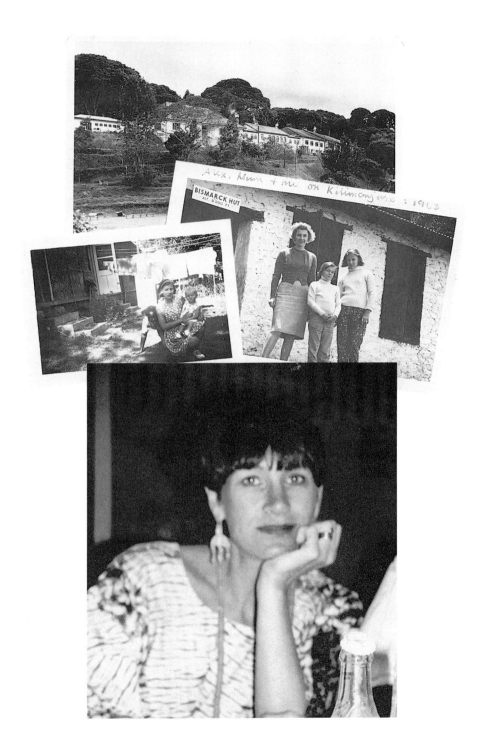

Alex, Mum + me on Kilimanjaro : 1963

BISMARCK HUT
ALT. 9,000 FT.

JANE BRYCE

White Child – Black Nation

When I was born, on February 8, 1951, I became the fifth generation of my family to be born in 'the colonies'. My father, though Australian by birth and by descent, spoke impeccable Oxford English, and used to recount with pride how his mother sat on his bed when he was a child and drilled him in his vowel sounds. Another point of pride with him was the fact that the progenitor of our family, though of humble Irish origin, was one of the original non-convict settlers in South Australia. In Australian terms, therefore, we were almost aristocrats.

It was all just a fairy-tale to me. I was born and grew up in what was then the British Protectorate of Tanganyika, East Africa. I first visited Australia when I was five years old, and we all travelled for what seemed like days on end on a succession of aeroplanes to Adelaide to stay with my grandmother, my father's mother. Her name was Katie Lucette, known to her numerous grandchildren as Yum Yum, and she was born in 1883. She had married George Bryce, a Scotsman, who served as an Agricultural Officer in the Colonial Service. With him, she travelled to postings in Malaya, Ceylon and Nigeria between the 1920s and 1940s. In 1951, the year I was born, at the age of 68 and long separated from her husband, she flew from Adelaide via Sydney, Singapore, Karachi, Aden, Nairobi and Dar-es-Salaam to Lindi, the coastal town nearest to where my parents lived, to visit us in Tanganyika. The journey took 4 days and nights by 4 different airlines and 5 planes. On her return, my grandmother, who was something of a journalist, gave a talk on her visit to the Lyceum Club, a ladies only club for professional women in Adelaide. The notes she made for that talk, in the cursive script of a previous era, came to my father after her death, and provided me with the clearest sketch I had yet received of the world I inhabited before my memory produced its own images.

Of course, there were the stories my parents told. They met through mutual friends in England after the war, while my father was studying forestry at Oxford. He had been an RAF pilot, was shot down and spent 4 years as a POW, first in Italy, then Germany. On my 19th, 20th and 21st birthdays, he pointed out to me that at the same age, he had celebrated his birthday in captivity. I never understood what he expected me to feel, and settled for feeling resentful. After the war, he said, he looked around for a profession that would keep him unenclosed and out-of-doors, and chose forestry. He did not anticipate that he would end up in charge of a scientific research unit dealing with tropical hardwoods, spending much of his time bent over a microscope. But that was later. When he and my mother came to Tanganyika in 1949, they were posted to the Southern Province, which my grandmother called 'the Cinderella Province', to a place called the Rondo Plateau, 64 miles from the coast at 4,300 feet. Here they occupied a house, built of mud and with a grass roof, which stood in small clearing on the edge of a canyon 500 feet deep. According again to my grandmother's notes, the plateau was covered in 'primeval forest', which had been kept as a reserve by the Germans, who preceded the British until 1917, and then by their successors. In 1951, for the first time, 'for political and economic reasons,' the Tanganyikan Government granted a concession of 1500 square miles to a timber firm, Steel Bros. of Burma. The remaining 32,000 acres was retained as a reserve, presided over by my father as Forest Officer. His job was to supervise British Government interests and establish nurseries for re-afforestation. He set out to map the area by measuring it on foot, usually accompanied by my mother. In her first year, before she became pregnant with me, she walked on safari with my father 'over 300 miles through man-eating lion and elephant country, nearly always in danger'. This greatly impressed my grandmother, who found the sombreness and silence of the forest on 3 sides of the house oppressive and frightening. Taking me for a walk, she confessed to the Adelaide ladies, was her 'daily zero hour'. On one occasion, she and my mother were half a mile from home when they heard elephants trumpeting and fled for safety.

It was not my mother's first experience of Africa. She had joined the WRNS during the war and been posted to Tanga, a northern coastal town almost as far up as the Kenyan border. Her photograph albums of the time contained dozens of pictures of dashing young men in naval uniform. When I was older, she used to turn the pages, pointing out the ones who had been torpedoed at sea. One particularly handsome one, whose picture cropped up more frequently than most, was called 'Creepie'. He was one of those who died. I found it intensely romantic and used to fantasize about what it would have been like if he had been my father. There was also one called Frank, whom my mother had nearly married. He was not as handsome as Creepie, but he had given my mother a silver filigree bracelet with a heart at the centre, on which was engraved a pyramid. He had been posted in Egypt at the time. On either side were little silver plaques with the words 'To Anne Love Frank'. I have it to this day.

Those old photo albums, black pages interleaved with tissue paper, with black and white photos held in place by photo corners which gradually lost their gum as the years went by, were another source of early images for me. A picture I particularly treasure is of my mother on foot safari, washing her hair in a stream. I grew up with this sense of a romantic past, full of adventure and excitement, though by the time I was 3, we were living in Moshi, an upcountry town at the foot of Kilimanjaro, and those early days were all behind us. I did not know it then, but the few years my parents spent 'on the Rondo', with their foot safaris with tents and porters, dinners served by servants in the bush, brushes with lions and elephants, were the fading years of the old colonial era. I myself, born 10 years before Uhuru, Tanganyika's Independence, was a child of the pre-Independence era, of a new consciousness and a new ideology of which, however, I grew up entirely ignorant. My outlook was formed by my father's benevolent paternalism, his deep sense of dedication and 'service' coupled with the conviction that Africans were children who needed guidance. Until I was 16 or so, this is what I not only believed but took for granted, like my own position as a young *memsahib* who could tell grown-up Africans, employed as servants, what to do. Nevertheless, I suspect I was the instrument of subversion of my parents' authority on more than one occasion. European children, cared for by an ayah, generally had close contact with servants and up to a certain age were allowed to play with the children from the servants' quarters. So it was that in early childhood I was bilingual, and once, aged 3 or 4, chanced to repeat to my parents something the gardener had taught me to say in Kiswahili: 'Mavi yako ena nyoka', or 'your shit stinks'. It is perhaps to my parents' credit that they found it funny and repeated it periodically over the years as a family joke.

Adding to the romance of my early memories was the story my mother told of my birth. My parents' house was 64 miles from the nearest hospital, in Lindi, and when my mother went into labour, they set out to drive there in their battered Bedford truck. However, it was the rainy season and on the road they would normally have taken, a bridge had been washed away. They had to do a detour which delayed them by a couple of hours. My mother said that by the time they got to Lindi hospital, she was sitting on my head, and nearly had me on the stairs. It always seemed to me that *that* was the proper way to be born, not to someone lying down quietly in a hospital ward.

I have never, since we left the Southern Province, been back to Lindi, but my grandmother dismissed it in her notes as 'a sordid little town', which I found terribly wounding as a description of my birthplace. Once, it formed part of a chain of towns along the coast, founded by Arab settlers from 950 AD onwards. They were part of an ancient coastal civilization which bequeathed a peculiar character, and a language – Kiswahili – to the eastern seaboard. Remnants of that civilization can be seen in the ornate wooden doors and dhows riding at harbour, or carrying cargoes of spices to Arabia, of Old Mombasa, and the ancient streets and buildings of the islands of Zanzibar and Pemba. Nothing of it, apparently, was visible to the eyes of Katie Lucette, Australian lady, as she touched down after her gruelling flight in 1951. The rigours of the journey began with her transfer at Karachi from BOAC to Air India. As she recalled: 'As the wife of a colonial government servant I had for over 20 years known what it was to be in a colour minority, but always with authority behind me and the priority it granted to those who were white and British. Without knowing it, I had shared the dying glimmer of British prestige and I was now experiencing the change.' As the only white traveller on a plane of 35 Indian passengers and 5 Indian crew, she was certain that in an emergency she would be jettisoned with the suitcases. Landing at Aden at 6 a.m., they were allowed to have breakfast. Katie Lucette was placed alone at a table for 20, while all 35 of the other passengers crowded into the farthest corner of the room, leaving her in stately isolation. It reminded my grandmother of her first voyage to Nigeria, where she was sailing to join her husband from Malaya. Among the 80-odd white first-class passengers was 'one young African negress of 18 returning to her homeland after 6 years at an English school, where she had been sent by her father, a lawyer in Lagos. In the dining saloon she sat for the 2 weeks' voyage at a table alone, and I never saw anyone but the captain talk with her.' I suspect my grandmother was unusual in being struck by what to most of the passengers would have seemed an entirely natural state of affairs. It did not stop her from feeling horrified when, over-nighting in Nairobi on her way to Tanganyika, the hotels were so full that 'I seemed in danger of being accommodated in a hotel for Indians and Africans.' But things were different then, and Kenya's white settlers operated a colour bar as stringent as South Africa's, even if it was 'unofficial'. Tanganyika, thanks to its different history – only becoming a British territory in 1917 and then not as a colony, so settlers were few – escaped the worst excesses of structural racism and Happy Valley self-indulgence.

I have today a photograph of our house on the Rondo from the air, marked by a cross, a tiny blob in the midst of forest. It was 12 miles from the river, which was the nearest water, and water supplies were delivered by truck to the house. My grandmother, coming from a meat-eating culture, cannot have been best pleased that she had to wait 3 weeks to taste fresh meat – an antelope. A Benedictine mission 15 miles away supplied vegetables, while eggs were brought 30 miles on foot. They lived largely on tinned food and grew vegetables and fruits with water saved from bathing. My mother used to recount to me how she would carefully sieve her precious home-grown tomatoes for me and I would spew them across the room. However, I survived, which is more than most babies under those conditions. African babies, if they lived that long, were weaned at 3 months onto an adult diet, as there was no milk. I was bathed in boiled water to prevent bilharzia, and slept in an iron cage as a protection against the lion and leopard that frequently visited the house at night. In the daytime, my crib in its iron cage, laid outside, was guarded by Ali, a young local boy. My grandmother's comment: 'When I failed to see what possible security he provided, Anne explained that a leopard would first seize Ali, whose screams would give them time to rescue the baby.' I think my parents must have coped with the privation and danger largely through humour. Certainly when they talked about those times in later years, it was always with nostalgic affection.

When I was 3, my twin sisters were born in Morogoro, another southern town, where we were then living. My mother did not know she was having twins till the second one was born. When they were still tiny, we moved to Moshi, where we lived until we left Tanganyika. Moshi is where my memories really begin, memories of an idyllic childhood of almost unlimited physical freedom, animals, friends, exciting trips to gameparks, holidays by the sea on the Kenya coast and great natural beauty. The people in whose world I was an ignorant interloper were nothing more to me than a backdrop to my own happy existence. Those with whom I came into contact were limited to employees and servants – my father's Indian carpenter, Mistri, who lived in a crowded tenement where saris hung to dry from the windows; the workers at my father's sawmill and office; the waiters at the whites-only club where my parents played golf and tennis; Indian shopkeepers and itinerant vendors who called at the house with eggs and fruit; and our own household servants.

This synthetic harmony was only marred by the inevitable incursion of school. Good European schools were few and far between, and after primary school in Moshi, the automatic next step for my parents was to send me, at age 8, to Lushoto Preparatory School in the Usambara mountains. This was a boarding school for mostly white children aged 8 to 13, situated in an old German army barracks in a region of the country where the climate was considered healthy because of its height. To me, coming from the dry heat of the plains, it was wet and cold and miserable, and the 12-week term could have been infinity. Old-fashioned discipline was practised, including beating for quite minor offences, the food was terrible and, for the first time, my freedom was severely restricted. The Moshi to Tanga railway, following an old Arab slave route, carried the Moshi contingent of children as far as Mombo, where we changed to buses for the climb up the mountain to Lushoto. The train journey itself was an event, with a large send-off party of tearful parents gathering at the tiny local station to see us off on our overnight trip. They were still steam trains in those days, and I remember my mother running the length of the platform as we hung out of the windows wailing and the train chugged slowly out in clouds of smoke. The buses from Mombo churned their way for what seemed like hours up the precipitous mountain road with its succession of hairpin bends, until the school and its playing fields came into view, and the prison gates clanged.

In spite of the extreme homesickness and the rigours of school life, Lushoto must have provided a 'good' education because nearly every child went on from there to top public schools in Britain, often winning scholarships. We learnt Latin from the age of 10, French, Geometry, English and Scottish country dancing and classical music appreciation. Singing 'Drip drip drop, little April shower', I used to watch the drizzle and wonder, why April? History was the kings and queens of England, Geography taught us to be proud of the red parts of the atlas because they were British, but Britain itself was a tiny island far away and I could never see the connection. Besides poems and stories I wrote plays, mostly based on fairy tales, and was encouraged to put them on for the whole school. I formed an acting company and bullied my friends into rehearsing. I also started keeping a diary. The earliest, for 1963, was a Letts School Girl Diary, with emblems and coats of arms of British institutions on the opening pages, followed by a list of 'Stories for Girls', a table of Latin verbs, photographs of Kent Oasthouses, Student Nurses and Cardiff Castle, and A Recipe for Quick Cream Ice. My main preoccupation that year was recording the age of the 3 ducklings my mother had given us: 'Jan.1: Ducklings age, 3wks. 1 day'; Jan 2: 'Ducklings age, 3wks. 2 days', etc.; up to 200 weeks, when I seem to have given up. The entry for April 2 records: 'Did the play – oh! –oh! –oh! Great success dwarfs sang "Heigh – ho!" Paf killed herself at the end with a knife. Box of chocolates from Mrs. Farrer. A day I shall never forget!'

Very little of the outside world intruded into our hermetic routine. We formed a Girl Guides Pack, and were thrilled at receiving a letter from Lady Baden-Powell with a picture of Hampton Court Palace. In December, 1961, we were issued with medals hung on ribbons of black, gold and green, the colours of Tanganyika's flag, but on the actual Independence Day, December 9, I was far away in Mombasa, where my father took me, in order, he said, 'to be where the British Flag was flying a little longer'. I therefore missed the bonfires on Kilimanjaro, the firework display and celebrations. I never quite forgave my father for the disappointment. I did not know what Uhuru was, but I knew it was a great occasion which had stirred up the whole country. As time went by, I understood it meant change, not always for the better. Our much-loved ayah, Martha Nairobi, who had cared for each of us from infancy, joined Tanu, the new political party, and started attending night school. We were all shocked when one day she informed my mother that she did not want to work for white people any more, and left us. I felt it as a personal betrayal, though if I had thought back I might have been less surprised. Long before Uhuru or politics or night school, Martha had roundly rebuked me for refusing to do something she had told me to do because, I said, 'I am white and you are black.' Her retort, 'God made both white and black', must have entered my subconscious and stayed there, one tiny seed of resistance to the all-pervading assumption of superiority in which I was immersed.

Behind my mother's bewilderment at Martha's behaviour hovered the unspoken word 'ingratitude'. Hadn't we always been good employers, looked after her and her child, remembered them at Christmas, loved them (almost) as family? Of the forces at work in the country, I had no idea, and no-one, neither parents nor friends nor teachers, was forthcoming with explanations. The new Vicar who took over our local Anglican Church sometime in the mid-60s was unpopular because of his views on Africans and his disregard for cherished long-established customs. He preached long sermons on equality and gave away our church bell to his mission because, I wrote in my diary, 'He cares more about them than he does about us.' On 23 January, 1964, I recorded in my diary: 'Rioting in Dar announced by Mr. Smith in assembly. No Europeans hurt.' I apparently remained incurious and in ignorance about the cause of the rioting.

In April, 1964, having passed the 13+ Common Entrance, I was sent to a big girls' boarding school in England. If I had been homesick before, I now underwent a kind of pining and emotional deprivation which coloured my entire 5 years at the school. Yearly holidays home were a 2-month interlude of intense sensual appreciation of all the aspects of Moshi life I so much missed in England. I hated the wearing of clothes, the hats and gloves and brollies and stockings, the livid green of the grass made me nauseous, the buildings gave me claustrophobia. On those brief annual visits I began recording with adolescent passion the details of my home environment. I wrote lyrically about the frangipani, the jacarandas, the flamboyants, the oleanders, the violence of tropical storms breaking the drought, the smell of the earth. It was as if I had intimations of the end, not only of childhood, but of my innocent belonging in a place that time would prove was not really mine. In July, 1967, I wrote: 'I read yesterday in a travel guide to East Africa, "Life in Moshi is inextricably entwined with Kilamanjaro." It is true, all the town's character comes from the mountain, its strength, its joy, its loveliness ... the cool blue slopes suddenly appearing through the morning mists, the glistening snow caps crowning them. It touches everyone who lives here. It becomes a part of each person's life, and remains with them wherever their destiny takes them. It is an unbreakable, intangible link.'

That was my last summer. Early the following year, when my sisters and I were safely back in our English boarding school, my parents fell prey to the policy of 'Africanization' then being implemented by the Tanzanian Government. After 19 years, they were given 10 days to leave the country. A letter from my mother dated March 15, 1968 reads: 'I am afraid I have news which will upset you very much. Daddy has been recalled to Rome (though still in his old post as Utilization Officer, he had recently transferred from government service to the UN Food & Agriculture Organization) and we are leaving Moshi at once. It all came as rather a shock and I know how sad and miserably disappointed you will be at the thought of leaving Moshi.... We have been so lucky with our happy life in dear old Moshi all these years it has been home to us.'

I had just turned 17. Surprisingly, I felt, not resentment, but empathy. I felt I understood why the Tanzanaians wanted us out and I did not blame them. Perhaps that abrupt deportation marked the start of my own long, slow process of decolonization, which, according to my Yoruba husband, is still far from complete.

Lauris Edmond

Lauris Edmond grew up in Greenmeadows, a small country town in New Zealand. She trained as a teacher and speech therapist and then went back to living in small towns as the wife of a school teacher and, eventually, the mother of six children. She has written poets in private since childhood, but did not publish her first collection till 1975. *In Middle Air* won the PEN Best First Book Award. She went on to publish nine other volumes of poetry, including the *Selected Poems* which won the Commonwealth Poetry Prize in 1985, and, more recently, *New and Selected Poems* from which she has been reading on a tour of Germany and England. In 1986 she was awarded an OBE for services to literature and in 1988 an Honorary Doctorate of Literature by Massey University, Palmerston, North New Zealand. She has published a novel, a number of plays, and a three-volume autobiography. She lives in Wellington, New Zealand.

LAURIS EDMOND

Membership of the Club

At school I believed everything I was told. When a teacher explained that the Australian aborigines were Stone Age men who would never learn to overcome their primitive nature I accepted this at once – all the more since, as she explained, you could plainly see their condition in the shape of their heads. Their foreheads were much lower than ours, with room behind for fewer brains.

In the same way the British had come to New Zealand to make us all British citizens and subjects of the King. At that time 'all' meant the Maoris, and the monarch they were invited to serve Queen Victoria, and the melancholy fact is that many Maoris, wrong-headed as they were, opposed this connection when it began to look like an excuse for wholesale confiscation of their land and villages. The 'Maori Wars' (as they are not now called) followed, but fortunately for everyone, especially the Maoris themselves, they were defeated by the glorious redcoats of the British army, a historical truth that has proved susceptible to massive re-interpretation by recent historians.

But not in time for me. I was at school during the Thirties, leaving high school to go to university and Teachers Training College in 1942. It was a time when a great many New Zealanders spoke of England as Home, even if, like my parents, they had no actual home to go to on the other side of the world. Both were born of parents who had themselves 'come out' on the immigrant ships of the 1870s and 1880s. As assisted immigrants they came to work, and eventually to marry, and unlike more affluent travellers left behind no establishment to which they might return, nor money to pay for trips 'home'.

But Home was there all the same, as an institution, a dream, a refuge, a model. All my reading was of English families, English schoolgirls playing hockey for the Upper Fourth or Lower Fifth at St Cuthbert's or St Joan's. Or, later, the provincial Victorian drawing rooms of George Eliot, the blasted heath of Hardy's rustic heroes and heroines, the Yorkshire moors and farmhouse kitchens of the Brontës, the Exeter valley where the Doone outlaws terrorized John Ridd and his neighbours in *Lorna Doone*. In all these magical worlds my imagination lived and flourished, and I did not wonder at all that none of their scenes were visible, that in fact outside my window the sun shone on paddocks, not meadows or fields, that the dark green New Zealand bush, *pohutukawa* and *rimu* mixed with pine and *macrocarpa*, all evergreen, was not at all like the copses and dingles of the English woodland. Christmas trees were made to look like snow-covered firs, while the summer sun blazed outside, and we stuffed ourselves with the unseasonably hot and heavy edible icons of roast lamb, mint sauce, roast potatoes, green peas and plum duff (in which we had earlier hidden the sixpences and threepences that were to clink miraculously on to someone's pudding plate).

My mother told us stories about Princess Elizabeth and Princess Margaret Rose, who were the same age as my sister and me, and thus very pertinent models. They were kind to each other (my sister and I often quarrelled), they obeyed their mother, Queen Mary, they were polite to visitors, they loved doing their homework, especially learning their Tables. The superior quality of their lives was assured, proven, by their advantages – their huge life-like dolls' house for instance. We had a small wooden contraption set up on the verandah by our moderately handy father.

My mother's view of society and one's chances of rising in it were as unassailably English as Arnold Bennett's; although I didn't know this till later, when I read his tales of the Five Towns. The dreadful gap between 'trade' and 'profession' affected us most deeply because our father was, alas, in the former, and we had been appointed by fate to share his misfortune. He was a painter and paperhanger, he worked with his hands, not in an office where presumably the use of brains, or the charging of fees, conferred high status. He came to be a 'master painter' who ran a business, employed other painters and trained apprentices, but as far as we could tell this did not, and could not, elevate him to the rank of the professionals. When my brother expressed a desire to learn engineering there was a consultation with aunts and uncles who collectively decided that this too was work you did with your hands, and trained for by being an apprentice (there was as yet no university course). He must be a teacher instead, an occupation for which even then he was manifestly unsuited.

Even if we were not the offspring of doctors or lawyers, or even teachers (my mother's occupation before her marriage, but that hardly counted), we had our own kind of class. We owned, and on rare occasions displayed and used, several pieces of English bone china – Royal Doulton, Royal Albert, Royal Stafford. English flowers and gardens, English woodland or hunting scenes decorated the fluted cups and fragile saucers, a jug and sugar bowl and a splendid coffee pot (which, since we didn't drink coffee, was never used). In the drawer in the sideboard where treasures lodged, there were also several silver serviette rings and a set of linen serviettes, used once or twice a year when relations came to stay or at Christmas.

When King George V died, Edward, Prince of Wales, was briefly installed as King Edward VIII. We observed with a mixture of shock and sorrow the performance of his abdication. He had fallen in love with an unsuitable American woman, and while love was beautiful to contemplate, we could see that she had a certain cheapness about her that made her unsuitable to be England's Queen, and ours.

All this was entirely consistent with the personal view I took of the characters in my English novels. They, simply, were me, I them. It mattered not at all that aunts in my family were not like Aunt Glegg or Aunt Pullet (from *The Mill on the Floss*) – anyway, perhaps they were, a little: didn't my mother and Aunty Alice have a solemn and protracted quarrel quite in the manner of George Eliot's ponderous aunts? Didn't we take our old clothes to give to a sister-in-law who was poorer than us, and thus a target for our mother's charity, and wasn't her manner of giving touched with a condescension Aunt Glegg would at once have recognized?

It is amazing now to realize how invisible was the reality of the 'here and now', and how it differed (despite a slight similarity in details like aunts) from the 'there and then' of my reading, not to mention the Royal Family and the Kings and Queens before them, and the history in which they lodged. We did, in fact, do some New Zealand history – we *did* the Maoris. Regularly, predictably, year after year at primary school I learnt the shape and purpose of the *pa* (a fortified village), the meeting house, the *pataka*, a storehouse where village food supplies were kept. Each year I waited for the familiar descriptions – like the details of how pigeons, cooked *hangi*-style in the ground, were preserved in fat and kept behind the wooden bars locking the *pataka* till the day for a feast arrived.

I learnt too about the *marae*, the open meeting place whose name has since entered the language, as its significance has become as great for *pakeha* as for Maori New Zealanders. Words like these – *mana* is another, the word for personal dignity, a kind of status that is more fundamental than the English kind, reflecting social position or income – give me a curious shiver of awareness still. It is really a quick glimpse of that early learning I did, showing its amazing artificiality. What an English child I was – and how thoroughly a New Zealander I have now become! Which is to say that mine is the generation in which this essential historical maturing has taken place. At school Maoris were a subject, quite distinct from the few Maori children who happened to be in my class (but whose families I did not know); I was a member of the 'little England' that New Zealand still was in the 1930s, and things Maori must have seemed as far away as the English countryside. Far further indeed; I came alive in one, was deaf and blind to the other.

There were of course Maori legends, and these were a pleasure, but only in the way that Greek tales were, or fairy stories from Grimm or Hans Andersen. All were collections of stories. What happened in England was *true*. I knew its population well – King John, the roistering Charles II, William and Mary, those strangely sober intruders on the royal scene; Victoria, whose austerely compelling loyalty to Albert, alive or dead, fired the moral imagination of good girls like me. A good deal of the compulsion was in the telling, I suppose. *Our Nation's Story*, for instance, gave as gospel a whole view of time and the world that was happily and unselfconsciously British imperialist. Our textbooks were written in the early years of the twentieth century; objectivity about Britain and its Empire lay in the social science-dominated future.

The Young Dominion, another of my authorities, explained that the Maori people, like the Australian aborigine, had suffered from a lack of the 'civilization that British rule could (and eventually did) bring... Cut off from their old home (the Asiatic Plateau) the Polynesians, as they are called, became a race apart. They did not share in the advance in civilization that took place in older countries.' Other authorities were inclined to see the New Zealand native race as, potentially at least, English under the skin. Reading *Our Nation's Story* in Standard Six (my last year before going to high school) I found the concession made that the Maoris 'were not without some of the qualities and graces to be found in a higher state of civilization. In some respects they were not very unlike the English at the time they were making their settlements in Britain. They had a great love for their homes and families, and lived in well-built, if simple houses...'

History was always associated with Civics, the study of citizenship, rules for achieving honour and virtue by keeping the law, standing up for 'God Save the King', saluting the flag, making wreaths for Anzac Day (when we honoured New Zealanders killed at Gallipoli and praised the British army which had organized their slaughter, though naturally we did not know this at the time).

I was a Girl Guide, and so were Princesses Elizabeth and Margaret. Like them, I learnt to tie knots, make beds with triangular folds at the corners, light a fire in the open (I never quite managed it in the rain, as the born Patrol Leader could do – I moved upwards in rank only slowly). I also earned badges – Needlewoman's, Camper's, Tracker's – and sewed them on my uniform; I mastered semaphore and the Morse Code on which it is based, and made my own signalling flags. In no other department of my life did I need to use this information, nor have I ever been asked to give or receive a semaphore signal since, but that had nothing to do with the satisfaction of getting it right in time to pass my test. I kept my lanyard washed and my whistle at the ready; on hikes and at patrol meetings I expect I was hearty and jolly as a good Guide should be, and as serious. I learnt by heart Longfellow's improving lines:

The heights by great ones reached, and kept,
Were not attained by sudden flight;
But they, while their companions slept,
Were toiling upwards through the night.

We met in a church hall round the corner, every week on Tuesday nights. Each time I entered it I felt again that peculiar dry draughty chill, smelling of dust and old wood, that belonged to church halls. A physical and moral strenuousness seemed to be implanted in the walls, the austere furniture, the swept wooden floor. There we went to our corners, assembled and saluted, formed into patrols, performed our various virtuous antics in the blue britway uniforms that always diffused the same cottony, blue-britway smell. If anything made me a living cell in the body British it was the grave, semi-military, robustly healthy rituals of obedience that Girl Guide membership required.

In my public life, there and at school, I was 'the average New Zealander'. This meant of course British settlers, and somehow counted in (or counted out) the Polynesian occupants of the nation. 'The average New Zealander is well able to think and act for himself', said *The Young Dominion*. 'He is proud of his country, and he is a staunch Imperialist. This was never better exemplified than during the Great War, when all classes of the community sprang to the aid of the Motherland, and eagerly did their part in preserving the Empire. In those dark and difficult days the youngest Dominion sent overseas more than one-tenth of her entire population, a proportion higher than that of any other part of the Empire.'

I swelled with pride. A Preface to another of these beguiling expositions assured me that 'the pupil is first taught the story of his own country, a story which cannot fail to arouse his pride and patriotism. Having carried him thus far, *Our Nation's Story* seeks to interest him in the historical progress of the nation of which he is a citizen.' My country was, clearly, an outlying province, a Roman Gaul or Britain, administered from the Capitol and shaped in discussions held in the Forum. (As for the assumption that every citizen to be referred to was male, naturally I took this for granted, having never known any alternative.)

The map of the world was satisfyingly patched with red, 'our' colour. 'We' covered thirteen million square miles of the globe, 'they' (i.e. the Germans, who had 'strenuously but vainly attempted to gain the mastery of the world') had only two hundred and eight thousand square miles and a paltry seventy million people. Ours was glorious in its scope – four hundred and thirty-five millions (though a footnote did explain in very small print that most of these were 'natives of various races'). The British Empire was the 'greatest and strongest World Power ever known in history'. Even better, this vast territory was 'so scantily populated that there is room in it for her continually expanding population to live prosperously on for perhaps hundreds of years to come if she can only hold it against her enemies'.

I expect I was a smug child. Smugness indeed was my inheritance. New Zealand is a tiny country, a squiggly fragment on the world map, but I knew with perfect confidence that I was part of the biggest, strongest, noblest, *reddest* company known to man. Everyone else was, like the 'natives of various races' (if not British), merely a footnote. The actual distance between the King in his crown and Westminster Abbey (where in my early youth I believed he lived) was insignificant. Moreover, there was by the 1930s (or whenever my reassuring textbooks were written, a fact not usually disclosed), a 'new spirit abroad'. The people of the Empire were 'healthy and contented' and felt a 'new and wholesome pride in British institutions and the splendour of British civilization'. The English are said to be the most club-able people on the earth; the most expansive and compelling of its clubs must surely have been its 'far-flung' Empire.

It wasn't till after 1945 that any sort of European awareness entered my consciousness, and with it a view from the outside of the institutions of Empire, the emotional structure of its hold on power, and the rhetoric that served it. But by then I was growing up anyway. I was ready to take part in the new fascination with coffee drinking, European style, having tea late and calling it dinner – and drinking wine with it – going to restaurants where you were offered raw salads, barely cooked vegetables and *gâteau* for dessert. These innovations were practised at first by Jewish refugees from Nazi Germany, but gradually they, and the philosophies behind them, grew into a much wider knowledge of the possible models old communities might offer to our young one, and so to the beginning of cynicism and separateness. But that is another story, and one that has not by any means yet been finished.

Dorothy Jones

Dorothy Jones was born in Mosgiel, New Zealand, in 1934 and was educated at Otago Girls' High School, Otago University, Adelaide University and Oxford. She has lived in Australia for most of the past thirty-six years and has taught in English Departments in the Universities of Adelaide, New South Wales and Wollongong, where she holds her current appointment. Her principal research is post-colonial and women's writing, areas in which she has also published widely.

DOROTHY JONES

The Antipodes of Empire

Can I possibly be labelled a Daughter of Empire, even an unbecoming one? I have visions of large-bosomed ladies singing 'Land of Hope and Glory' in unison while they stand to attention draped with sashes resembling both the Queen's garter-ribbon and the more flamboyant insignia of beauty contests. But I cannot wholly reject the title. One of my earliest memories is holding a flag at the kerb-side as a procession passed celebrating George VI's coronation, though I no longer know whether the small flutter above my fist was a Union Jack or the New Zealand flag. There is a further memory – a heraldic moment as another procession passes headed by two Boer War veterans on horseback, hat brims pinned up with clusters of roosters' tail feathers, green and black. When I was five we were told the King and Queen were coming to visit and school children would assemble at the local race-course to see them. I remember an overwhelming sense of importance as, at the Infant Mistress's direction, we learned to sing 'God Save the King' and 'God Defend New Zealand'. But I never got to the race-course. Was the visit cancelled? Did I fall sick? Or did my Scottish mother, prompted by anti-royalist sentiment, decide I should stay home?

For me, the meaning of Empire was modified, or at least inflected by a Scottish heritage, imparted not only by my mother, but also through growing up in a district settled by Scots last century. The shiver of homesickness certain blanket brand names produce in the narrator of Janet Frame's novel, *Living in the Maniototo* – 'a memory of school days when places became their products – Onehunga, Mosgiel, Kaiapoi: the places with the woollen mills and therefore the blankets' – becomes for me a moment of recognition, since I come from one of those blanket towns, Mosgiel, close to Dunedin, principal city of the province of Otago in South Island. The town was originally settled with mill-workers from Paisley directed by Thomas Burns, nephew (or was it great-nephew?) of the poet, and named after his farm, Mossgiel, the extra 's' mislaid, presumably, on the twelve thousand mile voyage. Street names were Scottish. Tay Street, where I lived, ran off Gordon Road and led in its turn to Forth Street and Forfar Street, while Firth Street and Lanarch Street were close by. Pipe bands flourished and comic Scots monologues were always a hit at local concerts, along with songs like 'The Road to the Isles'. As a genuine Scot, my mother was dismissive about local assumptions of Scottish identity and scornful of those who referred to Britain as 'home' (which she herself never did) without even having been there.

My father, born in New Zealand, though of Scots descent, despised English and Scots alike, while the sound of an upper-class English accent aroused him to fury. At a time when New Zealand announcers sought to imitate their BBC counterparts, listening to the radio in our household was a chancy business, since Dad censored any voices he disliked by flicking the switch on the wall above his chair. He wore out at least three wall-switches that way. Sporting commentators must have spoken with more acceptable accents, for on Saturday afternoons in winter the house resounded to broadcasts of rugby football, rhythmic, repetitive mantras celebrating fractional men – half-back, five-eighths and wing three-quarters – assembling and reassembling themselves into rucks, scrums and lineouts. None of us, I think, recognized the bonds of Empire constituted through these sporting enthusiasms, although I certainly understood that rugby was a male imperium. My father erupted when the team he supported lost, accusing my mother and myself of secretly siding with their opponents. But we were not the heretics he assumed, merely unbelievers – we simply didn't care. He never tried to convert us, while continually raging at our absence of faith.

Nevertheless, I absorbed an awareness of national identity bound up with sport. At high school we were taken to the Leni Riefenstahl film of the 1936 Berlin Olympics (probably screened to arouse public enthusiasm for the 1948 Games). No one told us this was a fine film of great historical interest. What mattered was that we would see for ourselves a New Zealander, Jack Lovelock, run the race which won him a gold medal. I cheered with the rest as he sprinted across the screen in his black singlet to a result determined years earlier. Here was New Zealand making its mark in the world beyond. I grew up believing in both the importance, and the extreme difficulty, of being noticed as a nation.

Membership of the British Empire produced double vision. In my primary school years, which coincided with the Second World War, we expressed patriotic fervour by singing 'Maori Battalion March to Victory', and belting out, with equal enthusiasm:

> There'll always be an England
> And England shall be free
> If England means as much to you
> As England means to me.

What *did* England mean? I learnt by heart John of Gaunt's speech from *Richard II*, so frequently broadcast during the war years:

> This royal throne of kings, this sceptred isle,
> This earth of majesty, this seat of Mars,
> This other Eden – demi-paradise –

Romance, not patriotism, inspired me. England – 'This precious stone set in the silver sea' – was a literary creation, a work of fiction, part of the storybook world. Nevertheless, it was a fiction endowed with considerable authority. News heard directly on the BBC World Service seemed far more authentic than any read over a New Zealand radio station. A fictional England also governed my perspective on the seasons. Although, where I lived, April signified the approach of winter, in the books I read, it was a spring month, while November, with its bleak literary associations, actually heralded summer. I didn't realize I was seeing double, merely accepting the world as it had been constructed for me. In choral verse speaking at school, we chanted 'Go down to Kew in lilac time,/ It isn't far from London', without questioning Alfred Noyes' assumption that we could easily drop in to visit a place on the other side of the world.

In contrast to the fictional world of England, my own country lacked glamour. How could stories happen there? It is true that after I first travelled by overnight ferry to North Island at the age of twelve, I read, with delighted recognition, Katherine Mansfield's 'The Voyage',in which a young girl makes the same journey from North Island to South. But knowing the author had made her mark overseas somehow authorized my pleasure. I enjoyed reading about the arrival of the four Maori canoes from Hawaiki in New Zealand history, but the rest of it – whalers and sealers, the Treaty of Waitangi, Maori Wars, the gold rushes – seemed merely an addendum to *real* history, which happened centre stage twelve thousand miles away. The Otago Early Settlers' Museum, where pioneers stared forbiddingly from rows of photographs on the walls, also appeared dull in comparison to the Otago Museum, which housed such exotica as an ancient Egyptian sarcophagus and mummy along with a richly and beautifully carved Maori meeting house and canoe. Hostility to the Early Settlers Museum was also fuelled by continual representations of pioneers as role models of fortitude, hard work and self-sacrifice – a joyless ideal impossible to receive with the gratitude expected of us. Inwardly I asserted that they came to New Zealand out of self-interest, to better themselves not to benefit future generations. When I first lived in Australia, I was struck by the absence of early settlers' museums and tributes to pioneers. It was obviously harder to quarry authoritarian dogma to burden the young from a convict past.

Having grown up an unwitting daughter of the Empire, I went to study at Oxford, its imperial heart, to discover there that I had been constructed as a colonial subject. No doubt London was more truly the heart of the Empire, but during those first years in England it remained a scary, confusing blur where I ventured only occasionally. An image of Oxford had glowed brightly in the storybook England of my childhood imagination and it seemed that to live there would be to take up a yearned for residence within the world of books. But, having reached the centre, and Oxford had no doubts as to its own centrality, I could only define myself as a complete outsider, loathing the place which had formerly appeared so enticing. I didn't share my father's rage at the Oxford voice – indeed I took sly pleasure in observing people I spoke to as they tried to place my accent geographically so they could determine where I fitted socially. Nor did I feel that Oxford rejected me. What Louis MacNeice once called 'the city of the sneering spires' would take you to herself, with regular reminders of your outsider origins, provided you adopted its own perspective. The seventeenth-century emblematist, Henry Peacham, includes a woodcut in his *Minerva Brittana* representing Oxford as a walled city elevated above the earth by a cord dangling from God's finger, and the accompanying verse claims how the light of truth, 'Directing thousandes erring, in their way', radiates from it by land and sea. But I utterly refused to adopt a vision of the world that would have involved dismissing as irrelevant and insignificant the antipodean life which formed me.

Not all my memories of Oxford are negative. There were fine buildings, jewel-like paintings in the Ashmolean Museum, the delights of researching in a magnificently endowed library and the joy of watching a succession of flowers blooming just inside the gates of the Oxford Parks as, each spring, snow drops gave way to crocuses followed by fluffy white daisies tinged with pink and, in the height of summer, drifts of Queen Anne's Lace. But, despite all this, I still remain totally unforgiving and, although I have since paid one or two brief visits, cannot bring myself to stay there for more than a few days.

Not surprisingly, Scotland proved more comfortable and comforting than England. The moors of the Border country, where some of my relatives still lived, had a rugged, ragged appearance, reminiscent of the untidy-looking countryside I had known in New Zealand, in contrast to the more manicured landscape around Oxford. Edinburgh street names were a further reminder of home since streets in Dunedin, where I had attended high school and university, had been named after them. The Scots accent, too, was not only more familiar, but seemed a less heavy instrument for bludgeoning people into a sense of class identity. But it was that first overall experience of Britain, and Oxford in particular, which both prompted conscious awareness of my post-colonial identity (though that term was then unknown to me) and led me to take active pride in it. It is not, perhaps, possible to 'unbecome' a daughter of Empire, for part of my life has been shaped by the experience of growing up in a country which once belonged to the British Empire. But, though I have now lived for many years in Australia as an expatriate New Zealander, my view of the world is still thoroughly antipodean with my feet firmly planted opposite to what was once the imperial centre.

Jean Arasanayagam

Jean Arasanayagam is a Sri Lankan writer of Dutch Burgher origin. She attended a private Methodist Missionary School and is a graduate of the University of Ceylon and the University of Strathclyde, Glasgow. Poet, novelist and short story writer, her most recent work has dealt with the tragic events of racial conflict in Sri Lanka. 'My major preoccupation,' she said, 'has been with the vast, the immeasurable tragedy of a country at war.' She has, however, also been concerned, as she is in this essay, with her own personal bi-cultural experience. She has won major awards both for her fiction and non-fiction, and has been published both in Sri Lanka and abroad. Her most recent collection is a book of poetry, *Reddened Water Flows Clear*, published by Forest Books, London and Boston, 1991.

JEAN ARASANAYAGAM

School Memories: The Missionaries

Childhood often writes remembered episodes of the past in memory, episodes without strategy, that often in those long periods of time during which we grow, shape themselves into the completeness of the explorer's discovery whereby we recognize those landmarks we have journeyed through. We set up our habitations there and to go back to them, we retrace our steps. We follow a path, a signpost, whether of face, rock or stream, plant or tree and find ourselves traversing a landscape in which those once familiar figures encounter ours, their faces still recognizable, although we knew them in a different clime, a different season. Time has taken them away from us but we do not speak of them as the dead. They are still there, inhabiting those landscapes of the mind, that vast terrain in which we are often alone wandering over those solitary or crowded places. We glimpse the past as in that phase of silver that appears through a gap in the mountain, to tell us that a restless ocean lies beyond it. My aunt Nellie had once given me a book, beautifully illustrated called *Beyond the Blue Mountain* and this was that imaginary and fabulous land that I had to reach someday.

From the garden of the house where we lived in Kadugannawa, Dawson's Tower with its gleaming whiteness stands out starkly against the bluegreen hills of Belungala. Within its dark interior, a narrow spiral stairway with broken steps winds up to a circular platform with railings. From this vantage point the view offers you a complete landscape, both close and distant, of lush foliage fed by trickling streams, and steep precipices dropping into valleys, with a chequerboard of paddyfields, houses and temples with never a person to be seen. The green pelt lies spread beneath the blue hills, across which pass shadows of light and dark and the eye searches for the path that descends beneath its terraces and trees and where those truly ancient roots delve into the past of some forgotten beginnings.

Looking towards the township the view changes with its railway lines and railway houses, the Railway Reading Room and tennis courts, the huddle of shops – Podimahathaya's with its bead curtains and imported Japanese ready-made dresses which my mother bought for house-wear, and the neatly folded camboyas which Mungo, my ayah, wore. There was Cunji Moosa's too, where we dipped into large glass-stoppered bottles containing gold-covered chocolates like big round sovereigns. There was the barber's salon with its swing doors and clients who sat before large mirrors with towels tucked round their necks, their faces all lathered with Vinolia shaving soap. It was from here that the squint-eyed barber came to cut my hair and trim my fringe. And beyond the railway bungalows were fairy-tale 'Royden' and 'Paradise View', where we had parties with home-made ice-cream churned out with fresh milk and egg custard and aunty Gladys's ginger beer, on the surface of which fat plums floated. And there was my own home with the thumbergia bower and the honeysuckers, the grenadilla creeper and my father's thornless roses.

Inside Dawson's tower it is fusty and dark, the atmosphere fetid with bats and their droppings, but my brother and sister with their intrepid friends had dared to climb to the top of the tower, through the almost choking darkness, till they reached the light and drank in the fresh, pure air. Below them was the world of mosque minarets, church spires and the rubber and tea estates. The vast circle of the turntable with its shunting engine slowly revolved – it was an experience we sometimes enjoyed, climbing onto it and feeling the blast of heat from the inferno of the stoked fires, the coal shovelled in with great metal scoops. To wipe out the grease and grime we were given wads of coloured threads – my greatest joy was to try to unravel these coloured strands of red and green, blue, white and yellow, smoothen them out, try to thread them through the needle to embroider impossible and fanciful designs on fine muslin and cambric.

I remained below the tower. My brother and sister felt I was too young to go through the suffocating darkness. They were also old enough to escape adult sanctions, to explore their own freedoms. They could take any road they wanted, appear or disappear at will, climb tall mango trees, perch on a branch and eat half-ripe mangoes. And my brother taught me a delicious secret of taking ripe yellow limes, making a small hollow in the skin and filling it with salt crystals and finely sifted chili powder which we sucked as we sat on a rock overlooking the railway lines, away from my mother's watchful eyes. I had a treasured Kodak snapshot of my brother camouflaged in a world of fruit and leaves, with a felt hat perched on his head, on the mango tree above our house. But very often I was left alone. My view was hazy, dreaming through the garden, theirs, my brother's and sister's the bold ascent. As they walked round the tower they carried the view visually with them – perhaps they could see as far as Bible Rock even. I had to wait till my father led me up the summit of Belungala, to lift me high on his shoulders and show me his vision of the ocean, so distant, so beyond reach, through a haze of blue.

My mother takes me to school by bus early in the morning from Kadugannawa. I am then in the Upper Kindergarten at Girls' High School, the private Methodist missionary school which I have been attending from Kindergarten days, when we belonged to the 'Baby Class' as it was then known. Early in the morning I have been lifted off the four-poster bed and still in my nightgown I am seated on a small stool before a large enamel basin of hot water. While I sit there half asleep I am soaped, scrubbed, wiped dry in a fluffy white towel, dressed in my school uniform and after a glass of hot milk and breakfast, Quaker oats or soft boiled egg with toast and butter I am ready for school. While I am in the bus I discover that I have forgotten everything that is necessary for my school work. I have forgotten my pencils, eraser, books, everything and my mother has to explain my lapses to my class teacher, Miss Phyllis Oorloff. She is kind and never scolds. What special gifts did those trained teachers have in those days – gifts of patience, kindness and dedication which took them through those long years of teaching until their retirement. Miss Oorloff took all our subjects from English to Arithmetic and always found time to read us stories, which she continued every week whilst we would sit back comfortably in our little wooden chairs, absorbed in chapters from *The Pot of Gold* or *At the End of the Rainbow*.

Phyllis Oorloff choreographs childhood as if it were a ballet. She drapes us in diaphanous folds of blue gauze for the dance of the fairies, with great gauzy wings pinned onto delicate shoulder blades. We dance and dance on the High School stage tripping with pointed toes. Silver hairbands with stars glitter and our faces are delicately made up with lipstick, powder, rouge from Miss Oorloff's compact. We have many concerts and variety entertainments at the end of term and the students dance, sing, act. I remember the Sailors' Hornpipe, Spanish dances, The Kitchen Orchestra, 'Riding down from Bangor' and choir songs like 'The Ash Grove' and 'Down in the Valley', while there were piano solos and duets too. I am an Unborn Child in Maeterlinck's 'The Blue Bird' blowing bubbles in a different world to the real one. I am dressed in blue. I wear a blue vest and my mother, holding a cardigan, hovers anxiously on the school verandah at rehearsals, in case I get cold. The 'big girls' come and sit by me as I blow my bubbles and beg to have a chance. Nothing matters except that my bubbles should emerge perfect, iridescently floating into the air until they burst fragmented into the faintest wisp of froth before they vanish. At home too I sit with a small enamel bowl in which I have dissolved lots of soap, Palmolive or Knights Castile and blow bubbles through a papaw stalk. What a dream world I lived in. Within each bubble I caught the reflection of the real world around me, of trees, leaves, flowers, bits of sky, sunlight, before those images vanished leaving the faintest taste of fragrant soap on my lips. I love to listen to those sentimental songs, 'I'm forever blowing bubbles, pretty bubbles in the air' and 'Somewhere, over the Rainbow'. It was the age of Peter Pan and Wendy, The Wizard of Oz, Snow White, Judy Garland and Shirley Temple dolls. Childhood was like a Christmas stocking through which I could forever delve.

At Sunday School we were given beautifully illustrated picture post-cards on our birthdays – the artist was a famous Englishwoman who painted exquisite pictures of elves and fairies. Was it Katherine Tynan I wonder. Whenever I think back on the world of poetry I remember the innumerable poems on that world of fairies, a fantastical world of the imagination – 'Goblin Market', 'The Fairy Queen', 'Elfin Skates', 'The Elfin Artist', 'The Death of Puck', 'The Lost Elf', 'The Leprechaun or the Fairy Shoemaker', to mention but a few. I still read them with a sense of curiosity, lingering on the names of those poets who wrote them – de la Mare, Nightingale, Hamilton, Allingham Hood, reading that esoteric, archaic language. We learnt those poems off by heart, and then we recited them aloud either in a chorus or individually. Reading out aloud, reciting aloud 'with expression' was common in those days and we were given marks for this exercise. At that time we did have our own poets – Blazé, Keyt and our own High School poet, Sunethra Wickremasinghe – but it was only anthologies of English poetry we read. This began during our earliest days at school, when Miss Gladys Vanderstraaten read Walter de la Mare to us and asked us to write our own poems on animals and birds. 'Nicholas Nye' was one of my favourites and so was 'The Scarecrow'. I was so influenced at that early age (and all this began in Middle-Kindergarten days) that I decided to be the Scarecrow for a Literary Characters competition between the school houses. With an old tweed coat, a bashed-in felt hat, a shirt with missing buttons, patched breeches, old boots and a meerschaum pipe, I won the Lawrence House prize above all the Cleopatras and Henry the VIII's and Sigiriya Frescoes.

Miss Simithraarachchi, my Standard Two teacher, was one of the most dedicated and able teachers of that era. She was also a perfectionist, so that she had the reputation of being strict, but she was absolutely just and fair although she did have a soft spot for the intelligent ones. All her students were looked upon as her special flock. She was always impeccably groomed in her georgette Kandyan saree and lace-sleeved jacket, a gold brooch pinning the pleats at the shoulder with never a hair out of place. She could teach every subject from Arithmetic to Geography. For drill Miss Eileen da Silva and Miss Olga Wijewardena taught us English Country dances, such as Hunston House and Gathering Peascods. We twisted multi-coloured ribbons round the Maypole as we danced round skipping in a circle.

At the Methodist Church we had Harvest Festivals just as you would have in a country church in an English village. The altar was piled with fruit and vegetables. In church, we waved our palm branches as we walked down the aisle crying out our Hosannas. And when we began studying Latin, Mrs. de Mel draped us in Roman togas as we enacted a wedding processional on the stage at the same time as we sang and chanted the hymn in Latin, 'Hymen O hymenis'. What a culture-mix we experienced, eclectic, polyglot and in many instances alien to the indigenous culture of the students. It didn't matter whether you were a Buddhist, a Hindu or a follower of Islam; such was the strength of that colonial era, and of that missionary zeal, that all the students met for assembly every morning and prayed and sang Christian hymns and bowed their heads in Christian prayer. It was indeed a microcosmic, macrocosmic world of the British Empire and our lives were shaped and formed to a great extent by the missionary principals like Miss Elsie Shire and Miss Ruth Allen, exceptional and indomitable women. With their strong sense of integrity and moral values, they taught their lessons more through their own example than anything else. What they set out to do was dictated by the firm conviction that they had a mission, and part of that mission was to impart an education based on religious values, taught in an alien language, that 'other tongue'. We were completely immured in England, its history, its language, its literature, so much so that when we started writing poetry ourselves as students the natural forms of expression for us were the forms of English poetry: our models were the Augustans and the Romantics, our verse forms the sonnet, the lyric, heroic couplets. In spite of this, looking at the school magazines from the 1930s to the 1950s one can find real talent and an awareness of our own culture in poems like 'The Perahera' 'Ante Lucan' and 'The Muezzin Calls' by Sunethra Wickramasinghe and Fauzynne Sally, both of whom died tragically young.

Miss Elsie Shire christened our new mat-slide. White-haired, serious, yet with a smile on her face, her bobbed hair lifted as she whizzed down with a valiant look while we small ones looked on and clapped our hands. An Irishwoman and the principal of our school, she executed her slide along the polished wooden surface with such bravura and ended up with migraine. Miss Ruth Allen came to the hostel on a Sunday evening for prayers and we ended up playing games with her. We stood in a line and took part in her quiz. Each question answered gave you one step forward until you reached the winning post. I was ten years old but I knew the answers, all based on British history and literature. 'Who rules the waves?' she'd ask. 'Britannia rules the waves,' I'd answer. Book after book was opened by those teachers to acquaint us with that other country.

When I was in the hostel Miss Rita Kaul, the matron, once asked me to take a message at breakfast time to Ruth Allen. I walked up to her bungalow and found her on the lawn beneath the jam fruit tree, which was filled with early morning birds twittering among the fruit. She sat at her white linen spread breakfast table eating toast, butter and marmalade, and drinking tea. She was in the act of scooping out a segment of ripe, golden-coloured papaw. She appeared to me then not as a missionary school principal, but as someone whose senses were delightfully fresh, open and receptive to nature, to her surroundings, to the light and air and freshness of the day. She greeted me with a smile. At that moment, unbeknown to her, she inspired me with a poem which I was to write many years later. For it was that particular experience which led me to question my own ways of thinking, so embedded in the values she taught us. She was unconventional for that era, very emancipated, very feminist and yet tender and emotional with her love of poetry and music. She would read, at assembly, snippets of news from letters – letters from 'home', letters from all parts of the world, even prisoner of war camps in Germany and she sometimes brought soldiers to address us at morning assembly, homesick soldiers who were faced with the strong and novel experience of speaking from a school platform to young schoolgirls in a missionary school. Behind them loomed a solemn painting by Karl Kasmann of Miss Mallet, a former principal and two

90

Victorian prints of famous paintings from the Rossetti and Burne-Jones era. In my kindergarten classroom where we hopped, skipped and galloped to the music played by the gentle Ethel Wijewardane I was very conscious of the coloured lithograph that dominated the room, of Jesus Christ with brown hair and blue eyes with children from all parts of the world surrounding him, white, brown, black, yellow.

From my poetry book I recited with gusto 'Oki Poki Chinga Ma Ring, native wife of an African king ...'. With its racist overtones, it was certainly very different from the translations of African folk verse, with its revelations of each tribal culture, which I was later to read. Africa, in my childhood, was the Dark Continent, the continent of Stanley and Livingstone and pygmies. We had much to learn. Several cultures confronted me but at that stage the history, the language, the literature was from the point of view of the colonizer – during my childhood there were British governors and G.A's. I remember Sir Andrew Caldecott and a painting of his daughter in oils in a white gown and wide-brimmed, white gauzy hat. Where, except in memory, would those portraits remain? While I read and recited English poetry, Florence Paranagama, an excellent teacher, read and translated Sandeseya poetry and I, to this day, bear in my imagination descriptions of those cities nearer home with their familiar metaphor of swanlike women, their faces radiant as the moon and of their doe-eyes; the lotus ponds, the palaces, while we also sang *kavi*. It was Mrs. Weerasiri who introduced Sunil Shanta's songs to us and also brought Sri Jayana as a young dancer to teach Kandyan dancing at High School.

It was in many senses a protected way of life, behind the thick convolvulus hedge where we played netball and tennis-quoits, jumped over hurdles and did our zigzag races in preparation for the sports meet. We acted Shaw and Sheridan. We sang sea-shanties and Elizabethan lyrics, danced Spanish dances and 'The Sailors' Hornpipe'. We had yet to discover our true selves, to listen to the familiar tongue which we heard every day.

A Missionary Lady

In the garden,
Early morning,
The English missionary
Sits eating ripe papaw
Scooped out with her spoon.
Already the trees are fruiting
And purple magenta bourgainvillea
Cascades into her ordered garden.
Birds sing, marbles of sound
Clinking against each other
And the braids of her auburn-grey hair
Are shell-coiled round her ears,
As if to shut out the noise of birds
And human voices.

I think of you with nostalgia
And pity, single, lonely English lady
With no one to share your bed,
You looked into my submissive brown face
Often, but did you ever remember
The careful regard of my dark eyes
Burning a hole into your existence
Like sun-scorched paper.

You made us puritans
You preached a stern morality
And yet you wept, lonely
Over an exile's letters,
The hot sun left your skin dry, mottled,
Your patterned silk gowns
Clung with time, more closely, to your angular limbs,
Your fine-boned hands, sensitive as butterflies,
Yet so impersonal.

Enclosed within a safe garden
Among the lazy tortoises and purple lilac,
It took us centuries to break away
From that alien pattern of living,
Nor can I weep over, or regret
Its final disruption.

Yasmine Gooneratne

Yasmine Gooneratne holds a Personal Chair in English at Macquarie University, New South Wales, and is also Foundation Director of the University's Postcolonial Literatures and Language Research Centre. Her books include *Jane Austen* (Cambridge UP, 1970), *Alexander Pope* (Cambridge UP, 1976), *Silence, Exile and Cunning: The Fiction of Ruth Prawer Jhabvala* (Orient Longman, 1983), *Relative Merits. A Personal Memoir of the Bandaranaike Family of Sri Lanka* (C. Hurst & Co., London and New York, 1986); and, most recently, a novel, *A Change of Skies* (Picador Australia, 1991), winner of the Marjorie Barnard Award for Fiction in 1992.

YASMINE GOONERATNE

Family Histories as Post-colonial Texts

The word 'Australia' summoned up in my mind a single picture, one which I instantly recognised as having come straight out of the *Philip's Atlas* I had used as a schoolboy at Royal. On Philip's map of the world, huge areas of the earth's surface had broken out in the rash of washed-out pink patches which denoted British ownership. To the east of India and the island of Ceylon (also pink), south of Borneo and Sarawak, there Australia had been, a blank pink space shaped like the head of a Scotch terrier with its ears pricked up and its square nose permanently pointed westwards, towards Britain.

That doggy devotion to Britain is something that I, familiar with the colonial traditions of my own family, fully understand the reasons for, even though I do not, of course, personally subscribe to it.

A Change of Skies, 1991

What the principal narrator of my novel calls a 'doggy devotion to Britain' is an imperial legacy that has long survived the end of the Empire itself. It could surface in surprising ways. Falling in love during a colonial adolescence could often be, for example, a quaint and curious thing. Ours being a very conservative society in pre-Independence times, a lot of what we thought of as 'love' had its existence entirely in the mind and in the imagination. Most schoolgirls, for instance, collected pictures of their heroes, and stuck them lovingly into albums. A classmate who sat next to me through Junior and most of Senior school took as the objects of her affection most of the members of the British royal family, which meant that her albums were full of photographs of crowns, medals, dress uniforms and corgis. The rest of us had less elevated desires – our dreams were filled by film actors and sportsmen: indeed, one of my classmates fell passionately in love with the entire Australian cricket team, then visiting Colombo on their way to play Test matches at Lords.

At a different level, this peculiarly colonial devotion may be identified in the sentimental affection that made thousands of West Indians answer the Mother Country's postwar call for assistance in running her extensive transport system, and staffed Britain's National Health Service with highly qualified medical personnel drawn from the Commonwealth nations of five continents. In pre-Thatcher times, it ensured that hundreds of university graduates (of my own generation) from Commonwealth countries travelled to Britain – rather than to the USA or to Europe – for their postgraduate education.

The imperial outlook seems to have affected not only the attitude of ex-colonial nations to Britain, but regulated the relationships of their citizens with one another. In an earlier book, *Relative Merits* (1986), an account of the English-educated Bandaranaike family of Sri Lanka, I drew attention to this phenomenon:

Cultivating English modes of living and thinking, the members of my father's clan had imbibed a very proper English prejudice against Jews, 'frogs', 'Chinks', 'niggers', 'Japs', 'Huns', 'fuzzy-wuzzies', 'wops' and 'wogs' of every description. English upper-class scorn of the lower orders in British society was easily translated, in the context of Ceylon, into a whole-hearted contempt for merchants, traders, members of 'inferior' castes, and even of ... Sinhalese families such as their own who were not, unlike their own, 'out of the top drawer'. Tamils,

> Burghers, Parsis and Muslims were, of course, literally breeds apart: acquaintance with them was possible, friendship rare, and marriage unthinkable.
>
> *Relative Merits*, p. 100

It was inevitable, I suppose, given the intensive nature of the English education with which upper-class 'colonials' were endowed by generations of teachers drawn from Britain's public schools, that British prejudices should have influenced the attitudes colonial and, later, Commonwealth nations adopted towards one another. In *A Change of Skies*, I had my principal narrator, a Sri Lankan university academic, reflect on his own ignorance of a Commonwealth country that is geographically located much closer to his own homeland than Britain:

> Long before I saw Britain for the second time (as a postgraduate student), I knew London, its Dickensian fogs and its murky river, the Shakespearean Tower in which Richard III had had his nephews murdered, Brooke's church clock at Grantchester which stood for ever more at precisely ten to three. I knew, long before I ever ate one, what muffins tasted like. Where Wordsworth's inward eye had been polished by memory, imagination had burnished mine: upon it flashed like images in a video on fast-forward, not just the skittish daffodils of his description but all the meadow flowers of Chaucer, Spenser, Shakespeare and Keats.
>
> For generations my relatives had been either going to, or returning from, England. And so firmly had their gaze been focused on the metropolitan centre of a pale pink *imperium* that they had never so much as glanced in any other direction. To do so would have seemed the grossest lapse of taste.
>
> *A Change of Skies*, p. 12

Growing up in post-colonial times has involved, for most thoughtful persons of my generation, cultural re-thinking and, quite often, political realignment. In countries that were once part of empires, British or any other, a gradual but progressive shedding of 'colonial' attitudes has occurred during the latter half of a century that has seen more people on the move – in transit between countries, cultures and languages – than possibly any other period in the history of the world. Some countries, notably the USA, Australia and Canada, have been built on the physical and intellectual labour of generations of immigrants.

The two texts that have, for me, effectively marked off my own world's colonial past from its post-colonial present and future, are V.S. Naipaul's novel, *A House For Mr Biswas* and Derek Walcott's moving poem 'A Far Cry from Africa'. The personal experiences explored in these texts – each so different from the other – and in so many that have come after them, reflect the political and ideological struggles of the former colonies and dominions of the British and other empires as they moved with varying degrees of difficulty towards freedom. But it has never seemed to me that either of these texts was written to a political agenda: I regard them as expressions of human feeling, of small-scale heroism and large-scale love. The agonizing emotional struggles they depict are instantly recognizable by readers everywhere as recalling similar conflicts in their own experience.

Part of the post-colonial experience, an important part, is the history of exile. It is no accident that Yeats, probably the finest poet of the modern period, and the patron-poet of Ireland, chose exile as the theme for the Dedication to a book of stories selected from the Irish novelists that he published in 1891. The following stanzas come from the Dedication as Yeats rewrote it in 1924.

> Ah, Exiles wandering over lands and seas,
> And planning, plotting always that some morrow
> May set a stone upon ancestral sorrow!
> I also bear a bell-branch full of ease.

I tore it from green boughs winds tore and tossed
Until the sap of summer had grown weary!
I tore it from the barren boughs of Eire,
That country where a man can be so crossed;

Can be so battered, badgered and destroyed
That he's a loveless man: gay bells bring laughter
That shakes a mouldering cobweb from the rafter;
And yet the saddest chimes are best enjoyed.

Gay bells or sad, they bring you memories
Of half-forgotten innocent old places:
We and our bitterness have left no traces
On Munster grass and Connemara skies.

The family histories of post-colonial exiles that seem to me to best explore the post-colonial experience are those that, as Yeats knew, combine comedy and tragedy, laughter and loss. The temptation to nostalgia at one end of the scale, and to mere entertainment or bitterness at the other, is ever-present, of course. It has ruined the work of some promising contemporary writers, but part of the discipline of writing is surely the devising of strategies for overcoming such weaknesses and temptations.

For it is not merely aesthetic effect that is at risk, but accuracy, the post-colonial experience being not a simple but a complex one. Paul Scott, in *The Jewel in the Crown* describes the long relationship of Britain and India as an embrace so long-drawn-out and so intense that it had become no longer possible for the participants in that embrace to be certain whether they hated or loved one another. The language in which that relationship is described by contemporary writers is, at its best, correspondingly and appropriately ambiguous. A love story less fraught with politics might be written with simple directness, but a post-colonial love-story calls for something more.

Salman Rushdie refers in 'The new Empire in Britain' to a time when half the map of the world blushed a rosy pink as it writhed pleasurably under the weight of the British Empire; and David Dabydeen has stated more recently that 'The British Empire ... was as much a pornographic as an economic project. The subject demanded a language capable of describing both a lyrical and a corrosive sexuality.'[1] This creative ambiguity, by means of which writers are exploring compelling personal and political concerns, is to be found in the great post-colonial texts: and it is one of the qualities that focuses upon them the close attention of today's post-colonial critics.

Writing a family history of my own while working as an academic in the field of post-colonial studies has taught me to regard sceptically, if not cynically, the belief with which I grew up, and which I held throughout my undergraduate life, that historians – especially British historians – are the custodians of truth. I now know that the line between what we call 'history' and what we call 'fiction' is so thin as to be almost indistinguishable. This is not only because some eminent historians use figurative language and aural musical effects with the obvious relish that poets do (cf. H.A.L. Fisher's *History of Europe* or Churchill's *History of the English-Speaking Nations*) but because they, like poets and other writers of fictive texts, live and write as men or women in a particular place at a particular point in world history.

It seems to me only natural, indeed inevitable, that given the political situations in which historians (especially Commonwealth historians) compose their 'histories', their view of past events would be coloured by the various aspects of that situation. How objective, how truthful, are some of the eminent and revered historians of the past? How much have they been influenced in what they write by their desire to edit the past so that they produce a work which resembles not what it really was but what it might have been?

However praiseworthy their intentions, however disciplined their methods, are not historians as prone to error and self-deception as other writers?

Family biographies, in which an author seeks to uncover and present the history of his or her own ancestors is a department of historical writing that is surely especially vulnerable to the operation of fraud and fantasy. The English poet William Cowper noted how hard it is for a man engaged in the writing of his own life to write anything but good of himself. How much more must this apply to the feelings of writers who undertake the biographies of their own ancestors or the ancestors of some admired and venerated figure, those people now dead or ageing, to whom their own lives and their outlook on life are inescapably bound.

Some historians, intent on presenting an informative, accurate view of problematic events, cautiously dress their creations as fiction. An outstanding example of this appeared in 1860, in *Max Havelaar*, the classic work in Dutch by Eduard Douwes Dekker, the subtitle of which betrays its real purpose and aspiration: it is a history of 'The Coffee Auctions of the Dutch Trading Company'. The writing and publication of this book followed Dekker's stormy departure from the Dutch colonial service. It is set in mid-19th century Java, and it aims to tell the world 'what is going on in the East Indies' (modern Indonesia). The novel describes the frustrated career of an idealistic, reform-minded Dutch colonial officer who tries to stop the exploitation of Javanese rural folk by their own local chiefs in association with the ruling Dutch. Havelaar doesn't last long – he is restrained in his attempts at reform by his superiors in the colonial bureaucracy, and it is he, not the larcenous aristocrats, who is replaced. Dekker's wit and his colourful language and imagery have caused his book to be regarded as a classic of Dutch literature. Whether we regard it as history or fiction, it is an important post-colonial text for many reasons, among which are: its theme and subject, its intrinsic literary value, and its role in inspiring the contemporary family history-as-novel *This Earth of Mankind*, written in Indonesian by Pramoedya Ananta Toer.

Setting down the facts of my own life for this book, I realize how closely they must resemble and parallel the outlines of other ex-colonial lives in my own generation. I was born in the island once known as Ceylon, and went to school and university there, following this with time spent as a Ph.D. student at Cambridge, and in teaching English literature at my old University, the University of Ceylon in Peradeniya. The latter is an institution that is located in the heart of the hill country that produced the famous tea with which, from British times to the present day, the island is associated in the world's mind; a parallel instance could, perhaps, be found in the establishment (on the site of a former sugar plantation at the Jamaican centre of 18th-century Britain's slave trade) of the University of the West Indies' Mona campus. I have now lived and taught English literature in Australia for nearly 20 years, at a University that bears the name of Lachlan Macquarie, a Governor of New South Wales who, as a young officer serving in Ceylon, had received from the defeated Dutch in 1796 the keys of the Fort of Galle.

Such parallels, I find, come naturally to the mind of a post-colonial writer.

Throughout my adolescence in a society that actively discouraged education for girls as socially unnecessary (and, possibly, psychologically damaging!), I was writing poetry, stories, and sketches for pleasure rather than for publication. As an undergraduate I began to write articles and reviews for local newspapers, proceeding later to write for overseas journals, edit university magazines and, later still, to develop bibliographical skills by practice rather than by formal training.

From 1956 on, the position in Sri Lanka of English language writers such as myself became very problematic. During a period of feverish nationalist 'resurgence', English was officially down-graded and the indigenous languages of Sinhala and Tamil were elevated in what one must regard, however tragic for the country its consequences, as a well-intentioned attempt to redress earlier inequities. (Not unlike the thinking behind Affirmative Action legislation in the USA in the 1960s, except for the important point that the new regulations in Sri Lanka benefited a powerful ethnic majority of potential voters, and not historically disadvantaged and politically powerless minorities.)

My personal response to this was twofold. I tried, on the one hand, to deepen my linguistic skills and my understanding of my mother-tongue and the culture it supported by translating from classical and modern Sinhala poetry, and drawing images from it into my own writing in English. At the same time, I tried to assert, through the act of writing and publishing, my faith in the English language (in the form in which we spoke and wrote it in Sri Lanka) as a medium capable of accommodating a truly national, indigenous Sri Lankan literature.

In 1970 I established, with the collaboration of a colleague in the Department of Western Classics at the University of Ceylon who originated the idea, a literary journal that we named *New Ceylon Writing*. This little magazine came in time to provide a useful forum for English-language writers in Sri Lanka. In the following year I published my first volume of poetry, *Word Bird Motif*. I felt so strongly about both these projects that it is likely I would have continued and developed these interests vigorously in different ways had I remained in the country. But by 1971 I was not only teaching full-time as an academic, but I had become the mother of two young children. While political unrest in 1971 seriously affected schools and universities, and disrupted teaching, offers arrived for my husband and myself of academic positions in Medicine and English literature teaching at Sydney University and Macquarie. We decided to live and work for a while in Australia.

So it was that *The Lizard's Cry*, my second book of poems, was in the nature of a farewell. It was published in the week we left our homeland for a foreign one that, like my fictional narrator in *A Change of Skies*, we had never seen and knew really very little about at the time. There followed a period of comparative silence, during which I wrote no fiction and very little poetry, and published only literary criticism, bibliographical essays, and editions or anthologies of poetry and prose.

Then, in 1981, I was awarded Macquarie University's first degree of Doctor of Letters. My children, having grown up in Australia, knew very little about their Asian background, which includes a family in which there were, and are, a large number of writers, translators and artists. I began work on another book, a history of my father's family. It appeared in print in 1986 with the title of *Relative Merits*.

With hindsight I realize that working in the area of biography and family history gave me a push in the direction, once again, of fiction.

This came about because, in presenting family personalities, I had used some of the techniques of fiction – knowing beforehand from family gossip the patterns of certain incidents, I had been filling out characters, taking as my starting point certain known dates, places and events in their lives, and putting into dramatic form conversations in which family legend asserts that they took part. I also took a long, hard look at the biographies that were being published in Sri Lanka in the 1970s and 1980s. In the Sri Lanka of today, biography – especially of politicians – often becomes a self-serving exercise in flattery and image-building. The biographies that came under my eye were mostly eulogies of politicians. I knew I didn't want to write eulogies. I wanted to create – or recreate – real people for my children to think about, not just waxworks for them to admire (and occasionally dust) or icons for them to worship.

Writing *Relative Merits* gave me practical experience in making characters live and move convincingly. It also helped me to see where I stand in relation to the theories of politics, literature and gender that have become part of today's intellectual atmosphere. These perceptions were sharpened when I was invited to direct Macquarie University's new research centre for Post-colonial Literature and Language studies.

According to some critics working in the field, the term 'post-colonial' covers all the culture affected by the imperial process from the moment of colonization to the present day. According to another school of thought, the term 'post-colonial' relates exclusively to the contemporary culture of independent former colonies. My personal preference is for the first of these definitions. I prefer it because, as a writer of poetry and now of fiction, I am aware that British culture, no less than that of Britain's colonies, has been deeply affected by the experience of colonization and of imperial domination. In 'The New Empire in Britain', Salman Rushdie drew attention to the manner in which the colonial experience has stained and brutalized the English language. Listing in his essay such words as 'coon', 'nigger', and 'fuzzy-wuzzy', Rushdie pointed out that the raw material of literature – language itself – has become stained and diseased by the colonial experience to a point at which it is very nearly unusable.

Coming to the writing of fiction in these post-colonial times, I am forced, like all my contemporaries, to devise strategies which will allow me to use the stained and diseased language Rushdie describes as medium and raw material for an art that will, if I am fortunate, outlast my own life. My own interest in writing fiction is not, however, subject to a political agenda, post-colonial, feminist or other. I am interested in exploring human relationships as they exist between men and women, parents and children, teachers and students, leaders of society and the persons they lead. I find fascinating as a subject for fiction the human weakness for self-deception. It creates a gap between what people really are and what they pretend to be (to themselves as well as to others).

The hope of exploring that gap as honestly and imaginatively as I can, in the lives of contemporary figures as well as of colonial personalities, is the lure that draws me to the adventure of writing fiction. Having been born in Asia, partly educated in England, having settled in Australia, and visited and taught in the USA and elsewhere, I share my contemporaries' personal histories of exile and expatriation, just as having been born in colonial Ceylon and having lived through Independence in 1948 and the post-Independence years, I share with writers and academic colleagues in all Commonwealth countries the experience of post-colonialism. The raw material for what writers of our times are presenting as fiction is, in fact, our life-experience, and the 'colonial' past they evoke is our own family history.

NOTE

1. 'On Not Being Milton: Nigger Talk in England Today', in C. Ricks and L. Michael (eds), *The State of the Language*, 1990, p. 3.

Shashi Deshpande

Shashi Deshpande was born in Dharwas, India, and is the daughter of Adya Rangacharya, the noted Kannada writer and Sanskrit scholar. She is married to Dr D.H. Deshpande. They have two sons and now live in Bangalore. Her publications include four short story collections, four full-length books for children and five novels. A sixth novel, *The Binding Vine,* is to be published by Virago shortly. *The Dark Holds No Terrors* (Vikas, 1980) has been translated into Russian and German and *That Long Silence* (Virago, 1988) into German, Dutch and Finnish. She has won the several prizes for her novels: the Thirumathi Rangammal Prize for *Roots and Shadows,* the Nanjangud Thirumalamba Award for *The Dark Holds No Terrors,* and the Sahitya Akademi award for the novel *That Long Silence.*

SHASHI DESHPANDE

Them and Us

'Can you write me a story for the Independence Day issue?' the editor of a magazine asked me. Could I? In three days? Even as my mind was framing a denial, something made me say, 'Yes, I will.' Later I agonized. How could I write a story to order? And in three days? But that night, as if the words 'Independence Day' had set off some process in my mind, memories began creeping in through unknown crevices. The memory of the first Independence Day – 15 August 1947. Of us going in a tonga, almost breathless with excitement to be out at that time of the night, to witness the hoisting of the Indian flag at midnight. The torrential rains, the thunder and lightning at which the poor horse whinnied and reared in fright. It came back, with an almost eerie vividness, the cluck cluck of the tonga driver's tongue, as he tried to soothe the horse, the constant patter of reassuring words he spoke to us. I remembered too the packets of sweets and tiny flags which they gave us in school in the morning, the crowds that roamed the streets and the air of festivity that prevailed. I did write a story, using some of these memories as the launching pad, and for the first time it occurred to me that I'd seen and lived through a historical moment. The end of British rule in India. The beginning of the end of the British Empire.

But to the child that I was then, the change that registered, the change that mattered, was the departure of the foreign priest who had been Principal until then. He left unregretted for, not only did he never speak to the students, he trailed the obnoxious fumes of a loathsome cigar wherever he went. He had also sobbed loudly when announcing that the British were leaving the country. I have a vague memory of a stony silence encapsulating these sobs. After 15 August, however, something was released. So that when, as he was leaving, his car turned turtle and fell into the ditch, just below the wall where some daring souls had inscribed in indelible tar – Quit India – the students cheered before helping him out. In his place came an Indian priest, a gentle-faced man who not only spoke to us, but knew our names, specially of all the clever students. Yes, it was a change for the better. But the British Empire – what was that?

Perhaps it was the enormous colonial blinkers we wore that blanked out the rest of the world. There was only England and India. Them and Us. And though there were pockets, even in India, where the British did not rule – the Native States – it seemed that They were everywhere. They, of course, were white, while We were all shades of colour, mainly brown. Actually, there were scarcely any English sahibs or memsahibs in the small town in which we lived. True, we did have a 'King Edward VIII Park' in the centre of town, and a maidan, the centrepiece of which was a hideous monument called 'Thackerey's tomb'; but 'the English' were a remote entity. Yet the idea of the Empire somehow seeped into us, colouring our lives, giving them a distinctive tinge. It was all around us, most strongly in the English school we went to, where we did sums that went 'John has 10 apples and Tom has five', learnt poems about strange things like tuffets and muffins, daffodils and daisies. We found out that the history of our country began in a sense only when the British arrived, putting an end to chaos and decadence, and that it was the start of an era of benevolent rule. They – the British – did wonderful things like giving us railways, English schools and colleges and courts of justice, while we Indians did terrible things like the Sepoy Mutiny and the Black Hole of Calcutta. We also indulged in child marriages and sati, which the British with their superior wisdom put an end to. There were school concerts during which we sang 'Simple Simon met a pieman' (pieman?) and danced a vaguely Greek kind of dance, wearing flowing white dresses with coronets of paper flowers on our heads. We learnt to sing songs like 'The owl and the pussy cat' and on all ceremonial occasions we sang 'God save the King'. For some reason, this is the most shaming memory of all, though, yoked to it, comes a redeeming one of many of us, mainly the older children, merely moving our lips, not saying the words.

It was a long way back from school, and at the end of the narrow dusty road bordered by tamarind trees, along which we dawdled, was home. Here we kicked off our socks and shoes, shed our school uniforms and entered a different world altogether. There were neither apples nor daisies here; instead we ate mangoes and guavas and plucked jasmine buds off fragrant bushes to plait into our hair. We wrapped lengths of cloth round ourselves, flung the end over our shoulders and pretended we were grown up and wearing saris. Nobody spoke of the Black Hole or the Mutiny here; it was Jallianwala Bagh and Swaraj. And the Rani of Jhansi was not a traitor but a heroine, and Thackerey no hero but the man who died fighting our local heroine, Kittur Chennamma – the widow of a chieftain. We heard of Bhagat Singh and Lokmanya Tilak, whose words 'Swaraj is my birthright' were a most favourite quote. Every evening we sat with our father to learn Sanskrit, beginning with the recitation of the Amarkosa. We found enormous delight in the sonorous sounds of the Sanskrit words as they rolled off our tongues, came gurgling out of our throats and chests and tickled our palates and nostrils. Once a week a dance master came to teach us Kathak, and we danced to the accompaniment of the songs of Radha and Krishna. And very often we accompanied our parents to functions where girls, dressed simply in white saris with narrow borders, sang invocatory songs in praise of Bharat Mata – Mother India.

But were the two worlds so distinct and apart as I have made them out to be? Surely they met somewhere, overlapped sometimes? Of course, they did. Our father who had, like many brilliant young men of those days, gone to England to study for the Civil Service and stayed on for four years, spoke with affection and admiration of his English teachers, institutions, the people and their liberal and rational thinking. Yet he never got through the examination which would have made him part of the hallowed ICS because, we heard this story often and each time with the same fascination and indignation, he had argued with his examiners during his viva, insisting that it was the British who were, with their divide and rule policy, responsible for the Hindu-Muslim riots. And while the bookshelves at home were lined with English books and we heard a great deal about Ibsen and Shaw, our father wrote plays in Kannada and was forever, in moments of leisure, absent-mindedly and tunelessly intoning verses from the *Gita*, from Kalidasa and the songs of the saint-poets in Kannada.

The combination never seemed odd. We did it too. Shakuntala and Dushyanta and a princess who ate rice and curds were as familiar to us as Heidi and Alice; and the story of the child Rama crying for the moon as much part of our lives as Dick Whittington and his cat. When we performed a play at home – to an audience of four – we did a scene from *Pygmalion* (yes, *Pygmalion*. I can't believe it myself but the memory is too distinct to be misleading. And I was, I remember, Eliza Doolittle, adding, no doubt, another brand of spoken English to Shaw's list!) and another about an Indian princess and a beggar girl which we took from one of our school texts.

But it was not always such a smooth interweaving; at times there was a dissonance, a jangle that confused us. During the endless discussions that went on at home, people spoke of Gandhi, Nehru, Patel, Azad, Bose and so many others, all of whom were, we came to know, heroes. The man who was their enemy, Churchill, was therefore the villain of the piece. Yet, when the talk turned to the War, the other engrossing subject then, they spoke of a man called Hitler, who, it seemed, was the real villain. And Churchill was his adversary too. So was he then a hero, after all? And when it was so clear that everything British was bad for us, why were we sent to an English school? Why did so many people speak of going to England as if it was a paradise? And while everyone rejoiced that the British were leaving, why did some people say 'What will happen to us, what will happen to the country when They leave?'

The contradictions pile up. Yet one was never totally buried under them. It was more like a juggler deftly juggling different coloured balls. Somehow, by some miracle, they remained in the air. Not all of them though. One could not be ruled by foreigners and escape wholly unscarred. There was a sense of inferiority about being what we were. From where did this come? I cannot imagine. The colonial cringe – I hear the phrase now and know how rightly it fits the feeling we had then. That amorphous thing called the British Empire, which never was a solid reality to us, nevertheless impinged on us, it laid its dictates on us. It was as if we saw ourselves with the vision of that 'Other', the outsider. Therefore, we were not the norm; they were. This is to rationalize now, at this distance of time. Then, one only knew that to speak English (and not the way we did), to wear English clothes (I can still remember the topis of those days, surely more of a status symbol than a protection from the sun and rain), to be large, white and Christian was somehow to be superior. To be Indian, to be brown and to be a Hindu was wrong. Most of the time the feelings remained contained within, they simmered and occasionally, very rarely, exploded. I can remember a boy in school who threw himself on a master and almost choked him to death when he, with what surely was a deliberate provocation, said, 'Hindus are dirty, they grovel on their bellies before their gods.' The master, we learnt later, was drunk when he said this and the boy was let off. Now I can laugh both at the master's remarks and the boy's exaggerated reaction; but then there was a taste of ugliness that lingered in the mouth. And there was always an ambivalence. So that I wondered whether it was truly wrong and dirty to prostrate oneself in a temple instead of kneeling in a church. Was it crude to eat with one's fingers and low to run about on bare feet? Even our names, it sometimes seemed in moments of despair, were wrong. Why were we Suresh and Ramesh and Shanta and Kanta and not Mary and Jane and Tom and John (those old friends who so maddeningly kept getting and losing apples)? To go to an English school, to speak English, to passionately devour books like *Alice in Wonderland* and *Treasure Island* was not, it seemed, enough to save one from being inferior. Worse – children who went to nationalist schools and shunned the touch of anything English, jeered at us who went to the 'Padre's school' as traitors. Which meant that one did not belong to that world either. Did we belong nowhere?

No, that never happened. All contradictions were somehow resolved by a tiny figure that dwarfed everything. It was Gandhi, who made the British what they were – just an incident in our history, of which there was so much more than these 200 years. The moral overtones of his being, of what he said and what he did, conferred on the freedom struggle the clear simplicity of a battle of good against evil. Even a child understood this much – that Gandhi was good. His followers – all those men and women who wore home-spun (khadi) clothes, led austere lives, sometimes went underground, and said 'no' to tea when they came home – were the forces of good. Therefore the British who opposed them were put firmly in their place. They were the tyrant who had no right to be in our country. It was we who belonged here.

It was Gandhi who chalked out this place for us where we belonged. He gave us not only a physical area but a moral territory as well. When we stood in this space, it seemed right, not inferior, to speak our own language, to dress the way we did, to go to the temple and pray to our own gods. It was not necessary to straddle two worlds; one could stand in one and reach out to the other. What was the Empire against this man who somehow reached to our innermost beings, where colour and religion did not matter? What was the Empire but something superficial, a scab that could be sloughed off?

Independence came, the British left and the Empire, which had long been tottering, finally gave up the struggle. We have moved on since then, aeons away from Gandhi. It is no longer possible, even for a person like me, who for a very brief while breathed in the rarefied air of Gandhi's world, to look at the Empire with the Gandhian vision, which wholly denied hatred and anger. Distance, of course, helps to dilute strong emotions and passionate reactions. But I do not think distance can always give us a better perspective; it can only give us a different one. Textbooks have been rewritten and we have had a turnabout – heroes have become traitors and traitors heroes. And instead of being a benevolent, divine-ordained rule, British rule has been proved to have reduced a rich country to one of the poorest nations in the world. But it's not only historians who rewrite and reinterpret history. All of us are continually reshaping events and people mentally, according to what we are and what has happened and what is happening to us. I try to think objectively now of the British Empire as one founded accidentally by commercial adventurers, who did the best for themselves and, when it did not clash with their interests, for the people whom they were ruling. But no amount of objectivity can do away with the fact that self-interest was always paramount. And even if I look back without anger, a sorrow remains when I think of what was, of the erosion of self-esteem that still remains. Yet I can never forget that the Empire was for me the bridge to an enchanted world, one which opened up for me as soon as I read a book that began: 'It is a truth universally acknowledged, that a single man in possession of a good fortune, must be in want of a wife.'

Meenakshi Mukherjee

Meenakshi Mukherjee is Professor of English at Jawaharlal Nehru University, New Delhi. She grew up in Patna, in the state of Bihar in eastern India. After obtaining her M.A. in English she went to the University of Pennsylvania, Philadelphia to study for another M.A. degree, and then taught in the State University of New York for a year. She is married to Sujit Mukherjee, who was an academic and later went into publishing. While her two daughters were growing up she did a Ph.D. in English. She has taught at the Universities of Poona, Delhi and Hyderabad, and took up her present position in 1986. Her publications include critical works: *The Twice-born Fiction: Indian Novels in English* (Heinemann, 1971), *Realism and Reality: Novel and Society in India* (Oxford UP, 1985) and *Jane Austen* (Macmillan, 1991); and translations: *The Virgin Fish of Babughat* (Arnold Heinemann, 1974) from the Bengali novel by Lokenath Bhattacharya, and *The Naked King and Other Poems* (Writers' Workshop, Calcutta, 1977) from the Bengali poems by Nirendranath Chakrabarty, with Sujit Mukherjee as co-translator. She has co-edited *Another India* (Penguin, 1990) with Nissim Ezekiel, and *Narrative: Forms and Transformations* (Chanakya, New Delhi, 1987) with Sudhakar Marathe.

MEENAKSHI MUKHERJEE

Growing up by the Ganga

One of my earliest memories of school was a Victory Day lunch. Since it was 1945, the occasion must have been the celebration of the Allies' victory in the Second World War, but at that time I was already so awed by my first glimpses of the world outside home, the vast – so it seemed to me – buildings of the Bankipore Government Girls' High School, the wide expanse of the river Ganga next to it, the fluid day suddenly solidifying into seven blocks of study and games, the thrill of the school transport fetching me back and forth from home, that the victory feast seemed like one more feature of this exotic new life to be taken in my stride. In retrospect it seems to have been a great extravagance – not matched even by the distribution of sweets in school two years later when India became an independent country in 1947. For this Victory lunch, not only did all five hundred girls sit down in rows under a marquee, as one would for a wedding feast, and eat a fairly sumptuous meal served to us course by course by the staff of the school, but each girl was also given a packet of laddoos to take home.

At that time I had only a vague idea about the war and who was fighting whom. As far back as I could remember there were maps and pictures of the war in the newspapers, my father and uncles listened to the radio news avidly and had heated discussions at every meal about Japan and 'German' (I thought German was the name of a country and its people were called the Germany). In my imagination the disturbances in the transmission of the short wave radio news became the sounds of war – uncomfortable, because implicit in it was the threat of a bomb. I think Burma had been bombed and there was one bombing incident in Calcutta. Even in our non-metropolitan Patna, three hundred miles to the west of the scene of danger, air raid shelters had been built and black-out exercises carried out, much to the excitement of the neighbourhood children. The good guys and the bad guys were not clearly set apart in our minds, far less the thought of where we stood in this war game, and the jingle that we sang in the playground echoed this:

sa re ga ma pa dha ni
bom phelechhe japani
bomer modhye keutey saap
British bole baap re baap.

A rough translation from Bengali would be:

Do re mi fa so la ti
A bomb dropped by the Japani
In that bomb a deadly krate
'O, my god!' the British said.[1]

Not only was the war over before I became used to the school routine, British rule in India came to an end within a couple of years. Traces of the old regime remained in our curriculum for a while (we must have been among the last batches to study British history in as much detail as Indian history; I still recall the names of all the seven wives of Henry VIII) but we studied Mathematics, Geography and History (including the history of England) in Bengali unlike, say, my father, who had studied everything in English and was often at a loss for the right Bengali terms when he had to explain to us problems of geometry. We bought new atlases with new maps but the old wall maps of the school still showed India as part of the large red blob on the globe. In fact from 1947 the map of India had assumed a different shape, with two segments from the east and west snipped out to form the new country Pakistan, but our teachers were not used to this change. We grew up learning to draw a complete map of undivided India (there used to be a geometric formula by which you could draw a skeletal diagram of the subcontinent in straight lines, and then give fleshly contours to it with artistic flourish) and only subsequently mark out the boundaries of Pakistan by hand with green crayon. I sometimes think this may well have been one of the subconscious reasons why a whole generation of Indians had trouble getting used to the historical and geographical reality of Pakistan.

Although my adult reading in colonial discourse makes me sensitive to the scars that must have marked me for life, at the time I was growing up I was blissfully unaware of the trauma of cultural displacement that the British system of education allegedly caused. I did most of my reading in Bengali and hardly spoke any English until I went to college at the age of fifteen. In our English textbooks in high school we read the Romantic poets and learnt passages of Shakespeare by heart, but because I went to a non-elite school, we also read a great deal of Bengali literature. (The government schools were inexpensive and allowed the children to study in their mother tongue; the Christian missionary schools and the expensive private schools insisted on English and this system remains unchanged to this day.) Perhaps I read a little more than some of my classmates because we had books at home and my father took my sister and me on occasional book-buying sprees. I remember reading *Twenty Thousand Leagues under the Sea, Treasure Island, The Three Musketeers, A Tale of Two Cities, Ivanhoe* and a lot of such books in Bengali translation long before I got to know the originals, and I am ashamed to confess that some of the originals I actually never got around to reading. Instead of feeling alienated from my own culture by these books, as now I realize I ought to have been, I felt very much at home with them and did not think of them as in any way 'foreign'. Books were read indiscriminately and avidly, specially because we had few other forms of entertainment. Going to a movie was a very special occasion and the films we saw, like the books we read, were a mixture of English, Bengali and Hindi, Chaplin's *The Gold Rush* or Walt Disney's *Pinocchio* followed by Gemini's *Chandralekha* or New Theatre's *Mukti*.

There were very few Indian films for children, but books were available in plenty. There was a popular 'Kanchnjangha Series' which published scores of detective stories for adolescents, and there were the sumptuous illustrated annuals published every October that contained short stories, poems, travel tales, science fiction, jokes and riddles. I now realize how fortunate we were to be surrounded by different kinds of fiction meant for the young reader written quite often by well-known writers of Bengali literature like Buddhadev Bose, Ashapurna Debi, Bibhutibhushan Bandopadhyay, not to speak of the several members of the celebrated Tagore and the Roy families. These books not only told us of the people around us and of the world we recognized to be real – the streets of Calcutta, the rainforests of Sunderban, the lanes of Benaras, the sadhus of Hardwar but also introduced us to unfamiliar landscapes and climates through stories of adventure. A favourite novel of mine, *Chander Pahar (The Mountain of the Moon),* was about an ordinary Bengali boy with a great desire for seeing the world who manages to escape from the almost inevitable fate of becoming a clerk in a British-run jute mill in Calcutta by running away to Africa. He gets a job in Mombasa and works with the Uganda Railroad Constructions to encounter the mysteries of the forest and the magic of far mountains. Of course all Indian knowledge of Africa was mediated through the English language, and it is not surprising that this book and many other adventure novels about the Sahara or the Congo focused only on the flora and the fauna, the forests and mountains. The people who inhabited these areas remained a shadowy group in the background with their bows and arrows, the foreground occupied by a white man with a gun. We did study the continent of Africa in our Geography class, learning to draw its map, and feeling relieved that the dividing lines between countries were so straight and geometrical. The terrible history behind these straight lines which were drawn at a conference table in Berlin in 1888 struck me only in the 1960s, when as an adult reader I first came in touch with Chinua Achebe's novels. When I was in school I had never clearly thought about certain countries in Africa being part of the same British Empire that included us. About Australia or the West Indies, whatever knowledge we had was connected only with cricket.

In our daily lives we had no special awareness of the Empire. I grew up without ever meeting an Englishman. The only Englishwoman I came anywhere near was the wife of the last Governor of Bihar, who gave away the prizes on our annual School Day. I must also have been near an Englishman the day our grandfather decided to take my sister and me to a reception where the Governor was the chief guest. Mother in her nationalistic zeal dressed us in Indian clothes – since we were too young to manage saris, it had to be salwar kameez – but grandfather who was always very formal and correct, made us change into organdy party frocks with matching ribbons in our hair. I was six then; my sister, who was eight, recalls the incident much more vividly.

In the early years of Independence all of us in Bankipore Girls' High School were sentimentally patriotic and drew a sketch of the national flag wherever we could, on the protective covers of our textbooks, on greeting cards, on top of letters, meticulously numbering the twenty-two spokes of the blue wheel of dharma on the white section that separates the safron and the green of the tricolour, passionately inscribing it with slogans like Jai Hind or Vande Mataram. A friend of mine even embroidered the flag on a handkerchief and another girl had a sari with a flag border. We wore tricolour badges as we did our physical exercises in the school playground by the Ganga and vigorously sang Hindi and Bengali songs about national solidarity. The Union Jack I hardly knew because the last years of British rule were a period of rancour against the British and the emotional rejection of the Empire. A distant relative of ours who had received a minor title from the British government for loyal service kept a red and blue flag tucked away on a shelf in his house as a token of gratitude, causing much derisive mirth in our family.

In our family nobody had ever served the British government. My grandfather and father, both being lawyers, could afford to be independent in their views and critical of colonial policies. But whatever his political opinion, my grandfather was an anglophile in certain areas of his life. He dressed nattily in three-piece suits when he went out, and ate an English breakfast (toast, half-boiled eggs in delicate egg-cups, marmalade and cheese) every morning with a knife and a fork, although he wore elegantly pleated dhotis in the Bengali style when at home and relished eating elaborately cooked Indian food comfortably with his fingers for the two major meals of the day. Such inconsistencies were not unusual then, and continue to be a normal part of Indian life. For example, we never questioned the fact that while the boys in the family would graduate from short pants to trousers, retaining their freedom of movement, we, after a brief girlhood of skirts and dresses, would have to be swathed into the restrictive folds of a sari. Preservation of tradition was always the task of women. I felt quite relieved that by the time my daughters grew up the hegemony of the sari as the symbol of Indian culture was on the wane.

But the world that I knew in my childhood was not the only one that existed in India at that time. At college, I came in touch with the products of the other kind of education – girls who knew English better than they knew an Indian language. The college was a missionary institution run by Catholic nuns in Patna which attracted students from many parts of India because of the residential facilities. Girls who came from hill station boarding schools and expensive 'convents' possessed such casual elegance and fluency in spoken English that we felt like country yokels. Having never spoken English outside the English classroom, we were at a consider-able disadvantage when from the basketball court to the lunchroom we were expected to conduct ourselves in English. At the age of fifteen suddenly our biculturalism seemed more like an embarrassment than an asset; we longed to be as 'daffodilized' as they were, denying any acquaintance with the familiar champa or mogra. For me this was a passing phase, because the pull of Bengali literature was too strong and my English marks at the end of the first year helped me to regain self-confidence. But as I chose to specialize in English literature, and later went on to become an English teacher, this dichotomy remained an issue that interested me professionally. The different world views generated by the 'English medium' and mother tongue methods of education and their differential effects on the student's response to literature continue to fascinate me, now more than ever, because English today is far more important than it used to be in our far away colonial childhood.

In our student days the monolingual English speakers were very few in number, although their glamour and power gave them a disproportionate visibility. But today, in my English literature classroom in Delhi, the ratio is reversed. Among the Honours and M.A. students I rarely find anyone who is truly biliterate. They may be capable of conversing in their mother tongue, but would rarely read a book in that language. More and more urban parents invest great amounts of money in giving their children the kind of education that would ensure the loss of their mother tongue. There must be complicated sociological arguments to explain the inevitability of this shift – demands of market economy in the global context, homogenization of world culture through the CNN or what have you. But it saddens me to think that our daughters will be less rooted in their culture than their mothers who played under the tamarind tree on the banks of the Ganga forty years ago.

NOTE

1. I am grateful to my friend Rukmini Bhaya Nair, who not only translated this jingle for me but gave me two other versions:

> *Do re mi fa so la ti*
> *A bomb dropped by the Japani.*
> *In that bomb a snake so vicious*
> *Exclaimed the British 'Goodness gracious'.*

and

> *Do re mi fa so la ti*
> *A bomb dropped by the Japanese*
> *In that bomb a deadly cobra*
> *'O-my-god' the British blubber.*

Nayantara Sahgal

Nayantara Sahgal is the author of eight novels, two autobiographies, and a study of Indira Gandhi's political style. She is also a political journalist whose chief involvement outside writing is civil liberties. In 1990 she was elected Foreign Honorary Member of the American Academy of Arts and Sciences. Her novel *Rich Like Us* won the Sinclair Prize for Fiction and the Sahitya Akademi Award in India, and *Plans for Departure* was awarded the Commonwealth Writers Prize for Eurasia.

NAYANTARA SAHGAL

The Schizophrenic Imagination

First we were colonials, and now we seem to be post-colonials. So is 'colonial' the new Anno Domini from which events are to be everlastingly measured? My own awareness as a writer reaches back to x-thousand B.C., at the very end of which measureless timeless time the British came, and stayed, and left. And now they're gone, and their residue is simply one more layer added to the layer upon layer of Indian consciousness. Just one more.

Let me begin by explaining my title. I am thinking of schizophrenia as a state of mind and feeling that is firmly rooted in a particular subsoil, but above ground has a more fluid identity that doesn't fit comfortably into any single mould. A schizophrenic of this description is a migrant who may never have left his people or his soil. We are all somewhat divided selves, but I'm referring to the divisions that history and circumstance impose on the complex creatures we already are. Let me take the example of Jawaharlal Nehru, a product of colonial times who called himself a man of two worlds, but unlike the quotation describing one of these as dead, the other powerless to be born, both his worlds were alive and vigorous. He was not in any limbo. That was the trouble. His was a life lived in two-plus-one cultures, in many ways a story of assimilation, yet the times he lived in and the role he played in them placed his cultures in conflict and confrontation. The struggle for independence gave the conflict a historic setting, and his life and personality a very different direction from the one it would otherwise have taken.

Educated Indians had, of course, been in contact with western civilization since the British occupation, though most Indians, who lived by the sun, the rain and the seasons, were not touched by it. But many of the educated, too, were affected only in their outer lives. It had not become second nature except for those few whose class and opportunities made this possible. Of these, some related to the East-West encounter by discarding their Indianness to become brown carriers of the white culture they admired and adopted. But nationalism produced another breed of westernized Indian for whom his plural culture meant a bewildering reckoning with himself, a balancing act, where the priorities were never in doubt, but where 'Who am I?' remained an on-going search and question. Nehru was one such Indian, and it may be that many of his countrymen and women are still sorting out the meaning of this particular historical experience.

In contrast, Nirad Chaudhuri, a man of the same generation as Nehru, born when the words 'Empire' and 'colonial' still had benign associations, seems not only an unanguished product of the same period, but one who became a philosophical observer and erudite chronicler of the colonial framework he was born and bred in. After independence, at an advanced age when few people emigrate from choice to set up house and put down roots somewhere else, he could leave India never to return, and could flourish heart-whole in what perhaps was, and is, the real country of his imagination, teaching the English how to stay English. For those who did not cross swords with the imperial order, it was simply the order of the day. For many it had a mystique, the elemental rightness, and right to be there, of a natural phenomenon.

A strong element of mystique attached to Nehru's outlook too, but it was the mystique of the fight for freedom, though that is not all it was. It was also traceable to his peculiar involvement with India, as fact, as dream, and as possibility. He wrote in *Discovery of India*: 'For we are very old, and trackless centuries whisper in our ears.' He was aware of that whisper. One incident toward the end of his life sums up the quality of his involvement. The family was at the breakfast table. A nephew said the country was in a mess, its problems would never be solved, and he, for one, was getting out to settle abroad. Nehru's daughter was listening sympathetically. Suddenly Nehru who had remained silent, spoke in a rage, 'Go where you like, but if I am born a thousand times, a thousand times I will be born an Indian.' It was a statement of almost mystical emotion and power. It had an echo of the cult of the motherland, for in the early years of this century these had been the last words of more than one Indian martyr after he mounted the gallows for his execution. This was Nehru's subsoil speaking, though he was a man deeply identified with other nationalisms, as also with the science, learning and pleasures of the west, and was better known as an internationalist than perhaps any other figure of his time. He was also saying that to transform your society, you have to be in it. The ultimate battles, whether for freedom or after it, are fought on your own soil. He was implying 'My life is my message' as opposed to 'My text is my message'. But the impassioned ingredient in his make-up is common to those everywhere – from rebels against empire to iconoclasts in art and literature – who see that there are facts which must be denied, and that there is more than one way of looking at the world.

There is a story from the imperial era about an Englishman whose posting in the Sudan was over. He was to leave with his family for England and he was pleased when his little son begged to be taken to say goodbye to the statue of Gordon. The father was proud that his child remembered all he had been taught about General Gordon's magnificent defence of Khartoum, a heroic event in the annals of Empire, and deeply moved when tears ran down the child's face as they stood at the famous equestrian statue, until the boy asked, 'Daddy, who's that man sitting on Gordon?' It is those who in all honesty and earnestness are looking at the horse and not the rider who can fit neatly into no tradition except one that is in the making. If anyone wants to fit me into a tradition, it is this tradition-in-the-making they will have to settle for.

My own divided experience starts with belonging to North India, a region that has been spared no convulsion or folk experience, from epic marvels and a matchless metaphysics to repeated invasion and slaughter. My part of the Ganges plain is the cradle of Hinduism but it is home to Islam as well, and Indo-English by virtue of the continuing impact and fall-out of British rule. All three influences meet in the city of my birth whose original name, Prayag, figures in the *Ramayana*, while its present name, Allahabad, testifies to Muslim conquest and rule, and where every road in my childhood was named after an Englishman, the public park had a statue of stout old Queen Victoria, and down the road from our house two nights a week came dance music from a club that did not admit Indians.

Going to school was like arriving at the club that didn't admit Indians. My school admitted Indians but ignored India. As I was quite sure that India existed, I didn't place much faith in school. At home I was nourished on revolt. My elders were committed to rooting out foreign rule and had made a personal beginning by giving up their scholarship and their careers at the Bar to devote their lives and all their resources to the struggle for freedom. They were so enthraled with organizing for it and being imprisoned for it that I thought going to jail was a career. They had no regular incomes because they had given up their means of livelihood, but they found it so exhilarating doing without the comforts, amenities and certainties other people took for granted, that when I was introduced to what is known as normal life after independence, it gave me quite a shock with its very different priorities. I had never before met people who earned livings, took holidays, joined clubs, went shopping, and knew what tomorrow would bring, and they struck me as a quaint and exotic species. Above all the whole business of entertaining, of serving elaborate meals to other well-fed people, and then going to *their* houses to be fed elaborate meals by *them*, seemed to me an extremely curious way of spending time. There are several aspects of normal life I still haven't got used to. I think I started to write books as a retreat from it. I know I am ill-equipped to be part of it. I will forever be an outsider looking in through its windows, marvelling at the sequences and continuities of normal life. When I try to read them, they look like hieroglyphics, a fascinating language for which I lack the code.

In a childhood filled with the sights, sounds and folklore, and sometimes the furore, of the national movement, nothing estranged me from school more than the way history was taught. Its content and perspective were so different from what I learned at home that I soon put school history in the same category as Kipling's 'Gunga Din' – a rousing, rollicking white man's fable that had everything to do with the conqueror's image of the bullied, beaten Indian, loyal to his last gasp, and nothing to do with India. In short I didn't believe a word of it. I was also surprised to learn that ancient times began with Greece, that the world had been created in six days, and that all of religion was down in one little book. Though the nuns did their best with me, privately I suspected that God Almighty was my grandfather, and Jesus Christ must be my uncle, since he carried other people's sorrows on his back; that they, together with my father and mother, were special shining beings, and that the fight for freedom was the path to the Holy Grail. I knew I inhabited a huger, older universe of which school taught me only a meagre slice, yet paradoxically this little scrap filled the textbooks and ruled the world.

Home had its paradoxes, too, but they fell into place as part of a larger purpose. I can see my frail, spectacled, widowed grandmother sitting cross-legged on her bedroom floor reading in a low mutter from her enormous large-print *Ramayana*, and shrieking for a servant when a mouse darts across the floor, but she's the same woman who picketed foreign cloth shops not long before, and who once stayed firmly put at the head of a procession halted by the police. Let me quote what happened next from a written account. She was 'knocked down ... and hit repeatedly on the head with canes. Blood came out of an open wound in her head; she fainted and lay on the roadside.' Within these outer tensions there were inner tensions, for non-violence does not come naturally to the human race, and my father once got solitary confinement for knocking down a jail guard who insulted my grandmother when she visited him in jail. I used to wish the time would come when my parents would stay home like other parents. For one of them the time never came, for my father died of his last imprisonment. I'm not sure whether a childhood lived in this heightened state of national and world awareness was euphoric or wretched. It is probably best described by Pushkin's reaction when he read Gogol's *Dead Souls*. After laughing uproariously all the way through it, he exclaimed, 'Oh God, how sad our Russia is!' It has been said that a person who survives her childhood has enough information to last her for the rest of her days, and it must be true, or my novels would not have reflected the political idealism of an emergent nation, and its progressive destruction and decay. There is always an obstinate idealist hanging around in my fiction, usually with as much chance of success or survival as a snowball in Hades.

I did not set out to write 'political fiction'. I have no ideology except a vague sort that feels uncomfortable with title and privilege, with kings, queens and political dynasties. I have no message either unless it is the non-message that Europe is not the centre of the world. Politics for me was an environment in which every issue was a political issue, and personal and political fates were inextricably bound. If it has remained a continuing awareness, it is because I live in an unsettled order, one I am trying to change, one where I am witness to the public and domestic misuses of power. And politics was for so long dictated by other people's view of us that I have found it satisfying to give it Indian expression and interpretation. Yet though I use a political backdrop or events – since these happen to be the outer focal points that trigger my imagination, and also because I think we gain or lose significance in our relationship to events – I prefer to think of my fiction as having a sense of history, in a country where race, religion or caste can decide the course of a love affair, where it can take as much raw courage to choose a husband, or leave him, as to face a firing squad. The nuclear family with its attendant traumas is not for us. Our traumas like our families are built on a grander scale. From where I stand, looking at the horse and not the rider, it doesn't seem to me there *is* such a thing as a purely individual predicament. Too many other factors blur and burden it, including the weather. Fornication and adultery go on in India as anywhere else, but I'm not sure they can be given such free rein as in western fiction without becoming unrelated to a social condition where the individual is tied hand and foot, and often back-breakingly, to wider responsibility. For one thing he hasn't got the time. And she has even less. But as we approach western living conditions – as in my novel after next – there will be more time for adultery.

Then, societies that have lived long under foreign domination bring their own behaviour characteristics into play. Passivity can become an active choice, a strength, among people where invasion and re-conquest have been the pattern, because it is one's best chance of remaining whole. Sycophancy, too, is the hallmark of the survivor, and all cultures have sycophants. But when I wonder why *we* produce them in such abundance, and this struck me strongly during the 1975-77 dictatorship known as the Emergency – then I have to ask, as I did in my novel *Rich Like Us*, whether Hinduism inclines a whole society to the status quo. Does it put out the fires of rebellion? Does it incline women to victimization, to individual and mass acts of horrifying self-sacrifice? Has the cult of virtue (female) and honour (male) been so ferocious and merciless in any other society that prides itself on its humane values? How do we explain this aspect of ourselves? I have been much preoccupied with the effects of Hinduism on character in my novels.

All Indians are not Hindus but all Indians must reckon with Hinduism since it is the dominant setting, the social and psychological atmosphere. Yet what it is we are reckoning with is hard to say when Hinduism has no beginning, no founder, no church, no commandments, no single bible, no single prophet or messiah. There can never be a law of blasphemy against Hinduism, or any other concrete religious measure to bring all Hindus into line. But memory and imagination are much the most powerful of human possessions, and give us almost unlimited scope for both enlightenment and bigotry. This, then, is the sky I and my characters live under, and in one sense I am nothing if I am not a Hindu. On the Indian subcontinent there is no escape from the aspect of cultural behaviour we call religious.

Some Hindus solve their problem of how to come to terms with Hinduism by dumping it and calling themselves atheists, agnostics, or secular. But this is no solution for a writer. If I change my name today to Henrietta von Blinkenstaff, who am I trying to fool? Can I quick-change my bones, my myths, my grandparents? Can I forget that my great-grandmother became a suttee? So I find it more useful to say, Believe it, you are a Hindu. Now figure out, if you can, what that means, and fiction is part of the process of figuring it out. Even if I were so inclined, it would be futile to wish away a force that has moulded hundreds of generations, that governs some countries and is a governing force in others, and whose absolutism has crossed national frontiers to sentence a writer to death for blasphemy. There is no safe distance from such a force any more than there is from modern weaponry. Literature can hardly ignore this unfinished question.

I used to try to integrate my overpowering heritage, feel relaxed and easy about it, but I've discovered I'm not supposed to feel integrated and relaxed. It is not only inevitable, it is also perfectly natural for the inheritor of one of the earth's oldest and most complex inheritances to feel fragmented. And I have learned to treat my own particular muddle as a priceless asset. It is for my Third Eye to reconcile these fragments through fiction, and through my sense of plural self to produce a fiction other than that which a less ancient, more homogeneous, more settled society produces. Time itself – an important event of the novel – is not the same in the Indian, especially the Hindu reckoning as in other societies, including other ancient societies that have suffered uprooting shocks and made clean breaks with the past. The city I grew up in had co-existing time zones. The past is so much with us, in the beliefs and routines people live by, in conversations whose allusions can go from legend to modern in minutes, that no time is ever entirely past. It is modern times that strain my own imagination, and I don't think anyone has succeeded in creating a modern Indian character, if by 'modern' we mean a basic alteration or transformation from what went before. I'm not sure such a creature exists, so real life cannot be much help in providing examples. Is 'modern' the frame of mind that descends from the European Enlightenment? Is it the position you occupy in the race for European technology? Is the contemporary western world still The World, and all other peoples to be judged by its yard-sticks of progress? I've made some play with the word 'modern' in my last novel, Mistaken Identity.

One of the effects of coming to terms with my own dividedness has been to ignore chronology and to free myself from Indian locale and characters in my fiction. This has been liberating for me, and I expect it must be so for schizophrenic fiction in general. Not only is it time for interpretation to flow many ways instead of only west to east, but the question of direction is itself no longer relevant when the migration of cultures is leaving cultures open-ended, and when migration can take place without ever leaving one's soil. Where does one culture begin and another end when they are housed in the same person? There are powerful winds blowing through English literature. English is being assaulted by cross-currents of racial experience, by a vast expansion of its frame of reference, by new uses of imagination and language. The day of pure literatures, like pure or ruling races, is over, and English, at least, is in a new flowering – one that expresses a vision, a vitality, an expansionism that Sir Francis Drake and other English gentlemen never dreamed they would be unleashing when they set sail on their swashbuckling adventures.

To end with let me give you an example of the schizophrenia I am talking about. My father, a Sanskrit scholar, a fairly arrogant Indian, and a dedicated freedom fighter who was to die of British imprisonment a few years later, wept when London was bombed in the blitz, and when Paris fell to Hitler's armies. His answer to the question 'Who am I?' would have been, 'I am a member of the human race – and all the rest is rhetoric.'

Ishrat Lindblad

Ishrat Lindblad (née Hamid Ghani) was born in Lucknow in 1940. In 1947 her family chose to become Pakistani. In 1962 she married and settled in Sweden. Her husband is Professor B.S. Lindblad and she has three children. Ishrat attended school in England, and has a B.A. and an M.A. from the University of the Punjab, Lahore, Pakistan. In 1968 she obtained her 'filosofielicenciatexam' from the University of Uppsala, Sweden and, in 1971, her 'filosofiedoktorsexam' from the same University. She has taught at a number of different universities, including the University of the Punjab, the University of Uppsala, King Saud University, and the University of the United Arab Emirates. Since 1976 her permanent position has been Associate Professor at the Department of English, University of Stockholm, Sweden. Her publications include *Creative Evolution and Bernard Shaw's Dramatic Art*, (Uppsala, 1971), *Pamela Hansford Johnson* (Twane Publishers, 1982), *Dickens in Swedish: A Critical Bibliography* (Stockholm University, 1984), and articles on Shakespeare, Shaw, Beckett, John Fowles, Anita Desai, and Salman Rushdie. She is currently working on a study of Shakespeare in Sweden and a critical volume on Salman Rushdie.

ISHRAT LINDBLAD

The Irresistible Anglo-Filiation of Ishrat

I have never thought of myself as a daughter of Empire but very much as my mother's daughter. Despite the intensity of my filial feelings however, I proved to be a most unbecoming daughter. In the Muslim Indian culture into which I was born, daughters were models of obedience. Yet my becoming the disobedient daughter who fell in love with a 'Westerner' and insisted on marrying him, must, in some measure, have been due to the insidious influence of that intangible mother whom I did not even know I had. Unhappily for my mother, who suffered the most, *she* was the one who had been the most outspoken champion of a proper Western education for her three daughters. She ought to have known that the mother who educates you and encourages you to think for yourself is doomed to have you struggle against her. After all, hadn't the British provided the education that enabled her family to spend their lives successfully fighting the Raj? Several of my mother's uncles were active members of the Congress party and had been jailed by the British. *They* were the really unbecoming children of Empire.

Not so my father's family. They were loyal servants of the British Raj. Even though my grandfather, who rose to become a High Court judge in British India, had not been permitted to keep on his shoes when entering a white man's office, he couldn't help admiring the British – their incorruptibility, their sense of justice – and it was his cherished dream to have his only son enter the Indian Civil Service. With that end in view, he packed my father off to St. Paul's boarding school in London where he could get a solid public school education. Once my father had realized his father's dream, he was allowed to stay on and study engineering which was what *he* wanted to do. After spending eighteen years in England, my father returned home and opted for an arranged marriage without ever seeing even a photograph of the woman who was to become my mother. An anglophile young Kashmiri, educated abroad, who loved to sing the songs of Gilbert and Sullivan, and told us of queuing all night to get tickets for Covent Garden and the Albert Hall ... a young daughter of the Frontier freedom fighters, barely out of purdah, who quoted Persian poetry and read us the articles she wrote for Urdu magazines ... what could they have in common? They fell in love at first post-wedded sight. It was my favourite fairy tale. In later years when I asked my father how he could have chosen to marry as traditionally as he did, he cryptically replied that he had seen enough of Western 'morality' to know he wanted to have nothing to do with it.

As a child, 'Empire' meant no more to me than the high-waisted dresses I saw in fashion magazines and wanted my tailor to copy. I often wondered why adult conversation on the subject aroused such passion. You would have thought that they would have stopped caring about fashion at their age! By the time I learnt to connect the Raj that my mother's relatives had fought, with the British King that we, at school assembly, so fervently sang for God to save, both were things of the past. I had found out about the insulting second stanza of the British national anthem and preferred to sing *Jive Pakistan*. We had to wear white and green *shalwar kamiz* to school instead of blue skirts and white blouses. We were an independent nation.

For me, Independence Day was literally a rude awakening. I was fast asleep when the sound of a discordant brass band playing loudly beneath my window drew me out of bed. I saw masses of people who all seemed to be dressed in tinsel and the repulsive shade beloved by Indian sweepers that we call *jamardani* pink. 'What's happened?' I asked, and was told that it was 'Independence Day'. For months afterwards, conversation was dominated by something called 'the Radcliffe Award' and how unfair the British had been: 'You can never trust the British.' The Hindus had been smart and made friends with Lord Mountbatten. *They* knew how to curry favour. The British had hated Jinnah and seen to it that Pakistan would be stillborn: 'How can you expect a nation to survive with a thousand miles of enemy territory between its wings?' The next thing you knew the British had begun pulling out their troops thus making doubly sure that the country would end in a fire of communal hate.

Even as they vented their ire, my parents continued to send my sister and me to the local convent school. We loved and respected the nuns who taught us, and felt very privileged because they accepted my mother's invitations to tea. Of course it was unpleasant to have the white girls shouting 'brown rats, brown rats', from their special School Bus every time they passed us waiting to be fetched outside school, but we could always shout 'white mice, white mice' back. My elder sister continued to enjoy going to the Girl Guides and I, who was 'too young', would pretend I was one too, passing away the hours till her return with imagined rituals, or skipping rope energetically chanting 'I am a girl guide dressed in blue ...'

The continuity was suddenly interrupted as we packed and got ready to move to Lahore. I remember a nightmarish train journey when I was supposed to be named 'Mary'. The name had been painted in black letters on the tin trunk in which my clothes were packed. If the British were our enemies why was it an advantage suddenly to have a British name? 'Be quiet, just do as we say.' At one railway station I saw a turbaned Sikh stab an old man who was prostrating himself before Allah. I kept expecting an ambush and a massacre like the ones I had seen on *Movietone News*. I was terrified that at the critical moment I would forget that I was called Mary. Then equally suddenly we were safely installed in a fine bungalow along the Canal Banks in Lahore. Soon after that bloated dead bodies kept floating down the Canal. My elder sister and I would stand on the bridge and watch them bob past. Our garden began to swarm with refugees and flies. You didn't know who was buzzing loudest. My parents kept pitching tents for them in the garden, and tending to their fly-infested wounds. They had no time for us and it was shameful to complain. The cook was constantly cooking food for the refugees. There was no private place for us to be. It was as if with the country's independence we had lost our own.

Only a few years later my parents began to express some nostalgia for the 'good old days' when punctuality was a virtue; telephones worked; traffic was organized; bureaucrats were honest, and standards of education high: 'You really had to hand it to the British for knowing how to run things.' I remember the grudging admiration in my mother's voice when she told us what a stickler 'Auntie' Hinton Cooper was for table manners. Especially the time tea had been brought into the drawing-room on a beautifully laid trolley and Uncle Harold made a move to pour it out. Auntie immediately made him aware he had overstepped the line by asking with delicate sarcasm: 'Harold, are you pouring the tea or am *I*?' The Hinton Coopers were people we really looked up to because he was the General Manager of the North Western

Railway where my father was an officer. Till today, I make a point of always being the one who pours the tea in my own home.

I also loved to hear about the great style in which the banquets at Government House (to which my parents were lucky enough to be invited) were held. There were so many knives and forks that it was a triumph to know which was the correct one to use. The table napkins were folded like white swans, and rose petals floated in the finger bowls which were filled with warm water during cold weather. My mother was famous for the elegance of the dining table over which she presided and she never served fruit without finger bowls with rose petals floating in the water which was warm when it was winter. I used to laugh derisively at the stupid Indian, when told the story of how he had started to drink from the finger bowl which had been placed in front of him at the banquet in honour of Queen Victoria during her visit to India. How I admired Our Gracious Queen who tactfully picked up her own bowl and drank from it too! 'That's the kind of people the British were you know.'

I began to identify with these marvellous British. How unnecessary it seemed when, in the zeal of new nationhood, the municipality demolished the dear old grey stone statue of Queen Victoria in Empress Gardens. How unduly chauvinistic when they began renaming Elphinstone Street and Victoria Road and Lawrence Gardens ... Who had ever heard of Zeb-un-Nisa and Shaheed Illmuddin? Thank goodness, no-one had thought of renaming the Nicholson Memorial, which I dearly loved. I never failed to run up that hill near Attock Bridge when we motored up to Peshawar to visit my mother's family. What did I know of the fact that it commemorated the victory of a British brigadier against my mother's people?

I remember what a treat it was when Sir Francis Moodie's family came round singing carols and what a pity it seemed to me that we didn't have any such charming traditions ourselves. How sad I was they stopped having the annual Christmas party at the Gymkhana Club. No more could I enjoy dressing up like the English girls in a fluffy organza party dress and wait for the present my parents had made sure would be hanging on the tree for Father Christmas to give to me: 'The British they really knew how to enjoy life they did.' Of course, one of the compensations of gaining independence was that we could now join the prestigious 'White's Only' Punjab Club and begin to look down our noses at the children who were members at the inferior Gymkhana. Having been looked down on by the British made me enjoy looking down on others myself. Even the servants who applied for positions with us would suffer from this legacy. I remember how furious my mother once was when a prospective cook she was interviewing proudly declared that he had only worked in the homes of English sahibs. In such nameless unremembered ways did the experience of the Raj make us into 'mimic men' and rob us of pride in our own identity.

The magic of everything British was enhanced when my father had to go to England for six months in connection with his work, and my mother went with him. It was her first visit. She wrote me letters about the wonders she saw. How people simply put down their penny in a box when buying their newspapers and nobody stole the money or dreamt of taking a paper without paying; how clean the public lavatories were; how the roads were studded with something called 'cat's eyes' that shone in the dark and made night driving easy; how you could make 'phone calls from public booths and if a person answered, the machine swallowed up your coin ... They sent us parcels full of exciting gifts: of juicy fruit chewing gum, and Buckingham-Palace-Guard dolls, and of Shakespeare's house in china and Elvis Presley records. All of England seemed to be gift-wrapped and waiting for me to open it.

That was when my elder sister and I began to long to go to boarding school in England. I began devouring books about St. Clare's and nothing seemed more exciting than the world it represented. I would recite 'Oh! Granchester, Oh! Granchester, I would I were in Granchester' as if I were Rupert Brooke himself, and thought King Richard's speech about the 'jewel set in the silver sea' was the finest speech in all of Shakespeare.

Destiny was on our side. Soon after my parents' return home, the Pakistan government abolished the Senior Cambridge Examination. Ever since I began going to school, at the age of four, I had been sent to whichever convent school was considered the best one wherever my father, in his peripatetic profession, happened to be. Although my sisters and I had a *maulvi* coming to our house to every day teach us how to read the Holy Quran, and a music master to give us daily sitar lessons, our formal education was entirely based on the British school system. My parents wanted us to go to university, which, thanks to Lord Macaulay's minute on education, meant we would stand a much better chance if we had our basic education in English. The abolition of the Senior Cambridge Examination was a major disaster. We had memorized reams of English literature and learnt all about British history and the climate of the British Isles but not a word about our own country. It was virtually impossible for us to enter the vernacular school system and matriculate. 'How,' argued my elder sister and I, 'could we cope with the confusion of Indian history or start struggling with literature in Urdu and Persian, languages we could barely read?' (I had also heard that the maths courses in the vernacular schools were much more difficult and maths was not my strongest subject. The spectre of failure when I was used to coming first in class was truly frightening.) Like a fairy godfather, a very close friend, Uncle Sam, one of the representatives of Her Majesty's Government who had stayed on, suggested that my parents should send us to the same boarding school in England as his own daughters were sent to. Within a matter of months everything had been arranged. One day my father came home with the coveted air tickets and, escorted by my mother, my elder sister and I were off to England ...

It was Coronation year and I was thirteen: 'Earth has not anything to show more fair.' The streets of London were coloured red and decorated with monumental arches. Breakfasts consisted of strawberries and cream (I had only seen pictures of this luscious fruit before). One of my father's friends even lived like a lord in a grand manor house, with a gleaming mahogany dining table, elaborate flower arrangements, and a butler straight out of Wodehouse. This gentleman kindly put his Daimler and chauffeur at our disposal, so that we could make a tour up to the Lake District, which proved to be everything that Wordsworth's poetry had made me imagine it to be. I felt like Maggie Tulliver in reverse: for the first time the world outside corresponded to the world I had been reading about! The only really unprepared-for moment came when I visited the home of one of the 'grandest ladies in the colonies'. It was the tiniest house I had ever stepped into. I felt like Gulliver in Lilliput. Most shocking of all, she was actually preparing her own food and washing her own dishes. I could hardly believe my eyes! Was this the 'home' that the British in India were always sighing for in such superior tones?

Once my mother left, and school started in earnest, life became scary. My elder sister and I were the only 'foreign' girls at that school. We were used to school uniform, but wearing ties and bowler hats was something new and pretty uncomfortable. We overheard the English girls discussing us and allowing in condescending tones that 'the two little Indian girls' (we never succeeded in getting them to think of us as Pakistani) 'really spoke English surprisingly well'. Considering we had been speaking the language ever since we had been able to speak, it surprised us that they should be so surprised. But we soon learnt to accept compliments on our good English, and to play up to our schoolmates. It was fun telling them that we had never seen a knife and fork before, and begging them to teach us how to peel a banana with the help of these implements (it was absolutely forbidden to eat anything at Wentworth with your fingers). Easy to make them believe that 'back home' we had lived in a mud hut and combed our hair with twigs. We soon became authorities on everything foreign and it became quite common for them to ask us about the kangaroos in Australia or the pygmies in Africa. The insularity of the British schoolgirl was unlike anything we had met before.

Gradually, by telling them how different I was, I came to take pride in my own culture: I asked my parents to send me saris to wear at weekends. I began to long for home food. I was glad to be asked to play the sitar on a BBC TV programme called *All Your Own*, and laughed when the compère, Clifford Williams, could only call that wonderful music 'a beautiful noise'. I sat shivering on the school radiators and realized that the climate of the British Isles was better read about than experienced. For the first time the lines of an old rhyme that had puzzled me all my life made literal sense: 'In winter I get up at night and dress by yellow candle light/ In summer quite the other way, I have to go to bed by day.' It seemed so much more sensible to have roughly equal days and nights all the year round as we did in my country.

In spite of these stirrings of national pride, I was not able to resist the glamour of imperial Britain entirely. I was thrilled to be taken to the Queen's Garden Party (how tiny she was!) and to the Horse Guards' parade. I felt inordinately proud when Uncle Sam's name appeared in the Birthday Honours list and he was made a Knight of the British Empire. I also made it a matter of honour never to make a single mistake in writing out the twenty lines of English poetry that Miss Trace expected us to have memorized each week. And how I loved rolling those lines around my tongue! I still treasure a classmate's inscription in my copy of *Macbeth*: 'Straight got by heart that book to the last page.'

With time, however, I found friends and grew to love Wentworth. There is also no doubt in my mind I owed some of the best education I received to that school. One of my most memorable experiences was when the history teacher was telling us about the Black Hole of Calcutta – from the British point of view, of course. For homework I wrote my essay on the Indian Mutiny casting the British as the villains of the piece. Miss Lamb won my everlasting admiration by giving me full marks for the essay and reading it out in class so that the girls should know that 'there are always two sides to history'. I now began to study Indian and Islamic history on my own and sat up reading Nehru's autobiography till 'lights out'. When one of my favourite cousins, who had been studying at Oxford, decided to become a British citizen and settle in England, I felt badly betrayed. I righteously told him it was a moral obligation for us Pakistanis to return home and serve our own country. Ironically then, it was through living and studying in England that I became determined to reject cultural imperialism.

Upon my return home I was eager to become more Pakistani than the most thoroughly native native. I abandoned western dress and took to wearing the sari daily, a habit I have never shed. I prayed five times a day. I stayed wide awake through all night Qawwali sessions, actually enjoying the religious songs I had once been so bored by. I even began to frequent *mushairas* (a form of poetry reading where the leading poets improvise verses to cap each other's couplets). I took up the sitar again. I chose to study Persian as an additional subject at college, and persuaded a dear uncle to help me through the poetry of Saadi and Hafiz. I even optimistically discussed launching a National Theatre movement with Zia Mohyeddin, who had just returned from RADA and produced a very successful play in Urdu.

But try as I would, how could I get away from the fact that it was easier for me to act in English than in Urdu, and that my most prized trophies were won for my debating skills at pseudo-British inter-collegiate debates? Or from the sad knowledge that many of my college mates thought of me as an Anglified snob? Or that the only Honours subject the college offered was English? Or that when I wanted to do my M.A. the best teachers were the English teachers at Forman Christian College and the most inspiring one of them all was an ardent Leavisite?

Even events seemed to conspire against me. Our English teacher had to return home to England and I was offered her job. Four years later, on board a ship heading homewards after a trip to England, I was fated to meet and succumb, in a most un-Pakistani way, to the charms of an idealistic young Swedish doctor on his way out to India. My despairing father asked me if I hadn't read enough English literature to know what came of shipboard romances. I kept trying to convince everybody I was NOT a rebel against my own traditions and culture. But actions speak louder than words: he became my husband.

Thirty years later I am living in Sweden and still teaching English literature. True, I put in a word for more courses in New Literatures in English and teach them whenever I get the chance. But when it comes to the crunch, and we discuss changing the canon of our vital undergraduate literary survey course, I find it impossible to justify giving up Virginia Woolf for Anita Desai. Somewhere, so deep inside of me that I don't even want to start digging for its source, is the conviction that there is simply nothing quite as great as the great English authors. And so, in spite of my own best intentions, I think that the most unbecoming thing about myself is that I have remained a becoming daughter of Empire after all. But isn't it true, as Bergson pointed out that 'Being and not-being are joined in a process of becoming'?

Shirley Chew

Shirley Chew is a senior lecturer at the University of Leeds. She edited *Arthur Hugh Clough: Selected Poems* (Carcanet, 1987) and *Re-visions of Canadian Literature* (University of Leeds, 1984), and has published articles on British, Indian and Canadian writers in various critical volumes and journals. She is currently collaborating on a critical study of recent literatures from Commonwealth countries. Since 1992, she has co-edited with John Thieme *The Journal of Commonwealth Literature*.

SHIRLEY CHEW

'And there's another country
I've heard of'

The British were back in Singapore, and even though their credibility as an imperial power had been dented by their failure to defend the island against the Japanese in 1942, an English education was still regarded as a good investment in the postwar years. So it was decided that I should attend one of the colony's English schools as soon as they reopened their doors.[1] I do not recall objecting to the decision but I must have missed the Chinese infant school from which I was parted. Not that it could have been anything other than a makeshift establishment with a noisy pack of children whom the teacher continually yelled at and occasionally smacked. But I was happy there, did well at my lessons, and even enjoyed a touch of glamour because a number of the teachers were family friends, often with associations stretching back to bygone days in Fujian.[2] I had also got used to myself as 'Zhou Lan', my Chinese name in Mandarin, and did not much care for the English name written into my birth certificate and by which I would be known at my new school.

The school which I was to attend, the Convent of the Holy Infant Jesus, was one of the best schools in the colony. It belonged to a French order, was run by Irish nuns, and was also an orphanage for abandoned girl babies. It stood with its grey walls, its trees and its elegant chapel close to the heart of the city, in the midst of swirling traffic.[3] Perhaps my parents did not feel up to dealing with so much foreignness all at once – white women in forbidding black habits who spoke only English and often with an uncomfortable intensity. Perhaps they feared that in the scramble to enrol for places, one false step on their part would end in my being turned away – the nuns, so the rumour went, were unpredictable and my parents had none of the usual safeguards of being either Roman Catholics or British citizens or old pupils of the school. Whatever the reason, it was not my mother, as might have been expected, but a family friend who took me to the school, saw me admitted as a primary pupil, and handed me over to the nun in charge. Left on my own and with only a few words of English at my command, I was soon in trouble. It was announced that we would be moving to another classroom tomorrow. That much I understood. What I failed to grasp was the location of the room. Hopelessly lost the next day, I took refuge in a long gallery lined with benches, on which other strays were already perched, and settled down to wait for something to happen. Something did. A nun scurried along the red flagstones, shooed us from the benches, marched us off in two rows and tumbled us one after another into such classrooms as had places to spare. I landed in front of a new class and a new teacher, this one not a nun, and having told my name, was slotted into an empty desk and chair without further question. (But questions there must have been at some point or other, for not long afterwards the family friend was sent to the school once more and with suitable explanations. However, as I had been struck off the first register by then, and appeared to be doing reasonably well in the class where I had re-registered myself, I was allowed to stay there.)

School and family, it seemed, had fallen into separate compartments. I had friends home to play but rarely did I discuss my teachers or lessons or school activities with my parents. They on their part were not overly inquisitive as long as the report card at the end of the year was satisfactory. Nor, under normal circumstances, did the school show much interest in the families of its students. Parents were sometimes known to the nuns if they were Catholics or former students of the school. Otherwise we existed in a void, not unlike the babies left at the convent's gates. By and large I was not averse to this anonymity. Not being home, school meant freedom of a kind. It was a little world in itself but a recognizable one, for the Convent H.I.J. was exceptional as a mission school in that it reflected the mixedness of Singapore society with students of different races and social backgrounds, and many local teachers on the staff, not all of whom were Catholics. More important still, and helped by the fact that the nuns were educators first and proselytisers for the faith second, it was a manageable world. Its rules were clear and all it asked of me was that I should be clever at my studies.

In reality, to the extent that school and family were part of the colonial world and the immigrant world respectively, they never ceased to conflict with one another. This led to perplexities which tended to surface on such occasions as the start of every school year, when forms had to be filled in with details relating to nationality, race, religion, and so on. Needless to say the finer points of my racial origin had early been impressed upon me. I knew I was native to Zhongguo, two characters in the Chinese language which, even to a child of six, possessed a weight of significance pertaining to 'the centre of the inhabited world, the source of all culture and civilisation'.[4] A southerner, I also referred to myself as 'Person of Tang', but in contrast to southerners from other provinces and dialect groups I was 'Person from Fujian' or 'Person from Xiamen'. Finally, I was 'huaqiao', an overseas Chinese, a phrase with resonances of having travelled beyond the pale. Indeed, being English-educated too, I was sometimes classed with the red-haired 'barbarians' themselves, so that 'fan' was how the more traditional of my relations, who disapproved of my loud laugh, tactless remarks, and inelegant posture, labelled me.

Distinctions such as these vanished at school where I fell into the broad grouping of 'Chinese' just as the children of other races were simply 'Malay' or 'Indian' or 'Eurasian'. What really counted, it seemed, was the fact that we were, almost without exception, 'British Subjects'. If this was a relief it did not last long, for the sense of being out of place persisted. I was a colonial and did not know it. But as I moved up the school the British army wives, employed for brief periods at the Convent, became the touchstones of my unease. Through a tincture of mockery in their eyes and words as they instructed us in the vagaries of English grammar, the rudiments of Latin, the principles of Hygiene, I saw myself and my classmates as an outlandish lot. I saw too that the girls from Westernized families were more readily accepted, especially those whose vocabulary embraced familiar items such as nanny, afternoon tea, croquet, ponies. The rest of us clung to the edges, a great blob of blue in our gymslips, who might have told of uncouth things, like grandmothers with bound feet, cubicles for living quarters, a snack of noodles bought for a few cents from a hawker at midnight, death by tuberculosis.

School being the Convent, I grew excessively self-conscious in trying to explain what my religious leanings were. 'Buddhist' might have been a possibility but, although my grandmother had a small altar at which she prayed and offered incense and food on holy days to a benign-looking deity, both altar and icon were removed when she went away to Hong Kong. 'Christian' was too vague, even though an aunt, a fervent evangelist with a following in Malaya, would sweep us off to church with her whenever she came to stay. The truth was that as a family we were lax regarding matters of faith and I decided to seek the teacher's advice on what best to put down under 'Religion'. A young Chinese who might or might not have been a Catholic, she was kind but did not doubt I was anything other than a 'heathen'. So British Subject, Chinese and heathen I became for a couple of years until, tired of that particular declension, I took steps to elevate my image. Catholic friends (though never the nuns) made an attempt to convert me, but while I was disposed to attendance at mass, catechism classes and spiritual retreats, I balked at confessing my sins. Other friends suggested services at a non-conformist chapel, and thus I turned 'Protestant'. My religious zeal fading some years later, I fell back upon a laconic 'nil' and it was not until I was practically at the end of my school career that I had the sense to leave the space next to 'Religion' a blank.

The colonial and the migrant worlds were complicitous in another respect. They instilled the habit of looking away from Singapore towards other countries and places. In the maps we were given, the island was a mere dot above the equator or a fragment broken from the tip of the Malayan Peninsula. In the books we read, it was a wilderness, an impenetrable jungle, and at best an insignificant fishing village which was transformed by Sir Stamford Raffles into a great port and settlement. Progress here, as elsewhere within the Empire, was taken to have begun with the arrival of British merchant ships and gunboats. For even though Singapore's beginnings were exemplary, in that the island was secured by the East India Company through a peaceful exchange of treaties with the Malay chieftains, its story could not be separated from that larger one I found between the red covers of my thick history book, a dry-as-dust account of the stages by which Britain guided its colonies away from anarchy towards good government. True, my history lessons acquainted me with different lands and peoples. And equally true, they helped to distort my point of view. I was taught, for example, to think of Indian history after the Mutiny in terms of a series of Government of India Acts, issued from Whitehall, which prepared the country for self-rule. The result was that India's part in the struggle for freedom often looked to me to be of secondary importance, at times even unnecessary. Similarly the 'Mau Mau' I understood to be terrorists merely and not a force against colonialism. As for the history of Canada, it was so bound up with the activities of white explorers, trappers, settlers and Governor-Generals that, even today and with many friends and relations settled in that country, I am hard pressed to think of Canadian society as anything other than white. In other words, the myth of Empire was curiously powerful in the 1950s, precisely at a time when the violent dismantling of imperial rule was going on all around us. Admittedly Empire Day in the Convent was a drab affair compared with, say, a visitation from the Reverend Mother General. It meant some brief words from the Principal at morning assembly and the singing of the British National Anthem, but more importantly it meant that school ended early. Any attention paid to the occasion usually sprang from the initiative of individual teachers and took the form of reciting patriotic verses. Once called upon to deliver to the class Sir Cecil Spring-Rice's 'I vow to thee, my country', I was not conscious of having any specific country in mind but, even so, made much of the fine-sounding words and my empty vows.

Outside the classroom, however, the story of Empire was only one of the many stories that crowded in upon the island. Some of these I was to come across in later years consequent upon changing perspectives in South East Asian history – Singapura, Lion City, where lions were never destined to stalk; otherwise known as Temasek, late offshoot of the Malay Empire of Srivijaya and sufficiently robust even in the fourteenth century to provoke the hostility of its powerful Javanese and

Siamese neighbours; alluded to as Chiamassie by Marco Polo in his *Travels*, a city 'very large and noble' with 'a king and language of their own'; and recorded as Tan-ma-hsi by the Chinese, an inhospitable place and a dangerous one for rich junks crossing its pirate-infested waters. Then there were the stories I seemed to have known all my life. Part of the baggage of my immigrant Chinese parents and our Fujian dialect group, they made up a version of Singapore which existed, like other non-British versions of the island, at a tangent to the colony. This Singapore, which was mine in my Chinese dialect, had its own focal points and sprawling spaces, its large business firms and congestions of shops, rich suburbs and tenement houses and shacks. It resisted the municipal names that tried to pin it down to some alien notion of order, and favoured instead a digressive mode in speaking of itself. 'Chinatown' was an invention of foreigners and English language speakers. The native Chinese person inhabited real places, such as 'the back of the temple of the ancient mother goddess' or 'the mouth of the gambling houses' or 'the street of crockery shops'. Even imperial landmarks were apt to succumb to this circumlocutory approach so that the Esplanade was more familiarly known as 'under the five trees', Victoria Memorial Hall 'the building with the big clock', and Raffles Place 'the street of department stores'. As for home, when I wished to arrive at it in Chinese, it was always there 'at the foot of the Governor's hill, a little further along from the Chettiar temple and Tuan Mong school, in front of the Rediffusion building'.

Of course there was no avoiding the symbols of colonial rule, but among my Chinese acquaintances who spoke little or no English the esteemed figures were merchant pioneers and philanthropists, in particular the ones who began with nothing and rose to the heights of wealth and importance. The stuff of legends, their lives found parallels even in the middle decades of the twentieth century in home-spun versions of the rags-to-riches story. Of these my family, like others, had its share, with living friends and relations for main characters. The narrative pattern seldom varying, it was told how young men were driven by hardship or ambition or Japanese aggression in the 1930s to cross the seas and seek their fortune in Singapore. Here they were employed by local firms, first as menials, their job being to sweep the floors, empty spittoons, and fetch and carry for their bosses, then as clerks and accountants, until having learnt the business from the bottom up, they were ready to strike out on their own. At times one would hear of some sort of benefactor playing a role, but it was generally held that clean living and thrift were the main essentials, and that with these the final step across the divide from employee to big *towkay* would be free of obstacles.

Narrative realism troubled me little in those days. My difficulty lay in matching the characters produced by these stories with the flesh-and-blood individuals I met on social occasions. The genial but tedious and decidedly overweight *towkay* at the wedding dinner who got noisier and redder in the face by the minute as he and his male companions helped each other to brandy and ginger ale – was it likely that he had been driven by ambition to rise above the commonplace? As for the highly excitable and open-handed cousin who would ply me with ice-cold and dripping bottles of Red Lion orange squash when we called on him in his tiny one-room shop crammed with fuggy old boots, dank canvas and rusting iron – was it conceivable that this trader in junk had 'come far', as they said, and was in fact a man of large substance?

Such incongruities were of my own making. Had I been better informed, I would have realized that *towkays* might well spring from the solid virtues of practical sense and patient industry; that in the aftermath of the war a retail trade in army surplus, acquired cheaply and in bulk at auctions, did bring in sizable profits. Less explicable in retrospect was the currency of these success stories. Did they help to conceal the by far greater number of failures borne out by the dull faces, consumptive coughs and bad gambling debts? Did they hold out the promise of compensations for the traumas of uprooting oneself and beginning anew in a strange place? Were they a way of laying claim to an island which the majority would never have openly acknowledged as home? Whatever the explanation, their confident notes failed to suppress entirely the other story, the exile's story, with its burden of loss and yearning. That I heard at its most poignant in the songs which, rising above personal grief, voiced the bitter history of a homeland despoiled by cruel invaders – Mongolian hordes, European powers, and most recently, the Japanese army.

> The Wall stretches for mile after mile,
> Beyond lies the home of my ancestors.
> Sorghum burgeons in the fields,
> Bean flowers perfume the air.
> The earth is golden with harvest,
> No one need go hungry here.
> Since then calamities have befallen us.
> The whole land is laid waste,
> There is plunder, suffering and flight,
> Families are scattered and dear ones dead.[5]

Given the course Chinese history was to take, what return to the ancestral home could be hoped for by the families scattered overseas? Here then was another country known only in fine words and empty vows. The real China was something else. It was letters asking for cast-off clothing and food parcels and foreign exchange; it was rumours of the oppressive ways of the Communist government; it was newspaper reports of deportations under Singapore's Emergency Regulations; and it was Communist guerrillas in the Malayan jungle whom British troops were trying to stamp out.

A colonial and an immigrant, I was immersed in the nostalgia of worlds fast dying. But I had also come into contact with two rich cultures and had in my keeping words and images which spoke of the dynamism of change and of renewal as an urgent commitment. Part of the entertainment I received at home consisted of a mixed bag of fantasy, folk tales, and historical narratives; and whether the heroes were supernatural beings, or outlaws, or noble warriors, it was their untiring capacity to reinvent themselves and their world which captured my imagination. In comparison, I found the various English Readers we were given at school, with their accounts of clever animals and good children, extremely feeble, and it was not until Shakespeare and nineteenth-century poets and novelists came on the syllabus that literature lessons meant something important. Then I heard resounding in Tennyson's lines the contradictions that marked my own days, grappled with Browning's flawed characters, and met again the snake woman of Chinese folk tale who haunted my dreams in her other guises – Lamia, Jane Eyre and, most brilliantly transformed, Cleopatra.

The second half of the 1950s was a busy time at school with a succession of important examinations to be sat which, it was hoped, would lead to a place at the University. Meanwhile outside the school walls these were years of political unrest, and along with elections and constitutional reform, it seemed at times that Singapore's future was being fought out in the streets. On certain days, lessons had scarcely begun when school was dismissed and we were told to go straight home.

Then news would come through of protest marches, buses and cars overturned, riot squads, injuries and arrests. The lines of struggle were tangled, especially when disgruntled Chinese school-students and striking workers were drawn into the larger battles that were being waged between the colonial government on the one hand and pro-communists and left-wing leaders on the other. By the early 1960s when I was leaving the University, colonial Singapore was a thing of the past, but the drama of change was to pass through several episodes (including merger with Malaya, Sarawak and North Borneo to form the Federation of Malaysia, and then expulsion from Malaysia) before Singapore arrived at full independence in 1965. As to how fitting a citizen I would turn out to be in my new country, that is another story.

NOTES

1. 'English schools' refers to schools in which the language of instruction was English and which received financial aid from the government. 'Chinese schools', in which the language of instruction was Mandarin, were funded by private donations and even the most established of them suffered from lack of government support.
2. 'Fujian' is transliterated from Mandarin, as are other Chinese names in this essay. In my own dialect, the Chinese characters for 'Fujian' are pronounced 'Hokkien'. 'Zhou' is my surname in Mandarin whereas 'Chew' is the same surname in Hokkien.
3. The site is now 'State Land' and only the chapel stands as part of an urban development scheme billed as 'Renewing an Old Masterpiece'. The school, like others in Singapore, has expanded and now occupies a more spacious situation away from the city centre.
4. Wolfgang Franke, *China and the West*, trans. R.A. Wilson (Blackwell, 1967). 'Zhongguo' is translated as 'China' or 'the Middle Kingdom'. The latter is not very satisfactory since what it draws attention to is a relationship with the rest of world in terms of space. Another quotation from Franke underlines China's view of its own position: 'As the distance of [the foreign states] from the centre increased, the standard of their culture and civilisation decreased.'
5. It is my mother I must thank for this and other songs. I am also indebted to D.J. Enright for help with the translation here.

Shirley Geok-lin Lim

Shirley Geok-lin Lim was born in Malacca, Malaysia to a Nonya (Malaysian assimilated) family. She received a Ph.D. in English and American Literature from Brandeis University in 1973. Her first book of poems, *Crossing the Peninsula*, won the 1980 Commonwealth Poetry Prize. She has published two other poetry collections and a book of short stories, *Another Country*. Her critical volume, *Nationalism and Literature: English-Language Writing from the Philippines and Singapore* is forthcoming. She is co-editor of *The Forbidden Stitch: An Asian American Women's Anthology*, which received the Before Columbus American Book Award in 1990; co-editor of *Reading the Literatures of Asian America* and *One World of Literature*; and editor of *Asian America: Journal of Culture and the Arts*. She has published in numerous critical volumes and journals, including *The Journal of Commonwealth Literature, New Literary History, Feminist Studies*, and *Poetry Review*. She is currently Professor of Asian American Studies and English at the University of California, Santa Barbara.

SHIRLEY GEOK-LIN LIM

Chinese Ba/British Da: Daughterhood as Schizophrenia

Black and White

Why is it in my middle-aged dream
I talk to my younger father
openly, affectionately,
as I had never talked to him
when he was alive? He's his usual pale
self, thinner than I remember
when he was a man and I a child.
He's now a figure in a snapshot
taken in the zoo in Guangdong,
himself a specimen of cancer.
I turn to listen to the news
on television so I don't
have to remember my dream,
his mortal life. But it persists.
He is vulnerable, come alive
from the black and white as if
I had moved into a twelve inch
screen of the sixties, falling asleep
on the cool linoleum before
the flashing images. He would watch
American shows – John Wayne, Bill Haley,
the American Bandstand – saying,
look, meaning, the young kids rocking
and rolling, they're just like you,
suddenly seeming to understand
who I was, that girl doing the twist,
the cha-cha, all night in tight blue jeans
and give-away lipstick, moving
to the drums of the conga. That heavy
Malacca night I fell asleep in front
of his black and white television,
knowing, in my sleepiness, I was
not one of those swirling skirts, clean
bobbed hair and rolled down socks.
My body grew black earth. Rubbing
my elbow creases made small dirt
balls appear like opium shit. My hair
frizzed, dipped in permanent chemicals,
refused to bloom. Between my legs
a dangerous charm I never showed
my father, a feather talisman,
an inkling of my future. So he thought
me black and white, like an American,
his Peranakan daughter, who has tamed
her dancing body, till in my dreams
she is only a child, open,

139

affectionate, talking to her father
about love – his power to hold
his children in his power. No secrets
about my love for him now, who
in my memory is disappearing,
pound for pound, into the photograph
of a man, emaciated, hardly
middle-aged, with his good-bye smile,
and I want to weep, to hold his body
for once, as a woman holds a child,
that her caring can be cleansed.

When I read my poetry at readings, I frequently introduce myself as a father-obsessed daughter. The audience almost always laughs at this statement. They mistake my meaning. They look at the speaker and see a middle-aged professional woman, confident, articulate, and successful, and the words do not connect. Or they communicate at the level of comic incongruity. Obsession appears far from where I stand – seemingly separate and poised. I must have long ago released myself from a father's possessive clasp.

The possessiveness, however, is mine: I cannot let go of my father because as a child I had always betrayed him. Even now, living in the United States, thousands of miles from his grave-site, almost deracinated, I am haunted still by my Chinese father whose memory continues to mock and confuse my Western home.

Like all women I have one biological father. But, like many women from the British colonies, I have been separated from this birth-father; adopted by a Great White Father, whose approval of my talents, etc., has taken me out of poverty, etc., and given me a better life and so forth.

My Chinese father was small, intense, gregarious, with large appetites for food, play, and pleasure, fated to struggle with unrelenting work pressures, a person of deep affection and even deeper egotism. He was, in short, very much as some objective yet intimate observer may describe my self. As a young child I called him Ba, or Baba, the consonant not quite a propulsive 'p' as in the Anglophonic 'papa', but a softer opening of pressure, a gentle parting of the lips. 'Ba' is a Chinese sound.

As a Chinese male, my father was a forbidden love object for me. In the closed Hokkien cultural world of my childhood, a father was always too good for a daughter's love. His superiority as male progenitor removed him from any kind of simple affection. When a girl was no longer a baby, anywhere up to the age of three or four, and often as soon as she was able to walk on her own, physical demonstrations of affection disappeared. Hugs, kisses, touching, hair-tousling were forgotten. A father showed approval by a grunt, by silence instead of verbalized anger, by boasting to neighbours and relatives. The absence of disapproval implied the presence of approval. An extraordinary father demonstrated unusual affection through gifts of candy and toys, acts generally frowned upon as inappropriate in that they would lead to the girl's 'spoilage'. Acts of affection taken for granted in contemporary Western societies were presented as dangerous corruption of the girl's sense of self; she would begin to think too highly of herself, thus becoming a social misfit who lacked a proper notion of her (lowly) place in the world.

Yet I was a much loved daughter, the only girl after two sons, and the only girl still another six sons later. For most of my father's life, I was his only daughter. (A last child, a girl, was born two years before he died.) It was absolute family gospel that I was the favourite. In fact, on a number of occasions when I was barely six, my father took me out with auntie Fanny in the evening for car-rides. It was only much later, after the car was sold, after our mother abandoned us, after we moved from comfortable home to rented shack, that I was able to figure out that 'auntie Fanny' was my father's crush, a young warm efficient nurse who dated him when chaperoned by his daughter.

My father was not an extraordinary man. He was an unfaithful husband, and I don't remember that he loved my mother, much or little. Perhaps all parents become deficient to their children as they age and children come into their own powers. But from a very early age, I remember understanding that my father was weak. His weakness, moreover, was entangled with his power, with what made him charming and lovable. My father was a Chinese playboy. It wasn't until much later, after I had put myself through all the hoops of a colonial education and begun reading classical Chinese literature in translation, that I saw that he was not unique, rather a familiar type in classical Chinese culture. Twenty years after his death, a generation later, I see the resemblance between his character and that of Chia Pao-yu, the 'hero' of *Dream of the Red Chamber*.

The fifth son in a family of seven boys, his early photographs show him as a handsome youth, smooth-skinned, tanned, tight-jawed, and with a carefree smile under a jaunty panama hat. He was not like the elder brothers with their weight of Chinese learning and Confucianist-regulated psyches nor like the younger siblings with their British-influenced interest in training for the Civil Service, and he managed to arrive at adulthood with remarkably few constraints. The in-between son from whom nothing was expected and who expected nothing strenuous of himself, he was like an animal born for pleasure, a civilized sensualist in the way that Chinese civilization had constructed human desire, all things being equal: desiring many children, good food and other earthly comforts, a long life. In that way he was a good man, clear and unambiguous about his wants, a materialist without the unsettling spiritual pollution of guilt in the way of his happiness. In the traditional well-to-do extended Chinese family, he enjoyed an ordinary youth. Moreover, in Malay-influenced Malacca, the desire for a life of *senang* (ease, absence of striving, comfort) was seen as natural.

Becoming a Chinese father, however, especially one with multiplying children and no capital, he soon discovered that he had to earn a living. Life changed from enjoyment to endurance, from pleasure to pain, from being to doing. My father, like Adam, was driven from the paradise of his youth to hard labour. As the third child, I observed at close hand the consequences of economic necessity on his life, the inevitable frustrations leading to rage and violence, the good nature turning to selfishness and deceit.

By the time I was eight, I was defending myself from my father's deterioration. More treacherously, I was determined to be more than my father, to have a life as different from his as possible. I would not be Chinese, with all I experienced it to be of narrow prescribed morality, social hypocrisy, and economic impoverishment, those forces that governed my father's untidy life and threatened my own.

School, to which I escaped five days a week from 7.30 a.m. to 2.30 p.m., was that fantastical mobile space where a Chinese girl could be more than the position assigned to her in her family. We marched fiercely in the blazing playing fields to De Souza trumpet music, little convent girls in blue and white starched uniforms, unaware of the ironies of our colonial education that had us waving Union Jacks for Sir Gerald Templer, the High Commissioner and Commander-in-Chief of Malaya, who had arrived to chase away the Chinese Communists hidden in the jungles. We believed instead in what the good Convent of the Holy Infant Jesus Irish nuns taught us: that British rule signified democracy, justice, liberty, and progress. These were the mighty ideologies that prevailed in the brief excerpts from works by Edward

Gibbon, Thomas Macaulay, Bertrand Russell, Winston Churchill, the entire panoply of Great English Men that we 'comprehended' and summarized for our Senior Cambridge Examinations.

The Senior Cambridge Examinations set out a curriculum that kept the British cultural Empire intact even as the Empire fell apart into 'developing' nations. Outside our convent school walls, Merdeka (Independence) fever had swept the Malay prince-playboy, Tunku Abdul Rahman, into electoral power. Within our British missionary school, however, we read Shakespeare, Goldsmith, Dickens, Tennyson for the Literature paper; the Magna Carta, Elizabeth I, the English Revolution, the colonies, for the History paper; the various countries forming the British Commonwealth, dramatically coloured red in our World Atlases, for the Geography paper; and the New Testament according to St. Luke for the Scripture paper. Even as nationhood, a strange identity known as 'Malaysian', entered our terms for debating forums, we were assured that we were undertaking an educational enterprise that spanned the entire world. Schoolchildren in Nigeria, Ghana, South Africa, Egypt, Hong Kong, India, Burma, Trinidad, British Guyana, Ireland, Scotland, and England studied the same books. Never having met each other, we were nonetheless equal and the same before the marking pens of the examiners sequestered in famous Cambridge University.

An adopted daughter of the Empire, however, I was never sufficiently secure to question, as Virginia Woolf did in *Five Guineas*, the morality, the social make-up, and economy of this universal British family. Training my intimate eye on my father, himself rent by the contradictions between his Hokkien patriarchal privilege and his colonial abjectness, I kept my universal British Father at a respectful distance. Respect becomes a form of deeply embedded love when familiarity breeds contempt.

Many of my father's peers had already gone non-native. They sucked on briar pipes fashioned in English parishes, disguising their Asian faces behind clouds of brown tobacco smoke. They exclaimed, 'Good Lord!', wore leather loafers, lunched on lamb chops, and affected a stiff-upper-lip manly directness. They bought Carrows crackers and Cadbury chocolates for their children, drove Hillmans, and went home from their offices to three-bedroom bungalows.

In contrast, my father's good nature appeared servile; his pants, always fraying at their hems, the costume of chauffeurs, gardeners, and house-boys. His grin, marred by gaps between his teeth that remained unreplaced all his life for lack of money, signalled the shiftless, thoughtless, casualness of those masses that daily surrounded the British civil servant in his duties. And it was true that, unemployable by all, my father became self-employed, a petition writer, filling in British forms and translating British regulations for hundreds of Hokkien immigrants who were in transit from China to the British Empire. Visiting him some afternoons in the Chinese coffee shop where he had taken up unofficial residence, I cringed at his ease with vegetable hawkers, coffin makers, bicycle repairmen, trishaw pullers, all those Straits Chinese from the lowest social tier to whom English was impossible and the Empire a warren of hostile immigration offices in the red-coloured Staadt House. Among these illiterate poor he moved as a mandarin, his old Royal typewriter and sheets of flimsy carbon paper the technological keys to their entry into legal British citizenship.

The books I studied, however, opened a series of doors into fictional English halls and living rooms in which men completely unlike my father, and those he petitioned for, ruled and conversed. They opened a future into the West he could never enter. Adopting a British culture, learning English as my father-tongue, I deliberately allied myself with masters, not servants; estranged from the familiar circle of the powerless because feckless, feckless because powerless, I was a serious child in the constant company of English writers. I did not grow up in an indigenous culture so much as I felt myself marooned in an alien world with only the safety line of English literature to reel me out someday.

And yet.

It is two distances I am marooned in. At sixteen, I single-mindedly pursued the details of the geography of the Lake District, memorized Henry's speech before the Battle of St. Crispin, read all of Gibbon's *Decline and Fall of the Roman Empire,* became, in short, an anglophile, not so much to excel in the Cambridge Examinations as in the unspoken faith that such knowledge would rescue me from my father's world. What I did not ask was what was the other world that would receive me. Not the breezy society of my man Jeeves, nor the mannered civilities of Austen's small English towns. Nothing the Cambridge Senior Examination curriculum offered has taught me how to live in this fractured world. My British Dada, I now discover, was irrelevant, bankrupt, corrupt, and senile. In my present tense, American English holds the key to world grammar.

My obsession with my father has much to do with this belated recognition that I had betrayed him for some not-so-sacred texts. It turns on my self-argument that his Chinese past is a kind of text that I can now study in order to make sense of my life, to make my life meaningful, to understand why there has been so little understanding, so little love, in me. More accurately, however, it is fuelled by my middle-aged acceptance of how my father's love had been represented to me through Chinese familial oppressiveness as forbidden sexuality, and how in my flight from fear of incest I have adopted the sublimated emotionality of English literature.

The first time I remember being repulsed by my father, hating his Chinese body, was after my young stepmother accused him of having an unnatural relationship with me. An eight-year-old girl among a plethora of brothers and their playmates, I had fallen in love with a sickly puppy that one of my father's petitioners, a one-eyed lorry-driver, had given to me. The pup, a female, was a short-haired white mongrel, with brown clownish spots on its sad face. For the month that I had her, I carried her all day after I got home from school, and sneaked out at night to keep her by my bed.

The afternoon I could not find her, my brother and I biked through the town desperately calling for her; later, our neighbour, Mrs. Li, told us that our stepmother had thrown her into the river. It was then, crying in Mrs. Li's living room, that I heard my father shouting. I thought he was quarrelling with my stepmother for drowning the pup. Much later that evening, Mrs. Li reported that he had broken every plate in the house because my stepmother had accused him of being an unnatural father.

I cannot recall the feelings that must have absorbed me then, only the pain of the loss of the pup. I remember crying for weeks for the dead puppy. Somewhere among those tears I must have also cried for my father and for myself, for that accusation of incest frightened me so sharply that I could never bring myself to touch my father again.

Living for the next ten years or so in the same small house with my stepmother and father and ever increasing family, I saw my father finally settle into Asian domesticity. The issue of unnatural relations, of extraordinary affection between father and daughter, was never raised again. I entered into the world of school, sports, popular music and dances, conspiring actively in the erasure of the Chinese daughter for a British version of the individual, exchanging BaBa for my freedom, my self-respect.

And yet.

Examining the unspoken dynamics of our household, perhaps it would be more honest to say that as much as I sought to reject my Chinese father, he had already rejected his dangerous modern daughter. We never had a conversation that went beyond banalities, we never hugged, we were never ourselves with each other. By the time I was ten, he had persuaded himself that I was thoroughly westernized and independent; I was left alone to read, wander, accompany whom I wished. In giving me my freedom, he was abandoning me to the orphanage of the Empire.

I cannot tell how deeply my stepmother's accusation might have wounded him. Was she merely voicing the unthinkable that perhaps lies confused in those puddles of darkness that haunt every large extended Chinese family, made up of brothers and sisters, aunts, nephews, cousins, uncles, grandparents, in-laws, so much so that the taboos of consanguinity are liable to be forgotten in the close tumble of faces and bodies? Did she look to wean the mother-abandoned girl from her dependency on her father? Or did she jealously strike out in the surest way she knew to break her husband's love for her step-daughter?

These are now merely intellectual questions for me. My absorption into Western culture has trained me to behave ironically, to distance my emotions from the irrationality of the native subject, to always remain in control of a situation. Between the sometimes straitened horrors for daughters in traditional Chinese society and the isolating autonomy – perhaps an illusion but a persistent illusion – of post-colonial culture, the choice may be very narrow.

Still, in some dreams, where I cannot speak English but only Hokkien, before I have ever seen a white person, when the whole world is my family, I remember clearly the experience of being a Chinese girl holding BaBa's comforting hand. That was true once.

Grace Nichols

Grace Nichols was born in Georgetown, Guyana, where she grew up. She received a Diploma in Communications from the University of Guyana and worked as a reporter and freelance journalist. She came to Britain in 1977 and since then has published a number of children's books and three collections of poetry. Her first, *i is a long memoried woman*, was the winner of the 1983 Commonwealth Poetry Prize, and her second, *The Fat Black Woman's Poems*, was published by Virago in 1984. Her latest collection of poems is *Lazy Thoughts of a Lazy Woman* (Virago, 1989). *Whole of a Morning Sky* is her first novel for adults.

The Duke Coming

The Duke coming. The Duke of Edinburgh.

At school the teachers talk about the visit which is all because Guiana is part of the British Empire. You preferred if it was the Queen coming though, in her gown and crown.

Nearly every night your mother would take you and Anthony to see the lighting up all over Georgetown for the visit. All the flamboyant trees on Main Street Avenue full of electric bulbs, hanging like see-through pears of every shade from every tree, right and left of the avenue as far as your eye could see. St George's Cathedral which they say is the highest wooden building in the world is washed in floodlights, glowing tall and white as if someone had painted it in moonlight. The Town Hall looking like a lovely icing cake because it's so studded with lights. All the shops and stores bright with new lights too, the big ones and the small. Some flashing lights saying 'Welcome', others looking as if they're embroidered in lights.

...

Archie walked briskly from the cool interior of the Public Free Library into the brilliantly hot afternoon. He was wearing his grey flannel trousers today, white shirt tucked neatly in his waist, his old leather briefcase carrying the two books he had just exchanged at the library, *Puck of Pook's Hill* by Kipling and a collection of short stories by Alberto Moravia.

He crossed over on to the busy shopping junction in front of Bookers' Stores and made his way round into Water Street. As he walked along the narrow crowded pavement a stream of traffic moved sluggishly along with him. Yellow buses, cars and wobbling pedal cyclists, trucks, horses, pulling long, over-laden dray carts, huge sugarbulks which left odd little trails of golden brown crystals on the streets behind. Sweet Demerara sugar, brown as the Demerara River.

Most of the shops and stores were closing early today because nearly everyone wanted to see the Duke or had given their employers that impression. Archie himself wanted to get a loaf of wholemeal bread and to pick up a lock for the little cupboard fitted into his writing desk before the shop closed.

The sunshine permeated everything, a thin hazy vapour seeming to rise from the hot asphalt streets and he welcomed the cooling breezes that the Atlantic kept pushing in. Georgetown was at its most teeming on this Friday four o'clock weekend afternoon with shoppers and workers pouring out of offices and factories and people drifting off to different assembly points to see the Duke.

Archie stopped at a small cakeshop to cool himself down on a glass of mauby and ice. As he sipped the slightly fermented barky drink, he watched the jostling move of people going by, a *mélange* of people of different races and different shades and mixtures of races. Africans, East Indians, Portuguese, Chinese, a few Amerindians and, of course, the growing numbers of Mixed. He watched the hustle of the pavement vendors fastening on to prospective buyers, selling anything from a safety pin to a bottle of Shiling oil, an all-purpose remedy for colds, toothache, sore-throats and a heap of other ailments. He eyed a couple of young men going up to people with their usual 'Give me a raise nuh, man,' in the hope of scrounging a few cents.

Archie walked on, chin slightly lifted, marvelling how the years had flown. This afternoon, for some reason, the memory of Highdam had invaded his senses. It was exactly eight months since he had left the village. Eight months since he had retired after contributing nearly forty years of dedicated service to the teaching profession.

Today, Highdam was coming back as a vision of rural purity, and suddenly he wasn't consoled by the fact that he had left it for the sake of his children. Maybe he should have realized that he was a countryman and that his spirit was best in the openness of space and land. He would never grow accustomed to the close proximity of the Georgetown houses. To the noise. The thieves. The hooligans. The slums. Not to mention the growing political tension which was obvious in spite of the lights, the streamers, the other outward signs of welcome for the Duke.

'Anti-Working Class Budget', 'No Independence Under Mohabir', 'Budget of Sorrow', were some of the placards that caught Archie's eye as he passed groups of anti-government demonstrators who were seizing the opportunity of the royal visit to embarrass the government.

As he approached the corner that led to his Princess Street home, he became aware of the police detouring traffic; of the barricades and din of voices above the street; of the heaving mass of human bodies blocking off the corner for a glimpse of the Duke. Archie, who would not have gone out of his way to see the Duke, debated within himself whether he should try to approach his home from another angle. But this struck him as useless, or at best, too much trouble. He edged his way into the patchwork of bodies, and was immediately engulfed.

The sun had reduced its intensity a little but people were becoming restless. There was less laughing and more cursing. The police broke up a scuffle between a fat woman in a tight red dress and a wiry man, who had just 'grind me foot off,' as she put it.

Unmindful of the cantering white horses, barricades and restraining teachers, school children, carrying little replicas of the British flag, squeezed their way through to get to the shave-ice cart installed in front of the rumshop. The shave-ice man, hot and bothered by the growing cluster of children around him, shaved frantically, scooping the crushed ice out with his hand, dipping it quickly into one or two of his thick coloured syrups, and passing it to the crowd of children without looking. Working as much out of greed for the coins thrust under his nose as for the desire to get rid of them, his hands moved non-stop. But still the children cried, 'Mister, Mister, a shave ice. Look Mister, I standing up hey before she. Mister, Mister, a shave ice.'

Archie clutched his briefcase in the crowd. He knew that it wasn't so much the Duke as the thirst for spectacle and drama that had brought people out in the thousands.

One of the picketers, a thin-chested man, held his 'Budget of Sorrow' in a careless manner. The stiff cardboard picket grazed the cheek of a man in front.

'Mind how you holding you picket,' the man warned, as he pushed the placard aside, but the picketer was too occupied with himself and picket to take note.

'Ah say, mind how you holding you damn placard, man. All-you fanaticals don't look wha all-you doing.'

Further down a young policeman was having a hard time keeping the crowd from pushing down one of the barricades. He warned the pushers at the back and they began to taunt him mercilessly. 'You ugly son-of-a-bitch,' a youth bawled out from behind.

'You ignorant,' the policeman answered back.

'Is only the Police Force would tek all like you,' another voice taunted.

'I have the education up here,' said the policeman, pointing to his white cap. 'I have five subjects GCE and could get anywhere. The only place you got to go is lot 12,' Lot 12 being another name for the Georgetown jail.

But the people had already erupted into loud derisive laughter. 'Five subjects GCE, eh! eh! look at Mister-Five-Subjects-GCE.'

'Thank the Lord I only have me little ten-subjects-at-two-sittings,' exclaimed a middle-aged woman mockingly, pressing her hands to her two ample breasts. Above the laughter a siren was heard in the distance. A white police car flashed by.

Word passed around that the Duke had reached the head of the city, and the crowd, injected with new vigour, heard the unmistakeable muffled roar of the police outriders.

Slowly the outriders came into view, ebony faces covered in beads of perspiration, sitting painfully erect on two huge, droning white motorbikes.

School children waved their red, white and blue flags crazily, picketers thrust forward their placards, the whole crowd craning forward at the sight of the long, elegant black car bearing the Duke.

In spite of being hemmed in, Archie caught a glimpse of the white figure in close-fitting tunic, moving his hand from left to right.

'Eh, eh, but he look just like the picture on the almanac, eh?' one woman observed to another. 'Ah wonder if he does wear dem clothes all the time?'

'Man, watch de red, white and blue pon de shoulder,' said the other one.

Beside the Duke sat Governor Rothschild, taking refuge behind light-green sun glasses, his European eyes still unadjusted to the harsh light after three years in the tropics.

It was the sudden wave of boos that alerted Archie to the passing of the Premier and his wife, and shouts of 'Mohabir resign'. From behind the closed windows of their small grey car, the Premier, a good-looking man in his late forties, endured the boos with a resigned smile while his wife held up two defiant fingers in a victory sign. Georgetown certainly wasn't their stronghold.

At that moment Archie felt a hand slipping from his back pocket. His own hand shot around in quick protective reflex, but too late, his bicycle key, ball-point pen and a couple of coins were gone. Luckily he kept little or no money in his back pocket.

Archie was borne away by the sea of human bodies towards his home. He stopped for a few moments on the parapet to allow the crowds to lighten, then turned into his gateway. Just then the wind brought a fine spray of unexpected rain to his face.

...

Marching in your new white yachting shoes and white socks, the only new things you get for the Duke. Marching till your foot get a blister. Waiting and waiting in the hot sun at the Parade Ground. Waiting for the chance to wave your little red, blue and white flag. Then the siren noise and stirring and the Duke coming. Looking like the picture on your exercise book cover. The one with he and the queen together. Everybody waving flags. Afterwards going back to school to get a pepsi and sweetbread. Afterwards taking off your shoes and socks and walking home barefoot. Hearing your father say, maybe it wasn't the best thing moving to Georgetown after all.

149

Velma Pollard

Velma Pollard is a senior lecturer in Language Education at the University of the West Indies, Jamaica. Her major research interests are Creole languages of the Anglophone Caribbean, the language of Caribbean Literature, and Caribbean women's writing. She is also involved in creative writing and has published poems and short stories in regional and international journals. Her other publications include two volumes of poetry: *Crown Point and Other Poems* (1988) and *Shame Trees Don't Grow Here* (1992), both published by Peepal Tree Press; and a volume of short fiction: *Considering Woman* (Women's Press, 1989). Her novella *Karl*, which won the Casa di las Americas Literary Award (1992), is due to be published by Casa as a bilingual (English and Spanish) text.

VELMA POLLARD

Frog of Britain Proudly Waving

Frog of Britain proudly waving over many distances...

I sang the improbable until I found that map of the world in the MacDonald almanac (with no good reason for its being there). On either side was a red white and blue flag on a long thick flagpole and in bright pink, almost red, were shaded what my father told me were the countries of the British Empire (on which the sun never sets), countries all children of mother England. Thinking about it now, we must have had different fathers. And I would have regarded that as perfectly natural given some examples in the community around me.

My father said that the flag of Britain ruled over us and united us. For some reason, although he told me we were all brothers (and sisters) and supported it with 'Children of the Empire/ We are brothers all', I found it easier to think of us as cousins. Perhaps that was because in my own family the cousins were the numerous ones, not the brothers and sisters. And they were close to us the way my parents were to their numerous brothers and sisters. So I understood us all to be cousins – Canada, Barbados, Australia, Jamaica, Ghana, New Zealand, Trinidad, Nigeria.

> 'Flag of Britain proudly waving
> over many distant seas...'

I associated the Empire with verse without music and with music – those lines about being brothers I heard at home and school. I am not sure how or why I made the association but Empire was as much involved with those lines as it was with 'Come tumble up Lord Nelson/ The British fleet's a-looming' or 'Drake is in his hammock now ...'. And from part of a different sensibility, what might be called Oral History these days, sung with much verve by my irreverent mother:

> King George was sitting on the throne
> when him say to all contingent
> you better take up you half-a-foot and walk.

Something unfeeling about King George was left with me from that one. I could see hundreds of wounded old soldiers, all black (I think the word 'contingent' conveyed that), anxious to get back home to Jamaica and being told rather facetiously by a king who was safely sitting on a throne, that they should find their own way home. I saw Lord Nelson on crutches too, but somebody was encouraging him to 'come tumble up' and that was clearly different.

I had no notion of time or space then. It seemed that there was, somewhere in my imagination, a huge bin into which scraps of Empire material were tossed whenever they appeared. Some kind of tapestry would eventually be woven or at least an Empire patchwork spread be made. The largest chunk for the spread would of course be from Empire Day celebrations at school.

Weeks before Empire Day we were practising song after song of the Empire. And on the day itself we sang as we watched venerable citizens plant trees in the schoolyard. The tree planting was the big thing for Empire Day, on the serious side; the lemonade and bullah-cake being the important thing on the frivolous side (in High School it became bun and cheese). Of course there was the raising of the flag and the singing of the anthem, 'God save our gracious King'. And there was marching, in the schoolyard. The dignitaries of school and church always said how lovely we looked in our uniforms. By noon everything would be over and the rest of the day was ours.

While Miss Hannah or whoever was the local dignitary planted the tree, we sang in loud clear voices that 'Britons never never never shall be slaves'. And we, the children of slaves, were somehow, by implication, those Britons. (People my age and race in the French Caribbean were reading about 'Our ancestors the Gauls'!)

Perhaps we should have been singing that we would never *again* be slaves. Indeed we were closer to the 'nations not so blest as thee' who, the song said, were obliged to bend to tyrants ('mustin mustin mustin their turn to tyrants bend'). And somehow, in spite of the official Empirephilia, another consciousness was being nurtured. There was my mother's disrespectful song about King George. And there was the one I heard from the man washing his foot at the standpipe, with his khaki pants rolled up to his knee and an old cloth cap on his head. He sang merrily:

Twentyfourth a May
a di queen birthday
Maloney bands a go play
no badda beat no drum
for nobody naa go come
Maloney bands a go play

To this day I do not know what kind of band was a Maloney band. But from the context I guessed it could not have been any respectable band. Perhaps it started life as 'Baloney band'. Perhaps that was what Mass Miah had been singing and my child-ears had heard it wrong.

These were the sentiments perhaps that would take us from Empire to Commonwealth; from children of the Empire to independent citizens with passports that were no longer British.

I was very shaken, not so long ago, to hear the child of a schoolmate of mine say she did not want to read a day more of Caribbean History; she did not want to hear about slavery one more time. But it made me realize how things had changed. SHE had heard about slavery all through high school and certainly during first year at the University of the West Indies. Her father and I are twenty-five years older than she is. In a quarter of a century so much has changed! WE had hardly heard of slavery during our years at high school. We had sat papers for foreign examination boards, in European History and English History – the treaty of Utrecht 1713 and the jingoist foreign policy of Palmerston sometime later and Robert Peel, after whom the English police were called Bobbies. (I am not even sure now if some of that information is accurate but that is what I have in my head.) A generation laboured for local syllabuses and local exams and the children who inherited changes were saying they did not want them! They knew excess. Their appetites had sickened and died. Not all I hope. This young woman was only one. And besides we were not really fighting for exclusiveness. Not Caribbean History only, but certainly Caribbean History first.

And it was not only History that we children of the Empire had to come to terms with. Lorna Goodison, foremost woman poet of the Caribbean, certainly of Jamaica, says she started to write poetry so she could hear about herself. She had come out of a curriculum that led her to believe that all poets were male and white and lived abroad or had died. My psyche selected a different way to deal with the problem. I had seen most of them as black. I still have the rakish picture of my great favourite John Donne, which I thought proved that he was a red man (brown skin West Indian type) I might meet on any street. And even in biblical things, the habit of repersonification (rather like relexification) stayed with me. I was V-E-R-Y shocked to see Samson, played by some man who did not look like Joe Louis!

But I did not always recognize the problem, if problem it was. Only in retrospect, long after I was through with all that, did I see the Girl Guide Movement as an exquisite piece of Empire hand-me-down. It was a good movement, a worthwhile movement pointing to healthy living and clean fun, but some things should have been altered to fit the local shape. Why did I belong to the Margaret patrol when Poinsettia was a distinct possibility? And why did my friend belong to Thistle? Or why were the tasks we were set so foreign? A Tenderfoot had to learn to bake a potato under ashes – not a sweet potato, mind you, or a piece of yam, but the temperate potato we call 'Irish potato'; and as we camped and sang around the fire, we cooked not 'stew peas' from the local cuisine but 'Irish stew', which the song said we all liked ('Every Girl Guide/likes an Irish Stew').

Perhaps we were sisters after all, or cousins, under the flag. Long before I had ever set eyes on an Australian, we sang around campfires the ballad of the jolly swagman who camped 'under the shade of a Koolibah tree'. The Irish stew was cooked and eaten long before I was really aware of the Irish and their sad history and politics. And we had pen pals who were Guides from all over the Empire.

We went to Guide Headquarters one auspicious afternoon and actually set eyes on Lady Olave (not Olive) Baden-Powell, the founding mother, so to speak, of us all. And when the Princess, elder daughter of the ruling king ('heiress presumptive' is the term I think they taught us), visited Jamaica with her Greek Prince and husband, we stood for hours under the hot sun so the open jeep with their smiling faces and royal waving hands could pass between row on row of Girl Guides. I think she had been a Girl Guide too. We were proud in our uniforms with well-badged sleeves (some more so than others), and we found out what a Greek nose looked like, so when we read about it in the next romantic novel we were well able to visualize it.

We wore our uniforms again for the celebration of the Coronation of that same lady, at night this time, at the same Up-Park-Camp which was the natural venue for such things. We were allowed to stay out late. We got to watch the military tattoo. I think the foreign detachment of soldiers was the Royal Inniskillins. I have no real reason for remembering the name, and the spelling is perhaps wrong, but then, I never had to spell it before. In any case both foreign and local soldiers performed surprising feats. And some of us, a few select ones, took part in a dance production. I was very happy to be a part of all that glitter, all that pomp and ceremony:

red white and blue
what does it mean to you
surely you're proud
shout it aloud
Britons awake
the Empire too
we can depend on you ...

We shared the joys and the sorrows of the Empire. I remember the deep gloom of a whole day given over to sombre classical music, Chopin's Funeral March for example, on the radio when George VI, the Princess's father, died. There was no TV then, so we couldn't see him stretched out in his coffin. But the music was enough. I had vivid pictures of him as a result of hearing it while my parents talked about the young girl who would ascend the throne.

Friends of mine, right after graduation from the University in the 1950s, went to London, to the seat of the Empire, and wrote back to me about hanging out in the pubs frequented by the literary figures whose work we had read. They also wrote about their hesitation in the presence of Buckingham Palace and Trafalgar Square; their uncertainty about their feelings. I was thirty by the time I visited. I had seen Canada and the USA. I had exorcised some of the ghosts of Empire. I enjoyed Trafalgar Square and Piccadilly. I was ecstatic about Stratford-on-Avon and the production I saw there. Oxford, Cambridge, venerable halls, if not of marble; rivers, the sites of the regattas mentioned in so many university stories. All these excited me. I had book-memories of everything. I fitted real pictures to them easily. Only the British museum offended.

I was glad to be able to see a mummified king. I was offered stores of information I might otherwise have missed. But I felt a great sense of loss on behalf of the real wonders of the artifacts. As if too much had been stolen for too long. I felt that things from the hot desert were cold and miserable in the British Museum. It all seemed very unfair. Just the way I felt outraged, years earlier, in Canada when I was taken to a reservation to look at Native Canadians, gawking at people as if they were animals in a zoo. And indeed they had been hounded and put away in these zoos on their own land or the fragment of it they had been allowed.

The Imperial Intention is the term I use for a kind of perception many First World people have of themselves in relation to the Other. The man/woman from the centre of the Empire is automatically better (prettier, brighter, richer) than the non-white children of the Empire. Even the best people seem able to function out of these presumptions if they are not on their guard. As a teacher I have had some very sobering experiences having to do with Empire. I remember, for example, stopping to apologize for imperial arrogance when, in a novel written by a usually gentle and considerate lady, reference was made rather disparagingly to every 'heathen' who ever bowed to Juggernaut. Half my class was of Indian ancestry. And very few were christianized. This attitude persists in many references to the Other. Sometimes it shows itself in a refusal to admit his/her presence on a landscape.

Of course the distinction does not always have to do with race. It is indeed the Other, not necessarily the Black Other to which the (hard) core reacts. For I remember being at Madame Tussaud's, and hearing an Englishwoman ask an Other whose accent she had recognized as different, if she was from the colonies. Somehow the term 'colonies', and the whole question, seemed remarkably strange and even rude there. But the Other answered quite simply, 'Yes, I am from Australia.' I have since met people from Ireland and from Wales who are proud to be different. And I ask myself what that says about the Empire connection and the Irish Stew. It is all so mixed up. Maybe my own post-colonial chip is too heavy. Maybe it is a huge log by now, weighing down my shoulder.

At Heathrow I felt vindicated. There were children of the Empire of every shade and vesture there. The stereotypical WASP in European clothes was the exception not the norm. Children of the Empire ... Brothers/Sisters not really searching for their parents were all liming[1] at Heathrow that day when the terrible truth struck me.

Afterword: Heathrow in Retrospect (from *Shame Trees Don't Grow Here*)

It wasnt the first time I was in Heathrow. It might have been the fourth or fifth. And I dont remember why I was there meeting somebody, leaving or arriving myself I dont know but I was at the British Airways counter and gazed out along the concourse to behold, and quite unexpectedly, the British Empire on which the sun never sets.

Well what a revelation! Suddenly I felt that I was England called upon after all to put my money where my mouth lie (accepting the pun). All those on whom the sun had not set were along the concourse – ladies with head covers like hats bee-keepers wear and mesh right down to the chin – people you were sure could never eat for all the tackle on nose and mouth nor go to the bathroom for all the skirt and trousers at their legs. There were dazzling saris there with brown love-handles smiling at ageing waists; black hair thrown open at the seam to accommodate one deep red spot and tall men each with his finely wrought fez walking as if flowing skirts and sandalled feet were help not hindrance to unreasonable speed.

No one had warned the British in their mad rush into Expansion that this contraction here at Heathrow would be likely. They had not then conceived of fast ships or of aeroplanes, linguistic skill and wild ambition that would bring all shades of black and brown (and white) to this one shelter and the cruel irony of children of the Empire, brothers all, at Heathrow.

And amid the bustle of Oxford Street, returning from the colonies to retire in England an old limey asks: 'Is there still space for an Englishman?'

NOTE

1. Trinidad Creole word for 'hanging about'.

Olive Senior

Olive Senior was born in Jamaica. She was editor of *Social and Economic Studies* (University of the West Indies) and of *Jamaica Journal*. She has published one collection of poetry and two collections of short stories — the first of which, *Summer Lightning*, won the Commonwealth Writers Prize. Her most recent publication is *Working Miracles: Women of the English Speaking Caribbean*.

OLIVE SENIOR

Colonial Girls' School

For Marlene Smith MacLeish

Borrowed images
willed our skins pale
muffled our laughter
lowered our voices
let out our hems
dekinked our hair
denied our sex in gym tunics and bloomers
harnessed our voices to madrigals
and genteel airs
yoked our minds to declensions in Latin
and the language of Shakespeare

> Told us nothing about ourselves
> There was nothing about us at all

How those pale northern eyes and
aristocratic whispers once erased us
How our loudness, our laughter
debased us

> There was nothing left of ourselves
> Nothing about us at all

Studying: *History Ancient and Modern*
Kings and Queens of England
Steppes of Russia
Wheatfields of Canada

> There was nothing of our landscape there
> Nothing about us at all

Marcus Garvey turned twice in his grave.
'Thirty-eight was a beacon. A flame.'
They were talking of desegregation
in Little Rock, Arkansas. Lumumba
and the Congo. To us: mumbo-jumbo.
We had read Vachel Lindsay's
vision of the jungle

> Feeling nothing about ourselves
> There was nothing about us at all

Months, years, a childhood memorizing
Latin declensions
(For our language
– 'bad talking' –
detentions)

      Finding nothing about us there
      Nothing about us at all

So, friend of my childhood years
One day we'll talk about
How the mirror broke
Who kissed us awake
Who let Anansi from his bag

For isn't it strange how
northern eyes
in the brighter world before us now

Pale?

Margaret Atwood

Margaret Atwood was born in Ottawa, Canada, in 1939, and grew up in northern Quebec and Ontario, and in Toronto. She has lived in many other cities, travelled extensively, and held a wide range of jobs, such as cashier, waitress, summer camp counsellor, lecturer in English at the University of British Columbia, and Writer-in-Residence at the University of Toronto. She has published over twenty books, including novels, poetry and literary criticism. *Cat's Eye*, her seventh novel, appeared in Canada in 1988 and in Britain in 1989. Since then two new collections of short stories have been published: *Wilderness Tips* (Bloomsbury, 1991) and *Good Bones* (Bloomsbury, 1992).

MARGARET ATWOOD

Empire Bloomers

The school we are sent to is some distance away, past a cemetery, across a ravine, along a wide curving street lined with older houses. The name of it is Queen Mary Public School. In the mornings we walk across the freezing mud in our new winter overshoes, carrying our lunches in paper bags, and down through the remains of an orchard to the nearest paved road, where we wait for the school bus to come lurching towards us, up the hill and over the pot-holes. I wear my new snowsuit, my skirt wrapped around my legs and stuffed down into the bulgy legs of the snowpants, which whisk together as I walk. You can't wear pants to school, you have to wear skirts. I'm not used to this, or to sitting still at a desk.

We eat our lunches in the chilly dimly lit cellar of the schoolhouse, where we sit in supervised rows on long scarred wooden benches under a festoon of heating pipes. Most of the children go home for lunch, it's only the school-bus ones that have to stay. We're issued small bottles of milk which we drink through straws stuck in through a hole in the cardboard bottle tops. These are my first drinking-straws, and they amaze me.

The school building itself is old and tall, made of liver-coloured brick, with high ceilings, long ominous wood-floored hallways, and radiators that are either on full blast or not at all, so that we're either shivering with cold or too hot. The windows are high and thin and many-paned, and decorated with cut-outs made of construction paper; right now there are snowflakes, for winter. There's a front door which is never used by children. At the back are two grandiose entranceways with carvings around them and ornate insets above the doors, inscribed in curvy, solemn lettering: GIRLS and BOYS. When the teacher in the yard rings her brass handbell we have to line up in twos by classrooms, girls in one line, boys in another, and file into our separate doors. The girls hold hands; the boys don't. If you go in the wrong door you get the strap, or so everyone says.

I am very curious about the BOYS door. How is going in through a door different if you're a boy? What's in there that merits the strap, just for seeing it? My brother says there's nothing special about the stairs inside, they're plain ordinary stairs. The boys don't have a separate classroom, they're in with us. They go in the BOYS door and end up in the same place we do. I can see the point of the boys' washroom, because they pee differently, and also the boys' yard, because of all the kicking and punching that goes on among them. But the door baffles me. I would like to have a look inside.

Just as there are separate doors for boys and girls, there are also separate parts of the schoolyard. At the front, outside the teachers' entrance, is a dirt field covered with cinders, the boys' playing field. At the side of the school facing away from the street is a hill, with wooden steps going up it and eroded runnels worn down the side, and a few stunted evergreens on top. By custom this is reserved for the girls, and the older ones stand around up there in groups of three or four, their heads bent inwards, whispering, although boys sometimes make charges up the hill, yelling and waving their arms. The cement-paved area outside the BOYS and GIRLS is common territory, since the boys have to cross it in order to go in their door.

Lining up is the only time I see my brother at school. At home we've rigged up a walkie-talkie with two tin cans and a piece of string, which runs between our two bedroom windows and doesn't work very well. We push messages under each other's doors, written in the cryptic language of the aliens, which is filled with x's and z's and must be decoded. We nudge and kick each other under the table, keeping our faces straight above the tablecloth; sometimes we tie our shoe-laces together, for signalling. These are my main communications with my brother now, these raspy tin-can words, sentences without vowels, the Morse of feet.

But in the daytime I lose sight of him as soon as we go out the door. He's up ahead, throwing snowballs; and on the bus he's at the back, in a noisy whirlpool of older boys. After school, after he's gone through the fights that are required of any new boy at any school, he's off helping to wage war on the boys from the Catholic school nearby. It's called Our Lady of Perpetual Help, but the boys from our school have re-named it Our Lady of Perpetual Hell. It's said that the boys from this Catholic school are very tough and that they conceal rocks inside their snowballs.

I know better than to speak to my brother during these times, or to call his or any boy's attention to me. Boys get teased for having younger sisters, or sisters of any kind, or mothers; it's like having new clothes. When he gets anything new my brother dirties it as soon as possible, to avoid having it noticed; and if he has to go anywhere with me and my mother, he walks ahead of us or crosses to the other side of the street. If he's teased about me, he will have to fight some more. For me to contact him, or even to call him by name, would be disloyal. I understand these things, and do my best.

So I am left to the girls, real girls at last, in the flesh. But I'm not used to girls, or familiar with their customs. I feel awkward around them, I don't know what to say. I know the unspoken rules of boys, but with girls I sense that I am always on the verge of some unforeseen, calamitous blunder.

....

One day someone appears in the schoolyard with a bag of marbles, and the next day everyone has them. The boys desert the boys' playground and throng into the common playground in front of the BOYS and GIRLS doors; they need to come to this side of the playground, because marbles have to be played on a smooth surface and the boys' yard is all cinders.

For marbles you're either the person setting up the target or the person shooting. To shoot you kneel down, sight, and roll your marble at the target marble like a bowling ball. If you hit it you keep it, and your own marble too. If you miss, you lose your marble. If you're setting up, you sit on the cement with your legs spread open and put a marble on a crack in front of you. It can be an ordinary marble, but these don't get many shooters, unless you offer two for one. Usually the targets are more valuable: cat's eyes, clear glass with a bloom of coloured petals in the centre, red or yellow or green or blue; puries, flawless like coloured water or sapphires or rubies; waterbabies, with undersea filaments of colour suspended in them; metal bowlies; aggies, like marbles only bigger. These exotics are passed from winner to winner. It's cheating to buy them; they have to be won.

Those with target marbles call out the names of their wares: *purie, purie, bowlie, bowlie*, the two-syllable words drawn out into a singsong, the voice descending, the way you call dogs, or children when they're lost. These cries are mournful, although they aren't meant to be. I sit that way myself, the cold marbles rolling in between my legs, gathering in my outspread skirt, calling out *cat's eye, cat's eye*, in a regretful tone, feeling nothing but avarice and a pleasurable terror.

The cat's eyes are my favourites. If I win a new one I wait until I'm by myself, then take it out and examine it, turning it over and over in the light. The cat's eyes really are like eyes, but not the eyes of cats. They're the eyes of something that isn't known but exists anyway; like the green eye of the radio; like the eyes of aliens from a distant planet. My favourite one is blue. I put it into my red plastic purse to keep it safe. I risk my other cat's eyes to be shot at, but not this one.

I don't collect many marbles because I'm not a very good shot. My brother is deadly. He takes five common marbles to school with him in a blue Crown Royal Whisky bag and comes back with the bag and his pockets bulging. He keeps his winnings in screw-top Crown preserving jars, donated by my mother, which he lines up on his desk. He never talks about his skill though. He just lines up the jars.

One Saturday afternoon he puts all his best marbles – his puries, his waterbabies and cat's eyes, his gems and wonders – into a single jar. He takes it down into the ravine somewhere, in under the wooden bridge, and buries it. Then he makes an elaborate treasure map of where it's buried, puts it in another jar, and buries that one too. He tells me he's done these things but he doesn't say why, or where the jars are buried.

....

When the handbell rings we line up in front of GIRLS, two by two, holding hands: Carol and me, then Grace and Cordelia back behind us because they're a grade ahead. My brother is over there in front of BOYS. During recess he disappears into the cinder playground, where last week he had his lip kicked open during a soccer game and had to have stitches. I've seen the stitches, up close, black thread surrounded by swollen purple. I admire them. I know about the status conferred by wounds.

Now that I've changed back from pants to skirts, I have to remember the moves. You can't sit with your legs spread apart, or jump too high or hang upside-down, without ridicule. I've had to re-learn the importance of underwear, which has a liturgy of its own:

> *I see England, I see France,*
> *I can see your underpants.*

Or else:

> *Me no know, me no care,*
> *Me no wear no underwear.*

This is said by boys, while making faces like monkeys.

There's a lot of speculation about underwear, especially the underwear of the teachers; but only that of the female teachers. Male underwear is of no importance. There aren't very many male teachers anyway, and the few that do exist are elderly; there are no young men, because the war has eaten them. The teachers are mostly women over a certain age, women who aren't married. Married women don't have jobs; we know this from our own mothers. There's something strange and laughable about older, unmarried women.

At recess, Cordelia doles out underwear: lavender frills for Miss Pigeon, who's fat and saccharine; plaid for Miss Stuart, lace-edged to go with her hankies; red satin long-johns for Miss Hatchett, who's over sixty and wears garnet brooches. We don't believe any of this underwear actually exists, but thinking about it is a nasty joy.

My own teacher is Miss Lumley. It's said that every morning before the bell rings, even in late spring when it's warm, she goes to the back of the classroom and takes off her bloomers, which are rumoured to be of heavy navy-blue wool and to smell of mothballs and of other, less definable things. This isn't repeated as speculation or as part of the underwear invention, but as fact. Several girls claim they've seen Miss Lumley putting her bloomers on again when they've had to stay in after school, and several others say they've seen them hanging in the cloakroom. The aura of Miss Lumley's dark, mysterious, repulsive bloomers clings around her and colours the air in which she moves. It makes her more terrifying; but she is terrifying in any case.

My teacher of the year before was kindly but so unmemorable that Cordelia doesn't even mention her in the underwear game. She had a face like a dinner roll and blancmange-coloured skin, and ruled by wheedling. Miss Lumley rules by fear. She's short, and oblong in shape, so that her iron-grey cardigan falls straight from shoulder to hip with no pause in between for a waist. She always wears this cardigan, and a succession of dark skirts, which can't possibly be the same one. She has steel-rimmed glasses, behind which her eyes are hard to see, and black shoes with Cuban heels, and a tiny lipless smile. She does not send children to the Principal for the strap, but does it herself, in front of the class, holding the hand out flat, bringing the black rubber strap down in sharp quick efficient strokes, her face white and quivering, while we watch, wincing, our eyes filling with involuntary tears. Some girls snivel audibly while she does this, even though she isn't doing it to them, but this isn't wise: Miss Lumley hates snivelling, and is likely to say, "I'll give you something to cry about." We learn to sit up straight, eyes front, faces blank, both feet on the floor, listening to the whack of rubber on cringing flesh.

Mostly it's boys who get the strap. They are thought to need it more. Also they fidget, especially during sewing. We are supposed to sew pot-holders, for our mothers. The boys cannot seem to do this right; their stitches are large and clumsy, and they stick one another with the needles. Miss Lumley stalks the aisles, whacking their knuckles with a ruler.

The schoolroom is high-ceilinged, yellowy-brown, with blackboards at the front and along one side and tall many-paned windows above the radiators on the other side. Over the door to the cloakroom, so that you feel you're being watched from behind, there's a large photograph of the King and Queen, the King with medals, the Queen in a white ballgown and diamond tiara. High wooden desks that sit two, with slanted tops and holes for inkwells, are arranged in rows. It's like all the other schoolrooms at Queen Mary, but it seems darker, possibly because there's less decoration. Our old teacher brought paper doilies to school in her many efforts at appeasement, and her windows were always crawling with paper vegetation. But although Miss Lumley observes the seasons in this way too, the plants we bring forth under her glittering steel-rimmed eyes are smaller, shrivelled-looking, so that there are never enough of them to cover the bare spaces of wall and glass. Also, if your fall-foliage leaf or your pumpkin is not symmetrical, Miss Lumley won't put it up. She has standards.

Things are more British than they were last year. We learn to draw the Union Jack, using a ruler and memorizing the various crosses, for St. George of England, St. Patrick of Ireland, St. Andrew of Scotland, St. David of Wales. Our own flag is red and has a Union Jack in one corner, although there's no saint for Canada. We learn to name all the pink parts of the map.

'The sun never sets on the British Empire,' says Miss Lumley, tapping the roll-down map with her long wooden pointer. In countries that are not the British Empire, they cut out children's tongues, especially those of boys. Before the British Empire there were no railroads or postal services in India, and Africa was full of tribal warfare, with spears, and had no proper clothing. The Indians in Canada did not have the wheel or telephones, and ate the hearts of their enemies in the heathenish belief that it would give them courage. The British Empire changed all that. It brought in electric lights.

Every morning, after Miss Lumley blows a thin metallic note on her pitch-pipe, we stand up to sing 'God Save the King.' We also sing,

Rule Britannia, Britannia rules the waves;
Britons never, never, never shall be slaves!

Because we're Britons, we will never be slaves. But we aren't real Britons, because we are also Canadians. This isn't quite as good, although it has its own song:

In days of yore, from Britain's shore,
Wolfe, the dauntless hero, came
And planted firm Britannia's flag
On Canada's fair domain.
Here may it wave, our boast, our pride
And join in love together
The thistle, shamrock, rose entwine
The Maple Leaf forever.

Miss Lumley's jaw quivers in a frightening way when we sing this. Wolfe's name sounds like something you'd call a dog, but he conquered the French. This is puzzling, because I've seen French people, there are lots of them up north, so he couldn't have conquered all of them. As for maple leaves, they're the hardest part to draw on our red flag. Nobody ever gets them right.

Miss Lumley brings newspaper clippings about the Royal Family and sticks them to the side blackboard. Some of them are old clippings, and show Princess Elizabeth and Princess Margaret Rose, in Girl Guide uniforms, making radio and other speeches during the Blitz. This is what we should be like, Miss Lumley implies: steadfast, loyal, courageous, heroic.

There are other newspaper pictures too, showing thin-looking children in scruffy clothes, standing in front of piles of rubble. These are to remind us that there are many starving war orphans in Europe, and we should remember that and eat our breadcrusts and potato skins and everything else on our plates, because waste is a sin. Also we should not complain. We are not really entitled to complain, because we are lucky children: English children got their houses bombed and we did not. We bring our used clothing, from home, and Miss Lumley ties it up into brown paper packages and sends it to England. There isn't much I can bring, because my mother tears our worn-out clothing up for dusters, but I manage to salvage a pair of corduroy pants, once my brother's, then mine, now too small, and a Viyella shirt of my father's that got washed wrong by mistake and shrank. It gives me a strange feeling on my skin to think of someone else, someone in England, walking around in my clothes. My clothes seem a part of me, even the ones I've outgrown.

All these things – the flags, the pitch-pipe songs, the British Empire and the princesses, the war orphans, even the strappings – are superimposed against the ominous navy-blue background of Miss Lumley's invisible bloomers. I can't draw the Union Jack or sing 'God Save the King' without thinking about them. Do they really exist, or not? Will I ever be in the classroom when she puts them on or – unthinkable – takes them off?

I'm not afraid of snakes or worms but I am afraid of these bloomers. I know it will be the worse for me if I ever actually catch sight of them. They're sacrosanct, at the same time holy and deeply shameful. Whatever is wrong with them may be wrong with me also, because although Miss Lumley is not what anyone thinks of as a girl, she is also not a boy. When the brass handbell clangs and we line up outside our GIRLS door, whatever category we are in also includes her.

Isabel Huggan

Isabel Huggan was born in Ontario, Canada, in 1943, and spent her life in that province until 1987 when, with her husband and daughter, she moved to Kenya, and then to France, where she now lives. A writer of short stories whose work appears in magazines and anthologies, and a teacher of creative writing, Isabel also writes occasional book reviews and a regular newspaper column. She happily confesses that her daughter has *never* been a Brownie. *The Elizabeth Stories* was published in 1984 in Canada by Oberon Press, and in 1987 in the USA and Britain by Viking-Penguin, and in 1990 in France (as *L'Echappée Belle*) by Gallimard. It won the 1987 Book-of-the-Month Club 'New Voice' Award. *You Never Know* is to be published in Spring 1993 in Canada by Alfred A. Knopf and in the USA by Viking-Penguin.

ISABEL HUGGAN

End of the Empire

Long ago, when I was young, I was in love with King George the Sixth. It was, as you might imagine, a rather lopsided relationship, but within its limitations so real that his death, in 1952, diminished for some time my expectations for happiness on this earth. Even now, all these years later, I sometimes suffer from a vague and aching sadness, a wandering sorrow in the halls of memory, as if my soul still mourns the day he died.

In King George, I recognized a soul very like my own – someone who had inadvertently, without having any say about it, gotten into the wrong life. In him I recognized such a gentle and bewildered dignity my heart was quite pierced through with arrows of devotion. Neither his daughter's anxious stiffness nor his grandson's self-deprecating wit can duplicate the winsome charm of his stammer, his long-faced sincerity and sweetness. Nothing can bring him back, he is forever gone; and without him, both the world and I have changed beyond recall.

The day he died I was so stricken with grief I had to be kept home from school that afternoon, my face swollen and purple from crying. We received the news of his death on the CBC at noon, from the small brown radio on top of the refrigerator. My father was on evening shift at the foundry that week so he was home and we were all sitting at the kitchen table eating lunch, our usual Campbell's chicken noodle soup and soda crackers and carrot sticks. As the announcer's deep rolling voice and the tolling British bells brought the truth home to us and the rest of Canada, I fell from my chair as in a swoon, and with a terrible gasp of 'Oh no, my King!' toppled to the floor at my mother's feet. My father, never one for emotional display, told me to straighten round immediately if I didn't want the belt, and my mother said, 'Now, now, there's no need for that,' but it was not clear whether it was to me or to my father that she spoke.

I gathered myself up and ran sobbing from the kitchen to the bedroom I shared with my older sister, whose jeering laughter I still heard as I slammed the door – cold, older-sister laughter. I flung myself across the white chenille bedspread, lay there face-down and felt the fuzzy ridges of its pattern pressing against my cheek as I wept out my despair. My hope for rescue was gone, gone to the grave.

My love for King George had been, until that moment in the kitchen, a private thing, a passion too rare to be shared with a family such as mine. I'd always known that, it was part of what made my royal life a necessary secret. My mother said she had no notion of what made me tick and whenever she said that, my father would mutter she had better be careful, because bombs tick too and then go off. It was meant as a joke, suggesting I was a tricky bit of business he didn't understand, and although it seemed rather a mean thing to say about his child – a bomb, indeed! – he was essentially correct.

Offsetting them, in fortuitous counterbalance, King George understood me absolutely. He and I were united at a deep and invisible level, as if connected by a silent underground river running beneath our lives. This became apparent the first time he saw me, the lids of his blue eyes fluttering momentarily and then opening with something like astonishment or delight. He saw me for the first time many

173

times, as I refined the pleasurable details of the scene. But always the heart of it remained the same: we belonged together, the King and I. Because of his age, and mine, the way in which we would fit would be father and daughter, but that was merely a matter of convenience and fate. Our destiny was interwoven, of that I was sure.

The events leading up to King George's happy discovery of me, Hannah Louise Clement, were always the same. I would have been found in a large green park by his younger daughter, Princess Margaret Rose, who would take me home to the Palace. Although I knew her to be a dozen years older, on this occasion she always appeared to be nearer my age, looking rather as she did in the photograph of herself and her older sister that hung on the dining room wall at my grandmother's house. She and Elizabeth were seated at a grand piano, wearing matching dresses of pink lace and tulle tied round with satin ribbon; they were smiling, and there were two small brown Corgi dogs at their feet.

Even in the park where it was rainy and chilly, dusk coming on, mist rising up from the lawns, Margaret Rose appeared to be perfectly turned out, as if royal radiance kept her dry. The park in my mind's eye bore a rather strong resemblance to Victoria Park a few blocks from where I lived in London, Ontario. A small and very ordinary city park crisscrossed with asphalt paths, it extended in my imagination far past its normal boundaries, became larger and greener, full of rose beds and statues and round ponds and decorative glass-globe lamps shining dimly in the fog. The weather was always English in this sequence, there was never sunshine, never snow. I knew perfectly well the climatic demands of my private mythology.

Although Princess Margaret Rose was always safe from the physical discomfort of ordinary mortals, it distressed her royal heart to see a cold wet creature like me, Hannah Louise, huddled on a park bench, hungry, outcast, alone. She would scrutinize me by bringing her dimpled face in its nest of curls very close to mine and then she would stand back, and pronounce her sentence very clearly: she must take me home to her Father the King.

Exactly how I knew that King George would want to adopt me as soon as he set eyes on me I am not to this day sure. I saw *him* only infrequently in black-and-white newsreels at the movie house on Saturdays, and in a few colour photographs in magazines or in the corridors at school. But I knew, with the intuition of the truly blessed, that he and I were cut from the same cloth. That is not to say that I had delusions of grandeur or that I believed myself to be of royal blood, my lineage lost and muddled over the years, my legacy denied because of some Dickensian nursemaid's foible. Rather, it was from the fine and innocent certainty that station in life meant nothing, a kind of childish notion of pure equality. Nobody gets to choose who her parents are, nobody gets to choose the time and place of his birth – we all start out the same, having no say in anything at all. It wasn't his idea to be royal any more than it was mine to be ordinary. I felt sure that King George was not any different from, and longed to be attached to, the real world of common people. Like me. And I sensed that he was, like me, a little scared. And I knew that he knew that I knew.

I was a thin, unadventurous child who preferred fantasy because less than a decade in this world had convinced me that reality was a punishing and difficult affair. Sometime shortly after kindergarten, perhaps as a result of a determined teacher insisting I use my right hand instead of my left, I developed a slight stutter, which had a way of coming and going so that I never knew exactly when I was going to stumble and fall over a syllable. The very random nature of this thing meant no one could find a way to cure it, and the family doctor simply assured my mother that I would, eventually, grow out of it. Which, of course, I did, except for occasional lapses when I am angry or afraid.

As a child, I found a lot to be afraid of. My mother used to say she thought I looked for trouble and she was probably right. In those years after the war, it was hard for a child to differentiate between the horrors one saw in the magazines and newsreels and the horrors one imagined. It was impossible to grasp the levels of hate and fear in the world and translate it all properly so that none of it applied to you. There were, for example, in our end of the city, several 'foreign' families known as the DPs, who'd come out of central Europe after 1945. Tough, hardened survivors ready to make a new life in the new land, these *displaced persons* did not fit into the already established patterns of London, Ontario and they were discriminated against at every turn, especially in working-class neighbourhoods such as mine where their presence was a threat, and a continuing reminder of the ups and downs of fate.

Their children, who went to my school were known as the Dumb DPs, and were mocked and scorned and treated with disdain. In my fearful heart, I knew how these kids felt, in their moth-eaten, hand-me-down cardigans, with their funny accents and garlicky breath and knobby knees. I felt like that when I was teased for my stutter or for being a beanpole or a smartypants. It was all the same, and it wasn't fair. And pity swelled within me for their awful plight.

It did not make me open my heart to them, you understand. I befriended not one solitary DP child. I turned instead for companionship and solace to the King of England.

Margaret Rose, on the other hand, had a heart of gold, and I feel for her still a grateful fondness. She did not hesitate to take home a wet little waif from the park and to share, with angelic generosity, her father and her life. Elizabeth, actually, I found a touch surly, a bit sulky in a self-interested way – much like my older sister. I could see she wanted to remain the apple of her Daddy's eye, unthwarted by any snotty-nosed stranger; and I always had the shaky feeling that if she had her way she'd whisk me out of Buckingham Palace quick as a wink, no matter what her silly sister said.

I would be led to the throne room by Margaret Rose who'd take my hand in a bossy but kindly way. As a rule the Queen was never present but her absence was easily explainable. A Queen was meant to be out and about, hovering by veteran's wheelchairs, offering sticks of candy to poor children, cutting ribbons, pouring tea, the impersonal, dutiful charities of *noblesse oblige*, requiring little of her but large hats and powdery smiles. I was not cynical but I knew the Queen did not matter.

The King, however, liked sticking closer to home and that was as it should be, a king on his throne, ruling. He didn't wear a crown, but he usually had on a peacock-blue smoking jacket, made of shiny, patterned brocade. It must have been handed down by his brother, I think. It made a nice, if surprising, change from the military gear one so often saw him in, and the informality of the costume made him appear relaxed, nearly jolly. He would be sitting with his hands folded in his lap, as if he'd been waiting for me to appear, and when I did, he would say to Margaret Rose, 'What's this, then?'

I would walk carefully up the long purple carpet to where he sat, and make a deep curtsey, and he would rise from his throne and touch my hair with his hand and say, 'There, there, child. Enough.' And I would look up at his face – the long, sad cheeks, the remarkable expanse from nose to lip, the thin lip itself – and see in his lovely eyes the perfect understanding of which I spoke earlier, and the flicker of paternal joy.

Bashfully, for neither of us was any good at making conversation, we would talk to each other about our lives. This episode would usually serve as a review of what I was doing in school at the time, and I would tell the King everything I knew. The routes of the explorers, the toughest multiplication tables, all the verses of all the poems I had memorized by Walter de la Mare and Christina Rossetti – all these things and more, without hesitation or stutter. And he too spoke clearly and calmly, in a voice rich and warm and even, in the voice a king should have. In the voice I gave him. And he would say, in this wonderful voice, that he was amazed at the depth and breadth of my knowledge.

'Why, I think you know more than either of my girls do,' he would say. And then: 'What would you think about coming to live here at the Palace? You are just the sort of girl I like to talk to.'

It was the kind of swift decision-making one might expect from a king. For although the invitation was phrased as a question, there was no doubt that it was a royal command, and that I would now live there forever, with him.

Conveniently, I was only recently orphaned, my insensitive family having perished in a car accident or a tragic fire or from food poisoning at a picnic, and so there were no obstacles to surmount. I would nod my assent shyly, and the court stenographer would be called upon to draw up immediately the adoption papers. I'd sign my name, Rebecca Louise, with a flourish, and King George would raise his eyebrows in appreciation of my fine hand, and then apply himself to his own signature. This would be followed by a hot wax seal, red and dripping, as the parchment would be lifted up, and the announcement made: 'Rebecca Louise Clement is now of the House of Windsor.'

Generally speaking, I never progressed beyond this point. The ceremony in itself was the culmination of all my hopes and dreams, and there was no need for denouement. And it was only the King's death that brought me back to the suburban street and two-storey frame house in which I dwelled with a father and mother who couldn't figure me out, and a sister who thought, if she ever gave me a thought, that I was weird.

Her name was Phyllis Anne, and in the weeks following my downfall in the kitchen she needled and teased me and made me miserable at every turn. Three years older than I, she was exactly the right age to take the approaching Coronation seriously, and she began a scrapbook, starting with the newspaper clippings telling how Princess Elizabeth had been given the news she'd be Queen while she was at Treetops in faraway Africa. Then she added to her collection the countless magazine articles and pamphlets flourishing in those days leading up to the event, full of Windsor family photographs, charts of royal succession, historical essays on the meaning of the Coronation, the symbolism of the orb and crown and ermine-bordered velvet robes. Etcetera, etcetera. All very cheery and positive, this business of putting that Elizabeth on the throne. Phyllis Anne purposely left this stuff out on the bureau, knowing I would see it and read it, knowing it would make me suffer. Well, perhaps she didn't do it on purpose; but the bitterness of my grief must have been apparent to her, she must have seen how I mourned.

I had longed for that name change with my whole being – I had heard in the King's last name the *win* and *wind* and *soar* of Windsor – and it made me feel strong and free, an eagle, a lark, lifted high above the ground where my unimaginative family congealed around me, dull and hard as cement. Clement, cement, stuck in my name forever. I felt so weighted with sadness I could not bear to think of it, and with some self-preserving instinct went off to the public library where I took books off shelves and flipped over pages, searching for something, anything to take me away from my life.

And by a chance as fortuitous as being found by Margaret Rose, one day I took from the top of a return cart a novel by Zane Grey, and within a few paragraphs had found what it was I'd been looking for. The words seemed to blaze from the page, so vivid and real I could feel the heat from the small campfire against my face and the dark prairie night cold at my back. I knew, as deeply as anything I had ever experienced, what it was to ride for hours across sand blowing with tumbleweed, through the cactus and the sagebrush and up into the purple hills, riding and riding and riding. And I turned to the Wild West with a passion.

It was only a small step from those novels to the cowboy comic books and movies suddenly surrounding me – how had I never noticed them before? Waiting for me, as if they'd known I'd be coming just at that moment, were Roy Rogers and Dale Evans, King and Queen of the Cowboys. They welcomed me into their movies – I spent every cent of my allowance on the Saturday matinees, often the only girl for rows around – and met me once a week on the little brown radio, which I was allowed to take upstairs for the precious half-hour of the Roy Rogers show. I would lie on the bed looking up at the ceiling where my imagination brought me the unfolding adventures of Roy and Dale. And I always took the radio back down to the kitchen feeling calm and contented, prepared to ride along my own happy trails until, next week, I would meet them again.

The universe expanded, allowing me to accompany Roy's sidekick Pat Brady in his jeep Nellybelle. And then, in no time, I found myself riding my own palomino Golden Girl, just a little behind Roy and Trigger. Often he would turn towards me rather than to Dale or Pat when things got tough and he needed a hand. Almost overnight I became a rip-snorting cowgirl who never rode sissy side-saddle, who could blast the eyes out of a rattlesnake with her six-shooter, who was vigilant in her defence of justice out there on the lone prairie. Roy and Dale said they didn't know how they'd ever managed before I came along, and I wondered myself as well.

My mutable soul transformed itself in all that sunshine and fresh air and my allegiance transferred itself too – effortlessly, painlessly – from one king to another. The hot dry winds of the desert swept away the chilly mists and the park bench and dear sweet Margaret Rose; and even Buckingham Palace receded into the distant fog. It had been easier to believe that things were all of a piece when King George was on the throne – England, Canada, Canada, England, hardly any difference, really – but now with Elizabeth up there, well, things weren't the same any more.

I didn't care. Once I'd discovered riding the range I was no longer waiting to be adopted in order to make life happen. I was becoming tough, brave, independent and prickly as a cactus. Maybe even a little dangerous. I was growing up. The Palace, if it ever did come to mind, seemed an awfully dull and confining place compared to sleeping out under the stars and listening to the coyotes howl.

One day, as I was riding on ahead of Roy and the sheriff's posse to show them the way, the entire Royal Family slipped out of my dreams and into the cold grey ocean separating their little island from my new American life. It ended just like that, as completely as if they had drowned. I crossed the border into the land of the free and the Empire dissolved behind me, gone with the ghost of King George back into the mists of time. And heartless as children are, I didn't look back, and I never said goodbye.

Daphne Marlatt

Daphne Marlatt, West Coast writer, was born in Melbourne, Australia in 1942, spent her early childhood in Penang, Malaysia, and immigrated to Vancouver with her family in 1951. Except for five years in the USA in the 1960s (during which time she received a Master's degree in Comparative Literature from Indiana University), she has lived on the West Coast. She has written a number of books of poetry and/or prose, including *Steveston* (1974, 1984), *How Huge a Stone* (1983), *Touch to my Tongue* (1984) and *Salvage* (1991). Her novel, *Ana Historic,* appeared in 1988, with a French edition, *Ana historique*, translated by Lori Saint-Martin and Paul Gagné, appearing in 1992. She has collaborated with Nicole Brossard in a pair of 'transformance' chapbooks (*Mauve,* and *character/jeu de lettres*) and with Betsy Warland (*Double Negative*). A collection of the Warland/ Marlatt collaborative texts is forthcoming from Guernica Press under the title *Words with You* (1993). Marlatt has co-edited several little magazines and was a founding member of the editorial collective which publishes the feminist bilingual journal *Tessera*. In addition, she has worked collectively to edit two conference proceedings: *In the Feminine* (1985) and *Telling It* (1990). She has been writer-in-residence at a number of Canadian universities, including the Universities of Manitoba and Alberta, and in 1988-89 occupied Ruth Wynn Woodward Chair of Women's Studies at Simon Fraser University. She now lives on Salt Spring Island with Betsy Warland.

DAPHNE MARLATT

Difference (em)bracing

In not the same person

What is it makes some words essential, relevant to one woman writer and irrelevant to another? and can we communicate then? what is communication but a sharing of our visions of what is essential? And by that i don't mean to refer to essence but to necessity, that which motivates us as writers. Sometimes in reading as in writing the shift from inessential to essential occurs in the same person (and is she, are you then the same?) – that certain space where words turn from abstraction and, not uncertainty exactly, but a kind of unspecificity where they have existed somewhere out there as objects in flight (UFO's even) in the world you read or listen in on, and then in a flash wing in to the core of your being and you recognize all that they stand for and that you have a stake in them, a share as speaker/writer/reader/listener, all of you there in that active complex. This is very different from being taken up by aliens, since it involves your own assertion of what is meaningful to you.

The difference writing makes where, caught in the act so to speak, you ask yourself questions and discover the words you can stand by are words that stand that ground you have a share in. Feminist, for instance, subject, mother, lesbian – words i recognize and have a stake in. They set up currents of meaning that establish this you i also am (not third person, as in totally other, and not quite the same as me). 'You' is a conduit, a light beam to larger possibility, so large it fringes on the other without setting her apart from me. Because we speak about 'her' in the third person, 'she' is where exclusion takes place. 'Feminist,' 'lesbian' take on other meanings then, even other qualities as words – they suddenly limit, they suddenly objectify. But in the first or second person i see who you are, feminist, lesbian: your historicity, your meaning-potential is what i grow into.

So i recognize certain words that constitute my body (not exclusive of the psychic terrain my body stands in) – the body of my writing. As any of us does over time. 'Getting to know you' words out there – maybe as other as the King of Siam – written from a white colonial point of view. Those dated words which excited my fifteen-year-old imagination under cloudy skies backlit by the foots and spots of Theatre Under the Stars in Stanley Park, still run through my forty-seven year old mind. But now i suspect a hidden imperialism in them making the other the same and therefore plausible, i.e., plausibly me. This script lies at the heart of fiction and is not what i'm trying to get at, which is the plausible implausibility of living difference as both other *and* not-other. Another besides me.

As Virginia Woolf has written of 'the sixty or seventy times which beat simultaneously in every normal human system' and how rarely we manage to synchronize them, or again of 'the perfect rag-bag of odds and ends within us – a piece of a policeman's trousers lying cheek by jowl with Queen Alexandra's wedding veil'[1] (this is a distinctly English cultural rag-bag). Or as Hélène Cixous has written of writing as 'precisely working (in) the in-between, inspecting the process of the same and of the other without which nothing can live, undoing the work of death – to admit this is first to want the two, as well as both...'[2] Women keep trying to write it, what we sense which language resists, structured as it is on the basis of difference as black + (read *or*) white, men or women, straight or gay, absolute difference which cannot bear the weight of both/and.

It is poetry which pushes the limits of this system, speaks in corresponding differences (differences which speak to each other). Not the same as 'same difference,' that childhood taunt of dismissal which collapsed difference into an identical same. How to find the words that will stand the corresponding differences of this complexity we glimpse ourselves living, despite the monocultural stereotypes that delude us into thinking difference means an opposition, the utterly singular on one side of a great divide.

Difference is where the words turn depending on who reads them and how we bring who we are to that reading. When we each bring our differences into that reading, the multiple nature of the real begins to be heard.

Arriving at Shared Ground Through Difference

It wasn't sharing but difference in a multiplicity of ways i felt first as a child in Malaya where i was taught the King's (it was then) English, to mind my P's & Q's, to behave and speak 'properly,' when all the while i was surrounded by other languages that were not proper at all for a white colonial child, but which nevertheless i longed to understand, filled as they were with laughter, jokes, calls, exclamations, comfort, humming. Sometimes rocked to sleep, sometimes teased or scolded, sometimes ignored by the sounds of Cantonese, Malay, Thai, i stood on the fringe and longed to know what the stories were that produced such laughter, such shakings of the head. When my Amahs spoke only English, they knew and i knew it was not the same, it meant we had to be 'proper.' O the complexities of the power dynamic between colonial children and their mother-substitutes, these women who had given up the possibility of families for themselves but who nevertheless led other lives, barely heard between the lines proper to their servant roles, and who illicitly imparted some of that culture, some of that life-experience to their Mem's children. I grew up loving the emotive sound of women's voices and distrustful of a system that dismissed women's experience in general, and some women's more than others', depending on the colour of their skin and the language(s) they spoke – and many spoke more than the single-minded ruling one.

Then there was my mother's mother tongue: English English with its many intensifiers, its emphatic sentence pitches, its ringing tones of boarding-school elocution lessons. Learning to speak properly – 'Don't drawl like that, it sounds so dreadfully American. Why can't you pronounce the ends of your words?' The trouble was i had become embarrassed by the language i spoke which branded me as both excessive (those intensifiers) and excessively polite in Canadian schoolyards. My speech sounded exaggerated: 'Wha'd ya mean "awfully sorry" You're not awful are you?' It sounded pretentious: 'listen, *nobody* walks on the *grawss.*' At first 'wanna,' and 'movies' and 'you guys' sounded funny in my mouth, as if i were trying to speak counterfeit words. But imitation cut both ways: there was now a whole new level of my own vocabulary, words that sounded false on the street: cinema, rubbish, being sent to Coventry, not to mention that give-away, Mummy, a world away from Mom. And so i engaged in long battles with my mother, each of us trying to correct the other, she correcting for purity of origin, while i corrected for common usage – each of us with different versions of 'the real thing.' The struggle over reality is a deadly one that cuts to the root of being. Words were

182

always taken seriously in my house because they were the weapons of that struggle. But a woman's sense of herself in the language she speaks can only be denied so long before it transforms into a darker (side of the moon), a more insistent ir-reality, not *un*real because its effects are felt so devastatingly in its subject and those around her. Her words, her very style of speaking derided by her own children, her colonial manners and English boarding-school mores dismissed as inappropriate by Canadianized daughters who denied any vestige of them in their own behaviour and speech, she withdrew into chronic depression and hypochondria. 'Unbalanced.' 'Loony.' But to deny: to completely say no to. A powerful mechanism. A form of colonialism at work within the family.

By the time I entered the University of British Columbia in the first year of the sixties, Canadian was something i had mastered – and i use that word deliberately. As a student of literature, almost all my literary models, quite literally 'the masters' of English (or American – at that time we didn't study Canadian) literature were men. As a young writer, the contemporary poetry other writers pointed me to was largely written by men. My own 'masters' (in that sense of mentors) were Charles Olson, Robert Duncan, Robert Creeley and their masters, William Carlos Williams, Ezra Pound, Louis Zukofsky. Somehow reading 'the poet, he' to include me, i trained myself in that poetic, the injunctions to get rid of the lyric ego, not to 'sprawl' in loose description or emotion ungrounded in image, to pay strict attention to the conjoined movement of body (breath) and mind in the movement of the line, though it didn't occur to me then to wonder whether my somewhat battered female ego was anything like a man's, or whether my woman's body had different rhythms from his, or whether my female experience might not give me an alternate 'stance' in the world (one that wasn't so much 'in' as both in & outside of a male-dominated politic & economy).

But there were cracks, fissures that led me to another writing world. Through Robert Duncan's prose poems and Charles Olson's essays i remembered my original delight in the extendable and finely balanced nature of the sentence ungoverned by line breaks (a different sort of sprawl). Duncan led me to Gertrude Stein and her play with emphasis, with difference in repetition, with the passionate nature of the loopy speaking sentence, peculiarly a woman's in her work. Duncan led me to H.D. too, another sort of passion, the passion of vision, of interwoven imageries lifted live from a wealth of spiritual traditions, the H.D. of her long poems and now the H.D. of her novels documenting the inner struggles of a woman living very much in her time.

Impossible to list here all the reading paths (as divergent as Anaïs Nin, Maxine Hong Kingston, Phyllis Webb, Marguerite Duras, Zora Neale Hurston, Nicole Brossard among others) which led me to the hidden and astonishingly varied tradition of women's writing – the other side of that man-in-the-moon face polished and presented to us as the shining side of 'Contemporary Literature' when i was in school. The dark side, a wonderful colloquy of women's voices writing about the 'trivial,' taboo and tacit: solitude verging on madness, women's social roles and loss of self, excessive passion, a whole female erotic, daily doubts that give the lie to philosophic certainties, companionship with animals and trees, women's companion-ship despite double standards in (and within) sex and race, double standards everywhere and women speaking of and writing on that double edge, in touch with one another's difficult balance there. And that was the excitement, the lifting of a horizon, that here was an ongoing dialogue where women were central, not marginal, where women were delighting in writing the complex i (fem.), not trying to write like 'the poet, he' in all his singular authority.

The Singularly Complex

This dialogue that our writing enters is a singularly (as in deviating from the norm) complex one because it includes, it must include, voices from so many fringes, not just that fringe, women (translated as white, middle-class, heterosexual, Anglo-Canadian/American) that has been gradually getting so legitimated it would seem to be moving into centre. Becoming aware of this dialogue on the (many) fringes, listening to other women's words / realities, is to engage in a delicate balance between recognition of difference and recognition of shared ground. The balance between i and we, neither capitalized nor capitalizing on the other.

To begin with, to write I, to assume our own centrality as ground, goes against all our gender-conditioning and is a frightening first step in autobiography and journal-writing. We do it because we must. But when we write I we discover that this singular column with its pedestal and cap, this authorized capital letter, far from being monolithically singular is full of holes a wind blows through, whispering contradictory images, echoing others' words. I am not myself, or we are not myself, *or* each of us is our selves in the plural, struggling to speak the difference we sense through rigid assumptions of sameness and identity in the language we have inherited.

I becomes a kind of shorthand for a complex of such fractured identity, with a corresponding urge to write we to include others. But at the same time this i, fraught with inner difference, cannot simply graph those inner differences onto others. A recognition of real differences of life-experience, privilege and accessibility to the centre is essential here. Without that, i simply co-opt others' experiences in attempting to make them mine in the writing, in attempting to make my we cover their i.

There are many we's which any i might feel included in, just as there are many we's which any i might feel excluded from, colour, class and sexual orientation being the broadest of distinctions/groupings. We cross over many borderlines, we inhabit many borderlands (as Gloria Anzaldúa[3] and Joy Kogawa[4] have both recently attested to). The complex of these for each one of us is not the same as for any other. This makes the differences in our language and in our sense of our selves crucial. It makes attention to difference in the work of others essential, and collaboration rather than assimilation an essential writing practice. Only then can we learn not to dominate one another with our claims to reality.

NOTES

[With thanks to Nicole Brossard, Betsy Warland, Joy Kogawa and Lee Maracle for their analyses.]

1. Virginia Woolf, *Orlando* (London: Granada, 1977), p.]91, p. 49.
2. Hélène Cixous, 'The Laugh of the Medusa' in *New French Feminisms*, eds. Elaine Marks and Isabelle de Courtivron (New York: Schocken, 1981), p. 254.
3. At the Third International Feminist Book Fair, Montreal, June 1988.
4. At Telling It: Women and Language Across Cultures, Simon Fraser University Downtown, November 1988.

Maggie Butcher

Maggie Butcher was born in 1946 in Woburn Sands, then a village, now designated a town, on the Bedfordshire-Buckinghamshire border. After a first degree in English at King's College, London, she did a PGCE at the University of York 'split' with a year teaching at the Arabic Teachers' College, Sokoto, in northern Nigeria. She taught in a comprehensive school in Leeds for three years before doing an M.A. in Commonwealth Literature and returning to Nigeria in 1974 to teach at Ahmadu Bello University, Zaria. After a four-year teaching fellowship at the University of Saskatchewan, Saskatoon, Canada, she returned to the UK in 1980 where a domestic flood provided the excuse finally to abandon her soggy doctoral thesis on 'The Development of the Female *Bildungsroman* in Commonwealth Literature'. Maggie was Deputy Chief Education Officer at the Commonwealth Institute in London, 1980-88, and International Education Coordinator with United World Colleges, 1988-91. She was appointed Academic Administrator of Gresham College in the City of London in November 1991. She edited *The Eye of the Beholder: Essays on Indian Writing* (Commonwealth Institute, 1983), and *Tibisiri: Caribbean Writers and Critics* (Dangaroo Press, 1989), and has contributed articles and reviews to various literary journals.

MAGGIE BUTCHER

Fireworks in May

Fireworks lit up the night sky above the South Saskatchewan River. Rockets rained showers of dazzling silver, green and gold on downtown Saskatoon. I was 30 years old and had survived my first Canadian winter. Any excuse would do for a celebration and, lacking Guy Fawkes, if the Canadians wanted to celebrate Queen Victoria's birthday, why not? It was only when I connected Victoria Day with Empire Day and with the descriptions of flag-waving schoolchildren in African novels that I began to realize I had been cheated. Back home in England I had never celebrated Empire Day. I hadn't known it existed.

Daughter: Mum, do you remember Empire Day?
Mother: Oh yes. I must have been three or four. It was 1918 or 1919. We paraded round the school playground and marched up and down to represent the countries of the Empire. I was a dairymaid with a three-legged stool. I represented England. I wore a smock and a white sunbonnet.
Daughter: What about the other countries? How were they dressed?
Mother: With whatever people could find. Everyone was very poor. Sheets or curtains did for India. And faces were blacked up.
Daughter: Had you ever seen an Indian?
Mother: No. That was much later. I think the custom died out, at least in Woburn Sands. In the next village they were much more Empire minded. It depended on the Headmaster.

Same school. 1955. Mrs Watts is taking the register. 'Yes, Ma'am; present, Ma'am.' Mrs Watts is a daughter of the Empire.
'She thinks she's the Queen,' our Mums giggled.
'Does Mr Watts have to call her "Ma'am"?' we wondered in private. In singing lessons her amber beads rose and fell above her lacy knit jumper. She pounded the piano and tried to keep us in time:

Hearts of oak are our ships,
Jolly tars are our men;
We always are ready,
Steady, boys, steady!
We'll fight and we'll conquer,
Again and again!

We pushed up the seats of our two-by-two desks and sang:

Some talk of Alexander
And some of Hercules,
Of Hector and Lysander
And such great names as these:
But of all the world's great heroes

There's none that can compare –
With a tow-row-row-row-row-row –
To the British Grenadiers.

1953. I am six and a half. I have paraded round the muddy 'Rec' dressed up as a plump ladybird in a red and black spotted outfit. It is pouring with rain and the dye drips down my legs. The pipe-cleaner antennae on my little cap droop in the wet.

We march up to the Institute where we are each given a Coronation mug and a five-shilling coin in a plastic case. A fat girl covered in newsprint and wearing a top hat, with a cigar clamped between her teeth, is awarded first prize. She is meant to be Winston Churchill. Someone dressed as Elizabeth the First comes second.

At home I had a golden carriage and scores of Life Guards and Household Cavalry in a book of cardboard cut-outs. They had tabs marked A and B and dotted lines where you were meant to fold. I was not very good at cutting and folding and gluing tabs together and my royal procession did not progress very far. We didn't have a television but I saw the pictures in the papers. Queen Salote of Tonga was the first black woman I had ever seen. She was large and smiling and looked very jolly and made everyone else look very small. Queen Mary was very severe and looked a bit like a sheep. She was wearing a special sort of hat called a toque on her head.

I read the newspapers lying on the floor. There is a coffin covered with flowers. 'Who was Stalin, Mum?'

A black man lodged at Mrs Preston's. He had a khaki bag over his shoulder like the one my Dad carried his sandwiches to work in. I don't know if anyone spoke to him.

Mrs Preston's front room smelt musty and peculiar. No-one ever used it except Doreen and me. Crystal prisms on the mantelpiece caught the light; the horsehair sofa scratched our legs and there were sheets draped over the chairs. Doreen was older than me and listened to Radio Luxembourg. There was sheet music in the piano stool lid, and we sang 'Three Coins in the Fountain' and hid when the bearded Sikh with his suitcase came to the front door. He was selling bright scarves and beaded jumpers. I felt a bit funny. I think if it had been my Mum she would have opened the door even if she hadn't bought anything. I didn't know why we had to hide.

In 1956, when I was nine, my father died. Mrs Hedges' daughter lived in Australia and my Mum, I know, thought more than once about emigrating. I think she wanted to go to Adelaide. But nothing came of it. We stayed in Woburn Sands.

The undertaker's wife in the next village was Hungarian. That year her family had to flee. There was a new girl in the school playground. She was older than me so I didn't know if she spoke English.

I go to play with a girl called Joan. Her mother is very tanned and wears earrings. They have a dog called Simba and have lived in Kenya. Another family came to stay with them. Elaine said they had had to leave Kenya because of Mau Mau.

I sit with my Letts Schoolgirl's Diary listening to the radio announce the results of the 1957 General Election. I add the name of Harold Macmillan to the list of Prime Ministers of Great Britain and Northern Ireland.

Each week I read *Children's Newspaper*, supplemented on Sundays with *The People* and Pop's copy of *News of the World*, which Mum doesn't think I ought to read. I spend my pocket money on stamps and packets of stamp hinges. My green Pelham stamp album gets fat as my collection grows. Turks and Caicos Islands, Sarawak, St. Kitts Nevis and Anguilla. Red and green oblongs with George the Sixth looking out on coconut palms and men heaving great nets into sailboats.

The Gold Coast became Ghana and I did a 'project' on Africa in my first year at Grammar School. I cut out pictures of Kwame Nkrumah and knew a lot about cocoa. I wrote to Cadbury's in Bournville who sent me a cardboard cocoa pod and lots of leaflets and a picture of two glasses of milk being poured into a purple chocolate bar.

I was always sending away for things. I filled in coupons and sent off stamps and postal orders. I pretended I was a housewife and received the recipes for BeRo flour; a 'nursing mother' and got bottles of Dinneford's Magnesia which I drank like water. I wrote off for holiday brochures from exotic places like Paignton or Torquay as though I were planning expensive sojourns in hotels called the Royal or the Excelsior. I used my name, my mother's name and my grandmother's, until Pop, my grandfather, said I should look out; they'd send someone round to check on me.

I liked the sound of letters coming through the letterbox, and waited expectantly for the postman each morning. I liked seeing my name and address typewritten on the envelope:

Miss M. Butcher
7 Chapel Street
Woburn Sands
Bletchley
Bucks.

It gave me a sense of who I was and where, but confirmed that there was a world outside Woburn Sands which I wanted to test for myself. Intimations of it already existed.

Pop had a hole in his chest from a bullet in the Boer War. He had been in the trenches in the First World War and he was so tall he had been shouted at: 'Keep yer head down, Perry.' He kept pigeons, and had looked after carrier pigeons in the War. Nanny had gone to Belgium with her sister as a cook to a family of tea planters from India who had settled in one of the 'Big Houses' in Aspley Guise.

The Misses Mowbray, shadowy figures in black bombazine and veils, carried an aura of mystery. Hard to imagine they had once been sprightly young women who had visited the Holy Land and ridden side-saddle into Petra. 'The rose-red city half as old as time,' intoned my mother. I didn't know she was quoting.

Later, Miss Stevens taught us geography, and I coloured great swathes of Canada yellow and drew the rail line going through Regina, and put Broken Hill and Kalgoorlie within a few thousand miles of their true location on a map of Australia. Miss Stevens was Canadian. She despaired of making me understand longitude and latitude, and left me to read *Wuthering Heights* at the back of the class.

1968, the year of student revolution across Europe, passed rather without notice for those of us in our final year at university in London. Those of us, that is, who were not at LSE. At the end of that year I applied to go overseas with VSO and was accepted, to the undisguised amazement of some of my friends who perceived that I possessed none of the skills or attributes that they considered essential to 'life in the tropics' (the forerunner of the expression 'the Third World'). I was posted to the Arabic Teachers' College in the historic city of Sokoto in the north-west of Nigeria. It was there that I first read Achebe's novels and, naively, first tried to teach them.

Formally posed photographs reveal unconscious and insidious assumptions. The sole white Englishwoman is given the place of honour next to the Principal. Inappropriate lighting renders the black faces of my male colleagues, Nigerians, Sudanese, Egyptians and Pakistanis, dark and totally featureless. Lack of fixer has, over time, blanked out my own face. The outline of black spectacle frames remains. I cannot recognize myself in them. Or so I maintain.

When I wanted to go to the lavatory and discovered that the only staff latrine is an evil-smelling hole in the ground, whose voice was it that despatched the school lorry to the 'canteen' for disinfectant and a supply of Andrex toilet rolls? And a tow-row-row-row-row-row for the British volunteer? Mallama Maggie. 'Call me Ma'am'?

Shades of all the teachers I ever had flit around me as I stand in front of the blackboard. Sometimes I am unsure if it is their voices or mine I hear speaking to the class. Shades of my childhood again when, on a long train journey, laughing mothers press their small children on me. The infants, taken by surprise, catch sight of my white face and scream in terror. To them white people are doctors who might inject them with painful needles, or something worse. Watch out or the *baturiya* will get you.

Baturiya, European, Englishwoman, Bogeywoman. Just so do our images of self become the sticks with which we beat ourselves and others.

Helen Niven

Helen Niven is now a senior administrator with the British Open University, having joined it in 1971 on the same day as the first students. She has written a study of Dickens's *Nicholas Nickleby*.

HELEN NIVEN

When the Sun was Setting: Individual Connections in a British Girlhood

I was born in England on Empire Day 1945.

Not, I am sure, that the Empire was in the front of my family's mind. Fighting in Europe had stopped only three weeks previously. International affairs preoccupied my family as everyone in Britain at that time, but it is certain that the focus was not the Empire as an entity, but the closing stages of the Second World War, and the implications for a new European order of the defeat of Germany.

Both my parents were teachers, in neighbouring public schools in Monmouth, a small town in the borders of Wales. Both were first generation university graduates and in the depression of the 1930s had enjoyed a congenial life in a close-knit school community. Indeed, my father used to say that he had been extremely lucky to have obtained a teaching job at all, particularly in a good school, and there was no question of looking to move from it. The picture I have inherited of those times is of a rather idyllic existence. My father had a large house with a big garden. He grew vegetables and kept chickens. Socially there were tennis parties, bridge parties, excursions by bicycle into the surrounding countryside. My parents had both spent holidays in France and Germany and had a well-developed international perspective, but at a day-to-day level their lives centred on the preoccupations that were generated by their schools.

Relatively speaking, life must have been fairly easy during the war. My father had not been called up because of poor hearing and had been a fire-fighter. Because of the relative safety of the area, several other public schools were evacuated to Monmouth, and at the end of the war my father got a new job at one of those schools and we moved when the school returned.

Felsted, where the school was, is a small village in Essex. Archetypally southern English – the houses, some 300 and 400 years old, the farms, the nearby small factory for processing sugar beet, the public school with its large buildings and spacious playing fields ringed by chestnut trees – the conventionality of the setting seemed to mirror our family life, which was characterized in recollection by regularity, stability, comfort, confidence.

I know now that life for my parents was not as settled as it seemed. The state of the economy in post-war England meant that middle class families had relatively little money to spare. My mother was at home with me and my brother. She recalls having no money left out of the housekeeping to buy herself a lipstick – a galling constraint for someone who had a career before her marriage. Professionally too my father had become dissatisfied with his job and decided to leave. He cast his net widely and was actively thinking of taking up the offer of a headmastership in Perth, Western Australia, when a move to Lancashire presented itself. How different my experience of Empire might have been!

When we moved north I started 'proper' school. However, my keenest memories of early schooling have nothing to do with the curriculum. I sat at a desk in the left-hand corner of the front row of the class. We may have been taught about the

Empire but if so it is overwhelmed by other recollections. Being left-handed, my pathetic efforts with a nibbed pen and inkwell brought down the sarcastic wrath of Miss Miles. Better that, though, than the slippering with trousers down and in front of the class, which was the punishment meted out to the boys.

My parents were determined to give us a rounded cultural and social upbringing. My father had a keen interest in history, and outings to churches, castles and stately homes were a regular part of life in the school holidays. In the post-war years a huge expansion of teacher training and further education colleges took place, and we used to go with my father on some of the many site visits he had to make. It was not much gadding about compared with the way most British children live now. Nonetheless, we had a car all through my childhood and used it for visits to the seaside, picnics and excursions, and an annual summer holiday which was the highlight of the year.

Despite a fairly full educational and cultural life, it was all very anglo-centric. Unlike many families we had no close connections of emigration which would have brought the Empire home to us. An uncle of my father's had emigrated to Canada in about 1900, and a cousin in Montreal used to write to him each Christmas, but otherwise we had none of the extensive colonial networks which some British families had. We had some exquisite carved and engraved ivory boxes that had come from Java and several kimonos from Japan, brought home by my grandfather, who had been a tea trader. However, when I later visited the home of my husband's parents, whose family had spent many years in India and Burma, I realized that for some British people the Empire was alive in its artefacts – the rugs, the china, the jewellery, the ornaments – in a way that simply did not impinge on my family. Nor, I suspect, was this unusual. I imagine that for many English people of my age the Empire and then emergent Commonwealth was a fact of accepted life which did not merit great comment.

It was in one particular point of detail that the Empire did make an impact on me personally from my earliest years. When I was a child the national anthem was played on the radio on Empire Day before the morning news. It was also – as it still is – played on the birthday of the Queen, then Princess Elizabeth, whose birthday was the same date as my father's. It was always a family joke that he and I were special because the national anthem was played for us. I can't remember when the national anthem ceased to be played on 24 May, but I remember being very miffed that I was no longer as special as my father.

Queen Elizabeth ... I was six when King George died, and like most British people of my age the Queen's accession and particularly her coronation are among the first and certainly most vividly remembered public events of childhood. A schools radio programme on music and movement was interrupted to announce the death of the King. The news seemed incomprehensible and had to be explained by the headmistress. Were we sent home from school? Some children were, but I cannot say I remember.

The succeeding year, leading up to the coronation, was a time of intense anticipation. Prompted by the feeling that there were momentous happenings to record, I kept a scrap-book of world events, consisting of cuttings and pictures from newspapers and magazines. Much was made of the Queen's youth and the beginnings of a new Elizabethan era. The echoes of expansionism and national confidence of the first Elizabethan age were deliberately encouraged and there was an optimistic mood which caught the public feeling at the time. When Sir Edmund Hillary got to the top Mount Everest (never mind that he was a New Zealander!) it seemed as though Britain had a bright new world future.

194

By the time of the coronation we had moved back to Essex. To commemorate the event, every school child in the county was given a book about life in Essex at the time of Queen Elizabeth I, again reinforcing the parallels. Like many other families we bought a television shortly before the coronation. All the imperial connections were no doubt carefully woven into the pageantry, but the image which leaps out of the memory, and which encapsulates the exoticism of the Empire, is Queen Salote of Tonga riding through the streets of London in an open landau with the rain pouring down.

Later in 1953 the Queen made a major tour of the Commonwealth. I must have been still affected by the patriotic fervour aroused by her coronation because I embarked on another scrap-book to record her progress. I still remember the pictures of her being carried ashore in a ceremonial chair through the surf on a tropical island in the southern hemisphere.

Around the time of the coronation I was enrolled as a Brownie. Despite the received liberal view of the scouting movement I, like my daughter today, enjoyed the parades, the flags, the working for badges. Later, as a Guide, I lapped up the opportunities for group activity and identity which were available. Corny it undoubtedly was, but camping and the camp-fire singsongs provided a link with the pioneering ethos which was key to parts of the imperial experience. Baden Powell's proclaimed wish was to foster links between young people across the Empire, but I have to say that, other than through romantic association, my own awareness probably stopped at national (not to mention nationalistic) boundaries.

When I was eleven I went away to boarding school. In my second year our form mistress was a Nigerian teacher, Mrs Solanke. She was the first black person I can remember having direct contact with. She talked to us about life in Nigeria, but if her experience was made use of within the school as a resource to open our eyes to some broader issues we should think about, it certainly did not leave any detailed impression.

By my mid-teens I had begun to think of some of the issues about global resources. I changed school again when I was fifteen and went to the local High School where our history teacher, Miss Johnson, strongly encouraged an interest in current affairs. There was a branch of the United Nations Association at school, and I was chosen to go with our headmistress to the memorial service for Dag Hammersjöld at Westminster Abbey.

Through Miss Johnson many of us joined the Council for Education in World Citizenship. We had meetings after school with speakers, but the highlight was the annual Christmas Conference. Hundreds of sixth formers used to attend the two or three day meeting which was held in Central Hall, Westminster. We stayed in the Youth Hostel in Holland Park and, in addition to attending the Conference, we took advantage of being in London to go out to the theatre in the West End. The format of the Conference was a mixture of lectures and cultural events. It was here I first heard a West Indian steel band and watched Indian dancing.

One of the conferences was entitled The Fourth Horseman, and was about the threat of famine in the world and the need for development. One of the speakers was from VSO (Voluntary Service Overseas). The impact of his talk was so great that the emotional response – the idea of becoming a VSO – stayed firmly with me throughout my three years at Durham University.

Newly graduated, with a degree in English, I was accepted by VSO. The heart of the organization was – and is – service as a volunteer. However, in the mid-1960s VSO was much less professional than it now is in its recruitment and in the skills demanded of the volunteers. The normal arrangement was for school leavers and young graduates with no teaching experience to go out to developing countries (especially former British colonies) as teachers. Although the concept could be regarded as patronizing, the motives of those who went as volunteers when I did were largely idealistic. Certainly we were well aware that the enterprise was a partnership and that the benefits of the experience were likely to be as great, if not greater, for ourselves as for those we taught.

I was posted to Ghana and spent two years teaching English language and literature to first year students at the University of Ghana. The first year literature syllabus, which had been introduced a few years earlier by the then professor, Tommy Dunn, was encouragingly broad, and in addition to *Dubliners* and the eccentric choice of Christopher Fry's play *Curtmantle* about Thomas a' Becket, the students and I grappled with Raja Rao's *The Serpent and the Rope* and enjoyed Achebe's *Things Fall Apart*.

At that time travelling was easy and cheap and the vacations were spent in every part of the country. I visited historical sites, such as the castles at Elmina and Christiansborg, and huge engineering developments at the Volta Dam and the harbour at Tema, and absorbed the rich cultural and artistic life of the country. Across the borders were also the heady delights of Togo and Cote d'Ivoire where delicacies such as green salads straight off the morning plane from Paris could be had!

However, the purpose of the travelling was as much to make the journey itself as to reach the eventual destination – the methods varied from tro-tro to boat to long distance coach; the diverse landscape from the dry coast to the lush Ashanti forests to the dramatic escarpments in the north.

Beyond all this, living in Ghana meant making the individual connections which for me are the essence of the Commonwealth. To get to know students well enough to be welcomed into their homes to meet their families, or to share in festivals and celebrations of other cultures, was to have my sensibilities developed and my horizons widened in a way which travel and tourism alone could never have achieved.

Once I returned to Britain some of the Legon students who did postgraduate work in England visited and stayed with my family. Opportunities to welcome students and others from Commonwealth countries have continued, so my children are now growing up used to, and comfortable with, people of different cultures and nationalities in a way that I did not have the opportunity to be. In my personal journey, that is what the Empire and Commonwealth have most importantly meant.

Marina Warner

Marina Warner was born in London in 1946. She is a novelist and critic, and has also published historical studies of female symbolism (*Alone of All her Sex: The Myth and the Cult of the Virgin Mary; Monuments & Maidens: The Allegory of the Female Form*). Her most recent novel, *Indigo: or, Mapping the Waters*, was published in 1992, and a collection of short stories, *The Mermaids in the Basement*, will appear in 1993. She is currently working on a study of fairy-tales, called *From the Beast to the Blonde*.

MARINA WARNER

Between the Colonist and the Creole: Family Bonds, Family Boundaries

My grandfather was born a Creole, but I didn't know it. The French include whites in the term Creole, and so do the Spanish, but to English ears, 'Creole' sounds foreign, French, or worse, native, but native of another place besides England. To my grandparents' generation, the word connoted an Elsewhere where foreign words were spoken as a native tongue, and various kinds of foreigners mingled and became natives in the process. And it was of course impossible, then, for an Englishman to be a foreigner at all, and perilous (though regrettably not impossible) for an Englishman to become a native. The Warners had been born in the West Indies for generations and lived there, mainly in St. Kitt's, Antigua and Trinidad, in ever-increasing numbers (this grandfather was one of twenty-one children). But they had still remained English-bred in the bone.

It was startling to me to realize, when the recent nationality laws were passed, that my family's Britishness would have been abolished. For nothing could have been more British than my father and my father's family. If they could have been bottled, their voices, their walk, their dress (the ties, the hats, the sticks), their phrases, their laughter (my father's boisterous British laughter used to help me locate his whereabouts when I was a child), if they could have been pressed and fermented and drunk, they would summon up, in a single draught, an era and a world that was thoroughly and indisputably English. And yet, as I say, they weren't exactly English; how it would have shocked my grandfather to be refused a British passport, as would happen now. (Though being white, and of ancient pioneer stock, the immigration police would probably bend the rules, I know.)

The Warners, like other planter families, maintained their connections to the mother country by a series of strategies. For the lime demarcation lines in the turf that divided Englishmen from foreigners and natives could be rubbed out in the climate of the islands all too easily by passing feet. Inviolate Englishness, in a family like my father's and his fathers before him, was kept up by methods both subtle and brutal, conscious and unconscious, acts of convenient memory and sins of omission; the field of memory, which is the writer's testing ground, was carefully laid out in a certain way, and returning there now in imagination, as the granddaughter of Pelham Warner ('Plum'), I chose different markers, boundary lines, posts and goals from the ones that had been handed down to me in the family history.

However, because contexts and definitions are always in flux, I still cannot say that the Warners were Creoles as a simple statement of fact; the relations of the former plantocracy to the islands which they colonised and inhabited for nearly three hundred years make it fallacious, even opportunistic, for a descendant now to grasp the label and wear it with new pride. It's too easy a solution to the problems of the past, to make a few realignments – like moving the furniture to improve the look of a room. The history of denial in the past has forfeited someone like me the right to own in the present to the inheritance, much as I should like to. Indeed, I sometimes felt that by writing *Indigo*, the novel I set partly in the Caribbean, I was interloping on territory from which accidents of history had morally barred me; but then I also argued to myself that it is important, too, for anyone and everyone to challenge received ideas, and that I had tried to do this before, in a book about the cult of the Virgin Mary and a novel about women in Fascist Italy, themes which sprang directly from my family history too.

My grandfather's memoirs begin: 'I was born in the Island of Trinidad, in the West Indies, where my father was, at one time, Attorney-General, and my earliest recollections of cricket are of batting on a marble gallery to the bowling of a black boy, who rejoiced in the name of Killebree.'[1] He begins the book with this memory because he went on to become the England captain of cricket, and then, for a long time, President of the MCC. When I was a little girl, Sir Pelham was still a famous figure, a slim, brittle old man with a piercing look in his pale blue eyes, the effect of the precision vision which had helped score him all those runs on the pitches of the Empire. The London flat in which he and my grandmother lived in their old age was entirely decorated with cricketing memorabilia: from the bookcases beamed the curious harsh yellow of the Wisden almanacs, the game's scrolls of the law, and the walls were hung with caricatures ('Plum brings back the Ashes') and photographs (Plum carried shoulder high off the ground after a particular triumph; Plum with the King George VI at Lord's; Plum with Queen Mary, receiving a trophy).

My memory may not be altogether accurate, because I was small during the time when both our families were living in London (1952) but in the dark, corridor-dominated, typically stuffy mansion block flat in South Kensington, with its smells of boiling vegetables and chlorinated waterpipes, there was an atmosphere of worldly glory that had been deservedly earned and relished to the hilt. Sir Pelham was a beloved figure: he had played the civilized game of cricket all over the pink parts of the map and deepened the warmth and wisdom of that rose colour. As C.L.R. James points out in his inspired account of cricket and Empire, *Beyond a Boundary*, there existed a deep connection between the game and British power. Remembering his schooldays, James passes seamlessly from his passion for cricket to the way history was then taught: 'I would fight and resist in order to watch the big boys playing cricket, and I would do this until my grandmother came for me and dragged me home protesting ... Later, when reading elementary English history books, I became resentful of the fact that the English always won all, or nearly all, of the battles and read every new history book I could find, searching out and noting the battles they had lost.[2] Cricket pitches would become, for James, a place where that balance could be redressed.

The image of Killebree – Creole patois for Hummingbird, which the French spell 'colibri' – stuck in my mind and helped inspire the reckoning I attempted in *Indigo*. Without that 'black boy' bowling to my grandfather again and again, perhaps he might not have learned to bat, so early, so well, been trained up to the game which made him a kind of national hero in the 'Home' country. It seemed to me that in this exchange, as the nicknamed servant bowled to the young master in the 'marble gallery' of his father the Attorney-General's house, I could see the crucible in which my grandfather's skills were sublimed, and through this vision, by extension, the whole relation of colonizer and colonized: the whiteness of the batsman unconsciously enhanced by the marble gallery in which he stands at the ready, waiting to hit; the 'boy' infantilized by the affectionate but nonetheless patronizing sobriquet of the tiniest bird in the world; the easy confidence with which the writer, my grandfather, acknowledges his debt to his childhood trainer, that 'old world courtesy' which makes up for what it takes for itself by a show of exquisite good manners ('breeding').

My father's favourite adage was 'Noblesse oblige' – he said it whenever we did anything disagreeable socially (a boring party, a tedious chore), making it clear that we had to do it, not because we needed to, or might gain thereby ourselves, or were in any sense dependent on the goodwill of others, but to confirm our superiority. He wasn't an unkind man, my father, nor an especially arrogant one, but he descended from a line of Empire servants and he had absorbed – and never re-examined, let alone repudiated – their intensely hierarchical view of social organisation, which grants importance to every stratum by teaching it to despise the orders beneath and defer to the orders above. Moving through life as his daughter became a complex dance, something like an eightsome reel, in which we were continually 'setting' to partners, ducking and twirling and curtsying as we passed along the files attempting to define their rank with respect to ourselves and make the correct steps accordingly. But above all, I found in Killebree's bowling a repeat of the pattern in the carpet, first figured three centuries before, of the hospitable helpfulness that the indigenous peoples of the Caribbean had offered the first settlers; the Indians of Guyana showed the English buccaneers who arrived there in the sixteenth century how to grow tobacco and other crops that were unfamiliar to them. Some were later taken to the islands to assist there; and were promised they would return after the plantings and first harvests. But that promise went the way of all flesh. Like many others.

My father was very proud that the Warners had been significant figures in this early history. Alongside the cricketing memorabilia which we inherited after my grandfather's death, we also were left documents about the family's story in the West Indies: a copy of the charter granting Sir Thomas Warner, founding settler of the 'Mother Colony' of St. Kitt's, governorship of the West Indies on behalf of King Charles I; a photograph of his tomb in the churchyard of Old Road on that island. A marble slab, protected by a fretwork canopy, mourns his death in 1648 and records his 'acts of fame', 'brave exploits', and 'large narratives of military worth' in fourteen lines of rhyming couplets. I heard, recently, the poet David Dabydeen give a paper on the English language, and he said that he had seen similar glowing epitaphs to the liberality and nobility of slaveowners in the graveyards of the West Indies. They had been made by stonecutters who did not know how to read and write, who were their slaves. When I heard this, I felt prickly shame creep over me. For of course the Warners became planters, and as planters, became slaveowners.

There was one way this Creole past was acknowledged in my family: my father went to Trinidad in the Sixties to sell the last piece of land the Warners still owned on the island. There were so many heirs (the descendants of all those twenty-one siblings) that the parcelling out of the rents from this section of Port of Spain was proving an expensive nightmare. It wasn't exactly lucrative land, anyway – I suspect the rents could not be raised as the quality of the housing was so poor. When my father returned from the sale, aglow with Carnival and other excitements, he talked a lot about our Warner cousins, and when he showed us a photograph, of one he'd taken a special shine to (Cousin Lucy), I was very surprised to see that she wasn't white, but black. My sister was too, and because times have changed and we are different, we were intrigued and pleased; it was a kind of secret, something that kindled the same conspiratorial pleasure as the contents of the treasure drawer I had in my bedside table, which I only showed to very special friends.

My father explained that Warner was a very common name in the West Indies because the Warners had been enlightened owners and so the slaves were happy to take the same name. This was how we came to be related to cousin Lucy, he implied. But when I started reading to research the background of my novel, I came across another story. Not only that no evidence exists which suggests that the

Warners were any different from the rest of the plantocracy, who on the whole were the sorriest crew of ugly, greedy and often vicious self-interested parties ever to lobby parliament, as they did in strength against the abolitionists, and even against the 'ameliorists', who merely wanted to improve the conditions of the slaves. But the story was different also because the breakdown between 'foreign' and 'English' happened from the start; and was always denied, though it was plain from the law records, as well as the early chronicles of the islands, and had not been expunged entirely from the history books. My great-uncle, Aucher Warner, my grandfather's elder brother, wrote a biography of Sir Thomas, the founding father, and in it, he tells the story of the colony's early years, including the episode which concerns a certain 'Indian' Warner, son of Sir Thomas.

Thomas Warner, when he arrived in St. Kitt's, 'married' a local woman, called Barbe, and had several children with her, including a son, who grew up to become Governor of Dominica, appointed by the colonial governor of the islands, and the active leader of the large surviving community of Caribs on that island. Another son, Philip, was born later, by Sir Thomas's marriage to the English wife who joined him once the colony was established, and in 1672, Philip was appointed Deputy governor of Antigua. In this capacity, he led a raid on Dominica, to punish the Indians for alleged harassment of Antiguans. The two half-brothers met in conflict, but it was agreed they should talk; there was a feast, discussion of their differences, a quarrel flared; the peace conference ended with the deaths of Indian Warner and all his followers. Philip was accused of serving rum in order to intoxicate his enemies so that he could kill them more easily, and for this treachery, he was transported to the Tower of London and tried.

The massacre and Philip Warner's imprisonment took place around 1675, and the story, with its Cain and Abel overtones of mythic violation, remains startling. It would be even more astonishing, however, if Philip had been found guilty. After many protests from his fellow planters, and many affidavits to his good name and character, many reports of the cruelties of the Caribs and accusations of Indian Warner's conspiracies with their raids and thefts, Philip Warner was transferred for trial to Barbados and acquitted. He was not however restored to the governorship of Antigua.

'This is a strange story,' concludes my great-uncle, who had found the documents to the case in the Colonial Office, and to his credit, reproduced them.[3] It was such a strange story, so uneasy-making, so full of bloodshed and strife, that my father never mentioned it: though he was a historian by inclination, an often brilliant chronicler, a flâneur who could bring breathing men and women from the past with all their struggles, their mess, their violence, into the streets of the different cities where we used to walk together, though he was a bookseller with a true reader's love of browsing and searching, the history of the West Indies in the pioneer years of the seventeenth century had to appear a graceful, controlled, law-abiding act of conquest in the interests of civilization. It had to be cricket, rather than this bristling and bleeding tangled mass of loose ends, betrayals, and fratricide.

Père Labat, the Dominican missionary who lived in the Caribbean from 1693-1705, wrote in his *magnum opus* that he once met Indian Warner's mother, the Governor's ancient first wife, who was then a hundred years old and bald, but had kept most of her teeth. The story of her son's life and adventures are more complex than can be related here, and a good history needs to be done of this period.[4] But the way that I was told his story, or rather not told his story, points to the edginess English Empire families felt about miscegenation, interchanges between colonised and coloniser, about the translations of one culture into another that happened even while the hierarchical blueprint denied they could. Cricket, when it became the game of the colonized, and one in which they could compete as equals and defeat the colonizers, provided an allegory of the future; it also in another way encapsulated the buried facts of the past, that buccaneer and maroon could be father and son, that governor and slave could be brothers – and their wives and daughters, sisters.

As I say, this wasn't the story I was told, and indeed, as the Creole, colonial status of my father's family was never admitted as such, the Empire was something that I took for granted as belonging to us, unproblematically. But in my case, I was given a lamp which I could rub to transport me far, far from this condition of British complacency: my father, during the War, married my mother, who is Italian and Catholic. In this way, I became a foreigner. The kind of foreigner it was permitted for me to become, too, because Italian women were exotic, reputedly beautiful and voluptuous and vivacious and conscious of their femininity, their obligations towards men and children. An Italian son-in-law would not have won such approval from Sir Pelham and Lady Warner in their mansion block that they lavished on my young mother. She stood within the permitted degrees of foreignness, and Catholicism, as my father once remarked – unforgettably – was a good religion for a girl. But it isn't the religion of the British Empire, though French and Belgian and other missions carried it far and wide through their empires, and the infamous French *Code Noir* of 1685 declared, in the same breath, that slaves were chattels, and should be given Christian instruction and baptised immediately on purchase and that unless this were done, the owner would be subject to 'une amende arbitraire' – a heavy fine.[5] Nearly three hundred years later, at my convent school in Berkshire, England, we were still 'adopting' Black Babies by making an offering, and following it up by regular prayers in order to earn, as sponsor, a photograph of the designated, newly baptised fosterchild.

My family's Creole past, gainsaid, erased, became the inspiration for *Indigo*. I wanted to call the novel 'A Deeper Bite' from the Spanish proverb I used as an epigraph, 'The tongue has no teeth but a deeper bite', because the book is about survival through language, in the face of military and other strengths; about the power of memory, transmuted into stories, to shape experience both fallaciously and truthfully, harmfully and helpfully. *The Tempest* gave me a structure to work with; it was first performed in 1611, twelve years before Thomas Warner arrived and settled in the West Indies, and was most probably inspired by a shipwreck of some Englishmen on Bermuda. The first folio, in which the play appears, was published the same year that Thomas Warner landed and began the 'Mother Colony' – changing the island of Liamuiga into St. Kitt's, the first of the British holdings of Empire. *The Tempest* has often been interpreted as a drama about colonialism by contemporary directors; it was recast as a cry of liberation by the Martiniquais poet Aimé Césaire in his play *Une Tempête* of 1969, and has been discussed and explored by numerous writers from the Caribbean, inspiringly by George Lamming, for instance.[6] But as far as I know, nobody had attempted to discover in Caliban's mother, Sycorax, another being besides the 'foul hag' Prospero invokes. Yet, in the play, Caliban says, 'This island's mine, / By Sycorax my mother.' It was she who ruled before Prospero came, and in my book, she becomes the embodiment of the island itself, of its inner life, as well as a woman of ordinary passions and skills who – I hope – grows to the dimensions of a full humanity.

Because our family was involved in an enterprise that so resembles Prospero's theft, that foundation act of Empire, I felt compelled to examine the case, and imagine, in fiction, the life and culture of Sycorax, and of Ariel and Caliban, whom I cast as her foundlings; I wanted to hear their voices in the noises of the isle.

NOTES

1. P.F. Warner, *My Cricketing Life* (London, 1920?), p.1.
2. C.L.R. James, *Beyond a Boundary* (London, 1963, rep. 1986), pp. 49-50
3. Aucher Warner, *Sir Thomas Warner: Pioneer of the West Indies. A chronicle of his family* (London: The West India Committee, 1933).
4. Père Labat, *Nouveau Voyage aux Isles de l'Amérique*, 6 vols. (Paris, 1724). Peter Hulme, author of *Colonial Encounters – Europe and the Native Caribbean 1492-1797* (London, 1986) is at work on a history of the Caribs seen through European eyes and will shed some light on these events.
5. Jean Meyer, *Esclaves et negriers* (Paris, 1986), pp. 140-141.
6. George Lamming, *Water with Berries* (London, 1971).

Illustrations and Acknowledgements

Cover illustrations
  Shirley Chew
  Ishrat Lindblad, Wentworth, Bournemouth, 1953
  Shaka, Zulu King
  Convent of the Holy Infant Jesus, Singapore
  Lauretta Ngcobo, school photo c.1946
  Cherry Clayton, Breda Street, Table Top mountain in background
  Jamaica ABC colouring book
  Marriage of Maharajah's daughter, India, 1932   photo Harald Lechenperg
  Geraldine Pears, Empire Day Queen, 1947. Age 7 years

2   Marion Halligan

12   Lyn Innes   photo Gillian Cargill
  Her home, Australia
  Her grandfather, c.1908
  Her grandmother

20   Anna Rutherford   photo Helen Tiffin
  At 17 months
  At 12 years

30   Ama Ata Aidoo

38   Buchi Emecheta, 1992   photo Matti Kivekäs
  My first school, Ibasa, c.1950
  Age c.16 years
  With her children, 1968
  At Pussycat Mansions, 1982   photo Anna Rutherford

48   Lauretta Ngcobo   photo Anna Rutherford
  Lauretta, age 7 years, with her brother and maternal grandparents,
  Webbstown (Zulu Cabazi, Ixopo District, Natal)
  Lauretta in front of her mother, Rosa Gwina, who for many years was also her
  teacher, Webbstown Primary School: built by Lauretta's grandfather.

56   Cherry Clayton
  Me and my pram, 12 Breda Street
  Modelling dresses, 1954
  Me as little shepherdess on the floor

64   Jane Bryce
  Lushoto School, c.1950
  Me with my younger sister and Martha Nairobi, ayah, Moshi, 1963
  Mother, sister and self (far right) at Kilimanjaro, 1963

72   Lauris Edmond   photo Robert Cross
  Clive, Lindsay and Lauris

80 Dorothy Jones, Canada
    At Hampton Court
    Age 5 years
    Age 6 years

86 Jean Arasanayagam

94 Yasmine Gooneratne
    Kandy, 1959

102 Shashi Deshpande   photo Anna Rutherford
    Age 4 years

108 Meenakshi Mukherjee, New Delhi, 1991
    Meenakshi (right) with sister, c.1946

114 Nayantara Sahgal
    Age 4 years, lying on floor, with mother and sisters
    Age 12 years, next to Mahatma Gandhi
    Age 15 years
    Age 19 years with mother Vijaya Pandit

122 Ishrat Lindblad
    In front of our house in Lahore, 1948
    My mother, my eldest sister and myself. First visit to England, 1953

130 Shirley Chew   photo Gillian Cargill
    Age 3 years, in front of Chinese scroll
    Age 9 years, in front of Buddhist Shrine

138 Shirley Geok-Lin Lim
    1987
    As a young girl, Malacca

146 Grace Nichols   photo Sheila Geraghty

152 Velma Pollard   photo Anna Rutherford
    Girl Guide, Jamaica

160 Olive Senior   photo Martin Mordecai
    Age 4 years
    Age c.14 years
    With schoolmates, Montego Bay High School, age c.14 years
    Montego Bay High School, age c.18 years

164 Margaret Atwood   photo Laurence Acland
    Age 12 years, 1951

172 Isabel Huggan   photo R.D. Huggan
    Elmira, Ontario, 1952

180 Daphne Marlatt   photo Perry Low
    As a child   photo Arthur Buckle

186 Maggie Butcher
    As a bridesmaid, age c.9 years
    On the beach at Bournemouth, age 11 years

192 Helen Niven
    As a child

198 Marina Warner   photo Gillian Cargill
    First Communion, London, 1952
    Marina, Laura and grandfather, Sir Pelham Warner c.1959